Pale-Face Came

es for Familiar Places

CAPILANO RIVER
HOMULCHESON
USTLAWN
INDIAN
RESERVE
TLATHMAHULK
ESTAHLTOHK
MOODYVILLE
UTHKYME
KWAHULCHA
SAHUNZ
PIPELINE-CHAY-THOOS
BEAVER LAKE-AHKA-CHU
WHOI-WHOI
BROCKTON PT - PAAPEEAK
LOST LAGOON
CHUI-WHAH-ULCH
DEADMANS I^D - SOUTSAHS
HASTINGS MILL
KUMKUMLYE
CHETCHAILMUN
HUPHAHPAI
SUGAR REFINERY
CEDAR COVE
PUCKAHLS
LUCKLUCKY
WATER ST
SHUN
HOWE ST
MAIN ST
KIWAHUSKS
SKWACHICE
C.N.R. YARD
FALSE CREEK
CAMBIE ST
BURRARD BRIDGE
SNAUQ

OR J. S. MATTHEWS. V. D.
CITY ARCHIVIST
VANCOUVER
information given verbally by aged
of the Squamish and Musqueam Tribes
1932
roved, Squamish Indian Council

Copyright

ND LANDMARKS
D ENGLISH BAY
AN CAME

Stanley Park's Secret

Stanley Park's Secret

The Forgotten Families of Whoi Whoi, Kanaka Ranch and Brockton Point

Jean Barman

Harbour Publishing

With the voices of the families and their descendants

Simon Baker
Mary Silvey Buss
Jessica Casey
Margaret Mannion Christie
Laurie Nahanee Cole
Robert Cole
Agnes Cummings
Tim Cummings
Rachel O'Connor Day
Anne O'Connor Fowler
Alfred Gonsalves
Joseph Gonsalves
Willard Gonsalves
Walter Keamo
Elaine Smith Kennedy
Elsie Kerr
August Jack Khahtsahlano
Ed Long
Marion Long
Michael Long
Maggie Eihu McCord McPhee
Norman McPhee
Joseph Mannion
Edward Nahanee
James Nahanee, known as Schay-tulk
Jerry Nahanee, known as Bulxatsa
William Nahanee
Olive Keamo O'Connor
Mary Nahu Picard
Rocky Sampson
Marion O'Connor Schick
Mary See-em-ia
Debra De Costa Stubbins Smith
Herbert Smith
Martha Smith
Minnie McCord Smith
Peter Smith
Ray Smith
Rennie Smith
Amber Stubbins
Tesamis, known as Ambrose Johnson
Maude Nahanee Thomas
Ruth O'Connor Ulrich
Elizabeth Silvey Walker
Robert Yelton
Rose Cole Yelton

1 2 3 4 5 09 08 07 06 05

Harbour Publishing
P.O. Box 219, Madeira Park, BC V0N 2H0
www.harbourpublishing.com

Text design by Roger Handling
Front Cover: Kwahama Kwatleematt and Joe Silvey, courtesy Jessica Casey; Front flap: W. Brand Young Map, City of Vancouver Archives, Map 198; Spine: Siwash Rock, City of Vancouver Archives, 677-116; Author photograph courtesy Martin Dee.
Endpapers from J.S. Matthews, comp., *Conversations with Khahtsahlano 1932-1954*, City of Vancouver Archives, Map P10N8
Title Page: Deadman's Island, City of Vancouver Archives, ST PK P332.1
Printed and bound in Canada

Harbour Publishing acknowledges financial support from the Government of Canada, through the Book Publishing Industry Development Program and the Canada Council for the Arts, and from the Province of British Columbia through the British Columbia Arts Council and the Book Publisher's Tax Credit through the Ministry of Provincial Revenue.

Library and Archives Canada Cataloguing in Publication

Barman, Jean, 1939-
Stanley Park's secret : the forgotten families of Whoi Whoi, Kanaka Ranch and Brockton Point / Jean Barman.

Includes bibliographical references and index.
ISBN 1-55017-346-4 / 978-1-55017-346-8

1. Stanley Park (Vancouver, B.C.)—History. 2. Indians of North America—British Columbia–Vancouver—History. 3. Hawaiians—British Columbia—Vancouver—History. 4. Vancouver (B.C.)—Ethnic relations. I. Title.

FC3847.65.B37 2005 971.1'33 C2005-903493-9

Contents

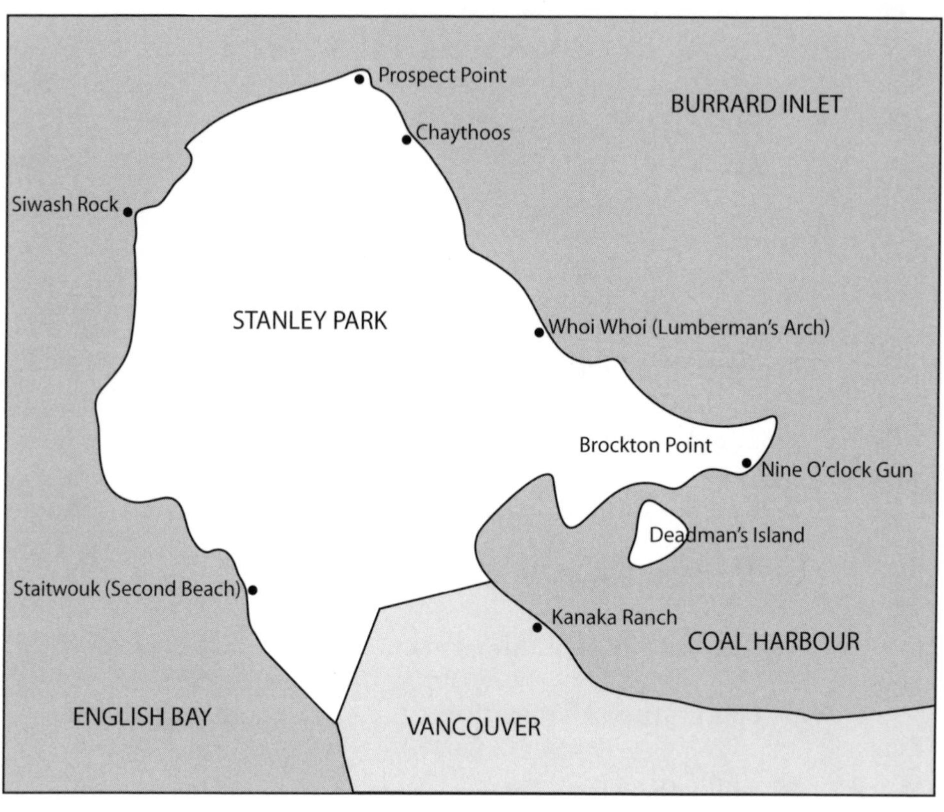
Prospect Point
BURRARD INLET
Chaythoos
Siwash Rock
STANLEY PARK
Whoi Whoi (Lumberman's Arch)
Brockton Point
Nine O'clock Gun
Deadman's Island
Staitwouk (Second Beach)
Kanaka Ranch
COAL HARBOUR
ENGLISH BAY
VANCOUVER

ACKNOWLEDGEMENTS

Many persons have helped to make this book possible. My greatest debt is to the descendants who have been my collaborators: Jessica Casey; Tina Cole; Llewella Duncan; Willard Gonsalves; Elsie Kerr; Marion Long and her son Michael; James Nahanee also known as Schay-tulk, his sister Laurie Cole, and his son Jerry Nahanee known as Bulxatsa; Olive Keamo O'Connor and her daughters Marion, Ruth, Rachel and Anne; Norman and Mabel McPhee; Mary Nahu Picard and her son Terry; Rocky Sampson; Herbert Smith, his sister Elaine Kennedy and daughter Rennie Smith; Ray and Marlene Smith; Amber Stubbins and her mother Debra De Costa Stubbins Smith; and Robert Yelton. I have also benefited from memories shared earlier with others.

Collaboration with descendants has been integral to every stage of this book. Among those who read and critiqued parts relating to their families are Jessica Casey, Laurie Nahanee Cole, Rachel Day, Anne Fowler, Willard Gonsalves, Elsie Kerr, Marion Long, Mabel McPhee, Jimmy and Jerry Nahanee, Rocky Sampson, Marion Schick, Herbert Smith, Ruth Ulrich and Robert Yelton. Family photographs have been shared by Jessica Casey, Laurie Nahanee Cole, Llewella Duncan, Willard Gonsalves, Elsie Kerr, Mabel McPhee, James Nahanee, Herbert and Rennie Smith, Marlene Smith, Amber Stubbins and her mother Debra Smith, Robert Yelton and the Keamo family, extending from Olive Keamo O'Connor and her daughters Marion, Ruth, Rachel and Anne, to members across the generations, including Brittany and Taylor Dennett.

My obligations go further. Randy Bouchard and Dorothy Kennedy shared insights and materials from their three decades of research on the Squamish people. Bruce Watson made available information from his fur-trade dictionary in process and Gail Edwards from her research on Protestant missionaries in 19th-century British Columbia.

Douglas Harris introduced me to the concept of adverse possession. June Mosher discussed her great-grandfather, Stanley Park's first park ranger, Henry Avison, Vickie Jensen Stanley Park's totem poles, Renisa Mawani her Stanley Park research and Sean Kheraj and Dick Lazenby their interest in Deadman's Island. Cheryl Wong painstakingly traced land records relating to Kanaka Ranch. Chris Hanna was, as always, invaluable in mining the British Columbia Archives. My husband Roderick J. Barman trekked Stanley Park and Coal Harbour with me, in searches for memories obliterated in physical form. We rejoiced together at finding the lilac tree in bloom at Brockton Point.

Archivists and librarians have been generous with their time. Retired City of Vancouver Archivist Sue Baptie and her staff were endlessly patient as I read through Major Matthews's collection of materials, Mike Steele's papers and Vancouver Parks Board records. I was also assisted by staff at the National Archives (London), Library and Archives Canada, British Columbia Archives, North Vancouver Archives, Vancouver Public Library Special Collections and University of British Columbia Special Collections.

Mary Schendlinger, Anna Comfort, Alicia Miller, Stephanie Sy and Marisa Alps at Harbour Publishing have guided *Stanley Park's Secret* to publication.

I thank you all.

Each spring the lilac at Brockton Point, overlooking the city of Vancouver, blooms as abundantly as ever. Courtesy the author

PREFACE

The Lilac Still Blooms

The lilac still blooms for the forgotten families of Stanley Park. Each spring at Brockton Point its flowers wax as abundant as they ever did, even though the families who gave it life have long since departed. Not only were they dispossessed, their presence has been erased. The lone lilac overlooking the city of Vancouver is the only trace of their long-time presence in one of the premier urban parks in Canada and the world. In a public place resplendent with statues, monuments and decorations of many kinds, no sign acknowledges the generations of men, women and children who lived at Whoi Whoi, Kanaka Ranch and Brockton Point.

Long before there was a Stanley Park, the thousand-acre (400 hectare) peninsula we know by that name was a locus of family life. Much of the history has been lost, but enough survives for us to acknowledge that the park was never the virgin forest its promoters would have us believe it was at the time of its imposition. Stanley Park's age—it is almost as old as Vancouver itself—obscures the complexities of its history. The city of Vancouver is often conceived as having sprung up on Burrard Inlet out of nowhere, emerging as the western terminus of the transcontinental railway that brought Canada together as a nation in 1886. The park became the city's signature piece almost immediately afterward, so it is easy to assume that the park was a pristine wilderness when it was created, being born alongside the city itself.

The language is powerfully persuasive: "primitive simplicity," "witching savagery," "the forest primeval."[1] Stanley Park is not alone with such designations. Parks are generally perceived to embody the natural world as it existed before the fall of the Old Testament, before a dissatisfied Eve bit into an apple and was thereby cast out of the Garden of Eden, along with her husband Adam. To venture into a park is to be permitted, for a brief moment in time, to escape the materialism of our workaday world. We put the imperfections of our lives behind us and reflect on what might have been. We experience the world uncontaminated by human beings like ourselves, before sin entered in.

Urban parks were established for precisely these reasons. As North America and Europe were rapidly industrialized in the 19th century, people migrated in droves from rural to urban settings. As cities grew, their proponents sought to retrieve the proximity to nature that had been left behind. They set aside oases of green as escapes from what were often unpleasant conditions of everyday life. Urban parks recalled a simpler, romanticized past, as well as offering a popular means of recreation. They were also good business, in that they kept people more content and encouraged still more workers to move to the city, to the advantage of businessmen and developers. Among the best known 19th-century parks conceived on this pastoral model are Tiergarten in Berlin, Regent's and St. James's parks in London, Central Park in New York City, Golden Gate Park in San Francisco and Stanley Park in Vancouver.

Not just in Vancouver, but elsewhere, people who already made their life in a site wanted for a park were cast aside. They had to be erased in order for the designated park to fulfill the purposes intended by its promoters. The space had to be made to appear natural. For Central Park in New York City, which preceded Stanley Park by a third of a century, the sequence of events was virtually identical. Much of the 850 acres (340 hectares) was occupied by modest Black, Irish and German families who raised vegetables, tended hogs and scrambled on the margins to survive. To justify evicting these people and to rally public opinion, authorities characterized the residents as "squatters, dwelling in rude huts." Histories of Central Park published as late as the 1990s characterize the residents as a "noxious element" that "lived in hopelessness."[2] As with the families of Stanley Park, they had no right to be there, certainly not in the face of the higher-minded venture that was Central Park.

No park is virginal, nor does it remain so. The natural world re-created there is just as contaminated by human desire and greed as the meanest street of the inner city. The pastoral settings of parks obscure their fractured histories, legitimizing elements of the story that those in control choose to share with visitors. These elements are almost always presented as the complete story, and as the natural order of things. The consequence is to make the silences in the history of parks—and there are always silences—all the more deafening.

Despite the rhetoric, and there is a lot of it, Stanley Park was not pristine. It was not even first-growth forest. Much of it had been logged, with the tacit consent of government officials. Trees grow back, but there was a greater, ongoing challenge to Stanley Park's virginity. The park was imposed on existing ways of life. It was intended from the beginning to serve one set of interests at the expense of others: its creation was a consummately colonial enterprise. The designation of the park was one small part of the process whereby Europeans from the 16th century onward sought to take control of all the world, subdue its indigenous peoples and reform their lands in the newcomers' image. The plan was a success, so much so that rarely if ever do we consider the possibility of other histories.

Yet other histories exist. Aboriginal people made use of the tongue of land we call Stanley Park for thousands of years. From their perspectives, the peninsula was not a Garden of Eden before the fall; it was their home. Other groups had their own histories. Some of the indigenous Hawaiians earlier employed in the fur trade took jobs at the lumber mills that dotted Burrard Inlet from the 1860s. A handful of these men set themselves down just outside the park's southeast boundary at what became known as Kanaka Ranch. Other newcomers and their Aboriginal wives settled at Brockton Point on the peninsula's eastern tip.

It took over two-thirds of a century from the imposition of Stanley Park in 1887 for the last of its families to be removed. In the interim, children were born, came of age, had families, grew old and died. The first generation became the second and then the third. These men, women and children occupied an intermediate space between societies. They were neither colonial nor colonized. In cultural terms they were liminal. It was for this reason that they were able to remain so long in Stanley Park and also for this reason that they could be ejected at the will of others.

The voices of the families of Stanley Park are less easy to erase than was their physical presence. However silent is the park itself, stories survive, in three principal forms. The earliest are hidden away in court records, principally of proceedings initiated against the families at Whoi Whoi and Brockton Point in the early 1920s but also from the beginning of the century. Summaries of the testimony are held in the Library and Archives of Canada in Ottawa. A carbon copy of the full testimony in the lead case was kept by the son of one of the defendants, and I am tremendously grateful to Willard Gonsalves for taking the initiative to share it with me and to Herbert Smith for lending me the Writ of Possession served on his grandmother in 1925.

Other stories originate with the exemplary commitment by Vancouver's first archivist, Major J.S. Matthews, appointed in 1933, to gather as much testimony as possible about the early city. During the interwar years, an era before tape recorders, he took notes of his conversations and typed them up. He then had the individual read through the typed copy to make amendments and corrections and to verify accuracy.[3] Sometimes his terminology peeks through the text, but the essence is what his conversationalists wanted him to hear. Because he was so attentive to the recollections of individuals who might be termed "old-timers," he made contact with many people at a stage in their lives when they were ready, and eager, to tell their stories.

Major Matthews was, quite remarkably for the time, determined not just to record a triumphalist history but also to tease out difference. Among his many conversationalists were people of diverse racial and socioeconomic backgrounds who either lived at Whoi Whoi, nearby Chaythoos, Brockton Point or Kanaka Ranch, or had stories to tell about those who did so. James Nahanee, whose grandfather was born at Kanaka Ranch, described for me how Matthews would sit in front of his typewriter and type along as Jimmy talked.[4] Matthews's informants became his friends: when the granddaughter of the first Hawaiian at Kanaka Ranch died in 1937, he attended her funeral. One of his longest lived conversationalists was an Aboriginal longshoreman and logger, August Jack Khahtsahlano, who had lived in Stanley Park as a child.

August Jack Khahtsahlano spent almost a quarter-century, from 1932 to 1954, in conversation with Vancouver archivist Major J.S. Matthews.
North Vancouver Museum and Archives, 4788

A third set of stories is held by the families themselves. It is now almost a decade and a half since Mabel McPhee first contacted me. She and her husband Norman so badly wanted me to understand and to acknowledge in print his birthplace of Kanaka Ranch and the Eihu family from whom he descends. I didn't have the confidence to do so, not then and not even after I got to know members of the Nahanee family of Kanaka Ranch and the Cole, Silvey and Smith families of Brockton Point. The turning point came when I was swept up by the enthusiasm of Olive Keamo O'Connor and her remarkable daughters Marion, Ruth, Rachel and Anne. Their stories, which they have shared with me in both oral and written forms, speak powerfully of the Cummings family of Brockton Point and also of James Keamo's interlude at Kanaka Ranch. In part through their initiative, I have come to know members of the De Costa, Gonsalves and Long families of Brockton Point.

Olive Keamo O'Connor with her daughters Rachel, Anne, Ruth and Marion in 1995. Courtesy Keamo family

Stanley Park's Secret tells the stories of the forgotten families at Whoi Whoi, Kanaka Ranch and Brockton Point, so far as possible in their own words. Factual details and sense of time sometime vary considerably between recollections. Memories are just that, gossamer threads caught in the brain that spill out through some impetus causing them to be recalled. The threads that come together in a story respond both to what the teller recalls, or has been told by others, and to the person to whom it is being told. The brain sometimes engages in a kind of mental shorthand, so that, inadvertently, time is truncated and several events are rolled into a single one. The nature of memory makes inconsistencies inevitable, even though, overall, the stories we each have to tell are remarkably honest.

Memories also exist in visual form. Descendants have kept treasured photographs across the generations and generously agreed to share them here. Others survive in public collections. Some of these commemorate important events in the life course, such as weddings and birthdays. Others speak to the world of work, especially to the collegial sense that can grow among co-workers. Yet others reveal the settings in which the families lived and played through the generations. Together the photographs speak as eloquently as words, perhaps more so, to Stanley Park's secret.

Among the generations of men, women and children who have shared in *Stanley Park's Secret*, some were never asked about their lives and others shared their stories very selectively. Memory is always partial. All of us make decisions every day about which parts of ourselves to reveal to whom under what circumstances. We recall what we want to remember. There is much about the forgotten families of Stanley Park that will remain just that—forgotten.

The task I've set for myself is to gather together the stories that do survive and want to be told. These I have woven into a narrative, incorporating other materials that testify to the stories' legitimacy and elaborate their circumstances.[5] To understand how families were erased not only from Stanley Park but from our collective memory, we need to understand the larger contexts. My search has taken me in unexpected directions, from the minutiae of Vancouver Parks Board meetings to the inner workings of Aboriginal residential schools to the camaraderie of longshoring to the partiality of the law. But it is the stories themselves that are at the heart of the book. They tell us about real people who are part of our common heritage.

On the advice of descendants, I have retained the spellings of Aboriginal names that were in use at the time the stories were told, rather than current orthographies. The process of rendering an oral language into written form is complex and ever-changing. Major Matthews was one of the first to attempt, as he once put it to August Jack, to "echo the words you say."[6] Since many of the earliest stories originate in Matthews's conversations, it is his written versions of names I use.

Stanley Park's Secret has another purpose apart from telling stories, as important as they are. The goal is to reclaim a place in the history of Vancouver, British Columbia and Canada for the forgotten families. Within Stanley Park the Aboriginal villages of Whoi Whoi at Lumberman's Arch and Chaythoos near Prospect Point need appropriate signage, as do Brockton Point and the nearby graveyard where families of all backgrounds were laid to rest. Kanaka Ranch at the foot of Denman Street similarly needs to be recognized. Not only were families dispossessed, the memory of them was erased. Only when the sites are returned to our collective memory will Stanley Park belong to all of us.

Chapter 1

The Aboriginal Presence

Aboriginal people told many stories about Siwash Rock, located on the western edge of the peninsula and here photographed in about 1898. According to Jim Franks, born around 1870, it is an Indian man who was turned "into rock so people see not much good to be too smart." Andrew Paull (Qoitechetahl) knew it by its Squamish name of Slahkayulsh, which means "he is standing up." According to Paull, the hole in the rock was where Slahkayulsh kept his fishing tackle.[1] City of Vancouver Archives, 677-116

Aboriginal people made use of today's Stanley Park for generations on end before the first newcomers reached the northwest coast of North America in the late 18th century. Some people went there on a seasonal basis; others remained for longer periods of time. Because the tongue of land was located somewhat inland from the principal trade routes up and down the coast, it gave those who stopped a certain protection from intruders. At high tide the peninsula became an island, its southern boundary a creek deep enough for a canoe to pass through. At other times, land access to the future city of Vancouver was by a log anchored in the mud across the highest spot.

The various Coast Salish groups are linked by language, and the peninsula lay between two of them. The Squamish inhabited the area to the north of Burrard Inlet into Howe Sound; the Musqueam lived to the south along the north arm of the Fraser River. Both groups drew on the peninsula's resources. In the 1930s Qoitechetahl, a Squamish man also known as Andrew Paull, talked about how "in bygone days my ancestors cut down many cedar trees in Stanley Park for making canoes and other purposes" using "nothing but stone chisels and a big round stone for a hammer."

Among the most useful sites Qoitechetahl described was Staitwouk, on the western shore, which later became known as Second Beach. According to Qoitochetahl, Staitwouk "is the Indian name for a clay material or muddy substance formerly obtained right in the bed of a small creek … which, when rolled into loaves, as the Indians did it, and

The shell deposits in middens that workmen unearthed in 1888 were hauled away for paving the road. J. Wood Laing photo, City of Vancouver Archives, SGN 91

heated or roasted before a fire, turned white like chalk."[2] The powder was whitened and applied to blankets made of woven mountain-goat hair.

The most populated of the sites whose name survives is Whoi Whoi, as it was spelled by Vancouver's first city archivist, Major J.S. Matthews. He and others wrote the word as they heard it, so spellings have varied, from Why-why to Qoiquo to xw'ay xway to x̲wáýx̲way. Whoi Whoi is located on the north shore of the peninsula between its northern and eastern tips at what is today Lumberman's Arch. The name translates as "a place for making masks," suggesting its use as an important spiritual component of Aboriginal life. In 1888, when the first road was built around Stanley Park, a construction crew unearthed near Whoi Whoi a large deposit of broken and crushed clam shells, as well as skulls and other body parts, about 8 feet (2.5 metres) deep and 4 acres (1.6 hectares) in size.

We know less than we should about the meaning of these archaeological findings because no one much cared about them at the time. Rather than exciting any interest, the shells were used to surface the road. The official report in June 1891 explained that "three miles [were] graveled ... the material used being clam-shells, which packed closely present a remarkable white appearance, adding greatly to the attractiveness of the park."[3]

The only interest in the finds came from an intellectually curious young Englishman, Charles Hill-Tout, who arrived in Vancouver in 1890. As an avocation he probed local archaeological sites, including the remains from road building. "In carting away the midden mass," he wrote in 1900, "numerous skeletons were brought to light. The bones of these were gathered up by the workmen, and placed in boxes for the Indians to take away, and bury in their burial grounds. [Some of the] boxes … were afterwards hidden in the forest where I discovered them a few years later. The crania had then fallen to pieces. I recall making selections of these bones, and sending them to … the Dom. Geol. Survey Museum in Ottawa." Hill-Tout claimed to have discovered eight or nine "old village sites" in Stanley Park, including Whoi Whoi and Staitwouk. He also pointed to "large numbers of spear and arrow heads" that "can be picked up on the northern shore of Stanley Park at low tide by the score." Much later, archaeologists located seven separate sites around the edge of the peninsula, each indicating extensive use over time.[4]

The first European colonizers to reach the northwest coast of North America in the late 18th century were few in number, and for that reason they were usually treated kindly, as guests. Some explorers stopped briefly, their principal legacy being their claiming through naming the bodies of water and such landforms as Burrard Inlet and English Bay. Among them was George Vancouver, a sea captain dispatched to ensure

Frederick Dally was one of the first photographers to visit Burrard Inlet and in about 1868 caught what he termed "Indian Ranches," possibly located on the peninsula. BC Archives, C-09568

that the area became a British possession. He described in his journal the peninsula and its inhabitants as they appeared to him in 1792.

> At five in the morning of Wednesday the 13th [of June], we again directed our course to the eastern shore and landed about noon, on the above-mentioned low bluff point ... (which in compliment to my friend Captain George Grey of the navy, we called POINT GREY) ...
>
> From Point Grey we proceeded first up the eastern branch of the sound [into Burrard Inlet], where, about a league within its entrance, we passed to the northward of an island [future Stanley Park] which nearly terminated its extent, forming a passage [First Narrows] from ten to seven fathoms deep not more than a cable's length in width. This island lying exactly across the channel appeared to form a similar passage to the south of it, with a smaller island [Deadman's Island] lying before it. From these islands, the channel, in width about half a mile, continued in direction about east. Here we were met by about fifty Indians, in their canoes, who conducted themselves with the greatest decorum and civility, presenting us with several fish cooked, and undressed, of the sort already mentioned as resembling the smelt. These good people, finding we were inclined to make some return for their hospitality, shewed much understanding in preferring iron to copper.[5]

A land-based fur trade operated across the Pacific Northwest from the early 19th century on, but no trading posts were established on or near the peninsula. The place we know as British Columbia got its beginnings in 1846, when Britain and the United States agreed on an international border running west along the 49th parallel and then around Vancouver Island, which three years later became a British colony. The Royal Navy steamships that docked at Esquimalt, just outside the capital city, Victoria, needed a reliable source of coal. Stories circulated about coal seams on the southeast shore of the peninsula. In 1859 a Royal Navy captain exploring the area named the bay Coal Harbour. The northern shore of Coal Harbour he called Brockton Point after his ship's senior engineer. The name Coal Harbour held despite the discovery that the coal to be found nearby did not produce sufficient heat to make steam.

By this time a gold rush was in full force. The discovery of gold on the Fraser River and north into the Cariboo enticed thousands of men, many from the United States, hoping to make their fortunes. In the fall of 1858 Britain declared the mainland the colony of British Columbia. James Douglas, who already had charge of Vancouver Island, was appointed governor with authority "to do and execute all things in due manner." Miners took advantage of the peninsula only in exceptional circumstances, as when, during a spring flood, "we could not get up the Fraser ... so we ... camped on the beach [at] the place now called Second Beach ... There was quite a settlement of men there, all bound for the goldfields."[6]

What with the influx of American miners and proximity to the expansionist United States, the onus was on Britain to provide protection for its colony. Late in 1858 the Colonial Office sent out a detachment of Royal Engineers with a dual mandate to keep order and to lay out infrastructure, including townsites. The colonel in charge, Richard Moody, was given the additional titles of chief commissioner of lands and works and lieutenant governor, but not the appointment he wanted most, which was to replace Douglas as governor. Having located the mainland capital at New Westminster on the Fraser River, Moody looked north to the peninsula to protect its flank. "At the rear of the position [New Westminster], and distant five miles, is Burrard's Inlet, any access to which would be rendered most hazardous, by placing a work on the island [*sic*—peninsula] which extends across it. There is also on that side a range of high ground [the future Prospect Point], from east to west, on which could be placed earthen works and intrenched camp, preventing any advance."[7]

In the summer of 1859, Britain and the United States came close to open warfare over possession of San Juan Island, near Victoria. Moody was convinced that the Americans were about to invade, and he saw the peninsula more critical than ever to defending New Westminster's flank. "The upper end of B. Inlet is the only access for our Ships of War and the base of support for ourselves," he wrote to James Douglas. It was "a matter of instant necessity" to run a "military road" from the

Royal Engineers' headquarters near New Westminster to "the upper end of Burrard Inlet." There, facing Burrard Inlet's narrowest point, he proposed to construct "landing piers & a simple block house containing a store." Douglas and the Colonial Office considered Moody's demands both impulsive and financially prohibitive, and rejected them one after the other.[8] Moody resented Douglas more than ever and increasingly acted on his own authority.

The Colonial Office ordered Douglas to raise revenue and to promote settlement, and so in February 1859 he proclaimed that all land in British Columbia belonged to the Crown. Once surveyed, Crown land could be sold, unless it was reserved "for such purposes as the Executive shall deem advisable," including roads, towns and villages, places of worship, schools and "public purposes."[9] Douglas followed up in January 1860 with a second proclamation permitting newcomers who were British or became naturalized to take up to 160 acres (64 hectares) of unsurveyed land so long as it was not reserved and there were no signs of occupation. By marking out and registering their pre-emption, living on it and making improvements, newcomers acquired first right to purchase once the land was surveyed.

The two purposes to which Moody put Douglas's land policy each had ramifications for the future Stanley Park. The first purpose was to reserve as much land as possible before it could be pre-empted by settlers. In December 1859 Moody requested that Douglas contact the admiral in charge of the Royal Navy's Pacific Station at Esquimalt about naval reserves. Decisions were made within the month, including the establishment of a naval reserve to the east of the peninsula.[10] Moody also made reserves on his own initiative both as chief commissioner and as chief military officer. He particularly resented any intrusion on his authority in the latter post. For reserves to become official, the policy was that they had to be publicly proclaimed or "gazetted," but Moody appears to have issued no notices or placed any in the press and kept no official record.[11] All that survives is an undated Royal Engineers map outlining "naval reserves" in blue and "military reserves," including the peninsula, in red.[12] However, the map was not signed by Moody, which was the accepted means of making it official. In other words, Moody used neither of the two accepted means—gazetting and map signing—that would formally have made the future Stanley Park a reserve, or so it seems from the surviving records.

Moody's second use of Douglas's land policy further confused the peninsula's status: he rewarded himself, his confidants and members of his regiment with large chunks of land around New Westminster and Burrard Inlet. Within two weeks of Douglas's pre-emption proclamation in January 1860, Moody ordered that 320 acres (128 hectares) of the future Vancouver, roughly Princess Avenue east to Clark Drive and Burrard Inlet south to False Creek, "be registered" in their absence to his former private secretary, Robert Burnaby, and to British Columbia Attorney General H.P.P. Crease. The remaining land abutting the peninsula was not to be "pre-empted, without reference to myself, as Chief Commissioner of Lands and Works." By the end of the year Moody was insisting that every land transaction on the mainland colony "pass through my own office."[13]

Moody's meddling became so notorious as to occasion fervent denunciations in the New Westminster press. He was accused of spending scarce public resources to build roads to his private holdings, which would eventually total 3,000 acres (1,200 hectares), and, more generally, of using "all the advantages which his office and situation afford him for his own special emolument." In April 1861 Moody was officially reprimanded by Governor Douglas for his subversion of both the reserve and pre-emption policies. Douglas ordered that "all spots of land now set apart as Government or Indian Reserves, are to be forthwith published in three different places in each District where there may be such Reserves, and also in the local newspapers … and His Excellency requests you will furnish him at your earliest convenience with a rough general map of the country, exhibiting the different Districts, and also, as near as may be, the land already alienated by the Government."[14]

In response, Moody sent Douglas a plan "of a few Reserves shewing the general manner in which they are laid out," but, despite assurances that "plans of other Reserves are in preparation," his letter books contain no additional correspondence on the subject.[15]

Nor do British government records relating to the colony of British Columbia contain any references to the peninsula being formally made a reserve.[16] The assumption that it must have been so proclaimed stems from Burnaby and Crease's needing to have their parcels surveyed so they could complete the ownership process while Moody still had charge of the Lands Office. By the early 1860s it was becoming clear that the Royal Engineers were too costly to be kept on, making it doubly important for Moody to clean up loose ends on behalf of his friends.

In early 1863 Moody dispatched Royal Engineers Lance Corporal George Turner to survey Crease's and Burnaby's properties and the adjoining naval and town reserves extending west to present-day Burrard Street, and to report any incursions. The instructions were relayed to Turner in a memo to "Captn. Parsons, R.E.," dated January 26.

> I wish Corporal Turner and Party to proceed by earliest opportunity to Burrard Inlet to Revise Posts of Govt. Reserve for [intended] town near Entrance [to Burrard Inlet], Do. Do. Naval Reserve and then to survey lands, property of R. Burnaby and H.P.P. Crease and from thence to lay out claims or survey lands 160 acres East, narrow side to shore point between such points and the Village which has been laid out "En bloc." In carrying out above the party is especially to mark on Plan and transmit the same as early as possible to me showing any clearances or huts or other "occupations" recently made by any parties.[17]

Survey complete, Crease and Burnaby purchased their 160-acre parcels on October 19, 1863.

Even though Turner's instructions began considerably east of the peninsula, he mapped its shoreline from the water as he travelled around it in March 1863. Along the northern edge where Burrard Inlet was at its narrowest, he noted a single "Indian house" on a verge later named Prospect Point. In his field notes Turner referred to the peninsula as a "military reserve." When later asked why he had done so, Turner responded, "I had no authority at all ... I must have had instructions." Harking back to Moody's determination to protect the flank of New Westminster during the San Juan excitement four years earlier, Turner explained that "this land was reserved for military purposes long before that; it was already a Military Reserve when I made that survey."[18]

Shortly after Moody departed in November 1863, Governor Douglas tried to sort through the mess he had left. He queried the acting land commissioner about publishing the notices required to make reserves official and was informed that "no record has been preserved in this Department of the formation of those reserves."[19]

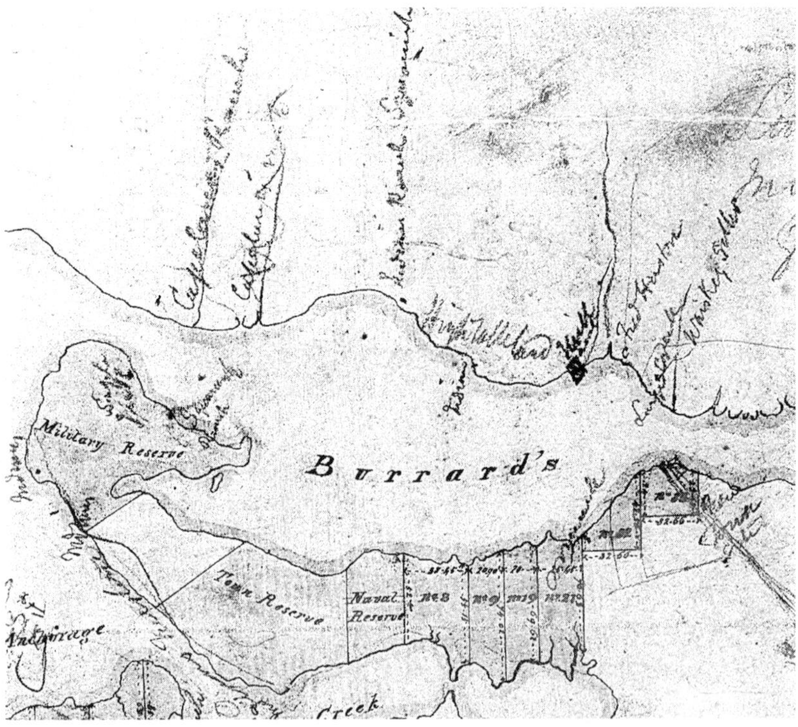

In August 1863, while passing through Burrard Inlet by water, Crease annotated a map of Burrard Inlet, made after the Royal Engineers survey earlier that year. He penciled in "Indians" at Staitwouk, "Suple Jack" at Chaythoos and "Squamish Ranch" at Whoi Whoi. On the north shore he wrote "Capilano Ranch," "Indian Ranch (Squamish)" and "Indians" west of the square indicating Moodyville Mill. BC Archives, CM/A1071

The same year, in August 1863, Attorney General Crease visited Burrard Inlet in connection with the opening of its first sawmill, constructed on the north shore. While passing through the inlet by water, Crease annotated a map drawn from Turner's field notes of his and Burnaby's holdings, which named the peninsula as a "Military Reserve" consistent with the verbal instructions Turner received. To the east of the tongue of land the map recorded unmarked land, "Town Reserve," "Naval Reserve" and then Burnaby's and Crease's property.

Crease was more attentive than Turner had been to the Aboriginal presence on the peninsula. At the location near Prospect Point where Turner noted "Indian house," Crease wrote in "Suple Jack." About a kilometre farther east, at the site of Whoi Whoi, Crease pencilled in "Squamish Ranch."[20] Newcomers typically referred to an Aboriginal settlement as a "ranch" or "rancherie." Along the peninsula's west coast extending north from Staitwouk, Crease wrote "Indians."

The "Suple Jack" whom Crease recorded as living on the peninsula was the father of August Jack Khahtsahlano, with whom Major Matthews conversed for over two decades, 1932–54. Supple Jack had already been there for some time. In 1859 Moody's private secretary Robert Burnaby, who was Crease's landholding partner and possibly his source of information about Supple Jack, had written to his brother:

> [We] were soon fairly into Burrards Inlet coasting along the Southern shore [of Burrard Inlet], which is sandy and covered with pine trees; every here and there an Indian hut or two is dotted on the Beach. Here the Squamish and other tribes come to fish during the season, lay up stores of salted and dried fish to last through the winter and then return into the rocky inland regions. We landed near one camp to feed, bought some fish and ate in the presence of a crowd of natives ... We were visited by an Indian named Supple Jack, who used occasionally to come with messages from the [Royal Navy ship] "Plumper," he was anxious to accompany us, but as he belonged to another tribe [than the Indians paddling our canoes], and was noted for his partiality to whiskey, we managed to convince him, after hard feeding, that we could get on without him.[21]

August Jack, born in about 1880, described to Major Matthews how his father, Supple Jack, and his grandfather, Chief Khahtsahlano, had lit on the tongue of land.[22] They were attracted by a high bank, a *chaythoos* in the Squamish language, about a kilometre west of Whoi Whoi near today's Prospect Point. Initially Khahtsahlano migrated to Chaythoos on a seasonal basis, but over time the family apparently settled down. In the 1930s, August Jack described their life on the peninsula to Major Matthews:

> Supple Jack was living at Chaythoos long before the Hastings Sawmill come [in 1865], and Chief Khahtsahlano lived there long before him. Chief Khahtsahlano at Chaythoos first; he came there because there's lots cedar there, and he makes canoes.
>
> Khahtsahlano and his brother Chip-kaay-am came down from [the] Squamish [River running south into Howe Sound]. He did not give up his position as chief at Toot-taak-mek. They simply moved back and forth, dried some smelts, salmon, clams, berries, and when the winter came on went back to Squamish.
>
> I do not know when it was that Khahtsahlano first settled at Chaythoos, or when his brother Chip-kaay-am settled at Snauq [False Creek, or Kitsilano, south of the peninsula], but they were both young men when they settled. Chip-kaay-am was the first man to settle and build a village at Snauq. He

> was known as Chief George by the whitemen and lived at Snauq all the time except when they were up the Squamish in the summer time drying salmon.
>
> [Khahtsahlano] died and was buried at Chaythoos. His house was close to a little creek at Chaythoos. I must have been about three years when he died.
>
> My father was Khaytulk or "Supple Jack." He had two houses, one at Snauq and one at Chaythoos. We moved from one to the other, from Kitsilano to Stanley Park and then back again as it suited us.[23]

The search for coal, the gold rush and the Royal Engineers' activity drew newcomers' attention to the peninsula, but did not much affect Aboriginal people's ways of life. Shortly thereafter, another development did so: British Columbia's high-quality timber was discovered by countries around the world. Burrard Inlet was surrounded by prime stands of cedar, fir and spruce, which were close to open water and therefore easy to transport to faraway markets. Sawmills operated at New Westminster and, from 1863, on the north shore of Burrard Inlet at Moodyville, named after an early mill owner. Another location that came under consideration for a sawmill was the future Stanley Park.

Shortly after Douglas's retirement as governor in 1864, a local entrepreneur applied to purchase 100 acres (40 hectares) of the peninsula. Edward Stamp acted on behalf of an English company

Victoria photographer Richard Maynard took this image of Moodyville in May 1872. BC Archives, B-0276837

among whose instigators and directors were both Colonel Richard Moody's former private secretary Robert Burnaby and Moody himself. Still hoping to be named "the govr," Moody dreamt of "living in B.C. as a Country Gentleman" on his far-flung landholdings. Moody had no concerns whatsoever about dismembering the tongue of land he once considered essential to defend New Westminster. "B.C. interests will be watched," he confided to Attorney General Crease about the new venture, but "of course, our object is to make money and no local feeling I think will sway the main point." As far as Moody was concerned, the peninsula was for the taking. Stamp, as company manager, made the request to purchase the Brockton Point area "at the customary price of $1.00 per acre," "to cut timber on reserves at Burrard's Inlet" and to have "the right of way for fresh water from the [Beaver] lake on the Reserve to the sawmill" in May 1865.[24]

British Columbia colonial officials responded enthusiastically. The only proviso made by the new commissioner of lands and works, Joseph Trutch, was that the province retain "the spot selected by Col. Moody for a Fort."[25] The rest of the peninsula was treated as if it were Crown land.

But there was a wrinkle. The government surveyor discovered that the property Stamp sought extended into the "Indian village" of Whoi Whoi and to nearby Chaythoos. He wrote to the Colonial Secretary in June 1865:

> In accordance with your orders of the 31st of May, I proceeded to Burrard Inlet arriving there at 3 p.m. and marking out Captain Stamp's Mill the same evening (June 1st). On referring to the sketch appended it will be seen that the N.W. corner [of the requested 100 acres] occurs in the centre of an Indian village to clear which would only give the sawmill about 90 acres. By the appearance of the soil and debris this camping ground is one of the oldest in the inlet. The resident Indians seemed very distrustful of my purpose, and suspicious of encroachment on their premises.[26]

Aboriginal people had every reason to be skeptical. In a follow-up report sent by the surveyor a few days later, the people he had described in his first dispatch as occupying one of the oldest sites in the inlet were transformed into trespassers. "I have the honour to state that a Squamish Indian called Supple Jack has squatted for the last three years on the land in question. There are two male relatives now living near him. Capt Stamp has no objection to their remaining where they are. They can at any time be removed, the ground does not belong to their tribe."[27]

In the end the project came to naught, but for other reasons than the peninsula being a reserve or the Aboriginal presence. Stamp changed his mind because of the strong tidal flows in the area and relocated the mill farther east on the naval reserve, at the foot of the future Dunlevy Street. Once again, when it came to the government's friends, land that had supposedly been "reserved" was up for grabs. In November 1865 the company backed by Moody and fronted by Stamp was given a Crown grant to 243 acres (97 hectares) out of what was now termed "the old Government Reserve."[28]

Hastings Mill began operating later in 1865, giving rise to the first sustained incursion of newcomers along the southern shore of Burrard Inlet. As did its counterparts on the north shore and at New Westminster, the mill spawned makeshift services for employees. A small settlement grew up to the west on the remaining town reserve, known officially as Granville, informally as Gastown. The Methodists were among the first newcomers to preach there, not just to other immigrants but also to the Aboriginal people living on the peninsula. Cornelius Bryant recalled:

> Sunday, July 17th, 1870, … Our first congregation … was wholly composed of Indians, who then, and for some future years, resided on the shore of the Narrows, a little to the west of Brockton Point and on the site of the present Stanley Park. These Indians had been visited by Bro. [missionary Thomas] Crosby and some of them had been savingly led to Christ and a class formed under a native leader … After my introduction at Moodyville, a deputation of Indians came in canoe [from the peninsula] and conveyed me to their camp at the Narrows [likely Chaythoos], where they expected me to preach. Although the hour was late, I did so to a full house through an interpreter; I had a time

> of gracious liberty as I knew the Word was being received with gladness, and wound up with an old-time fellowship meeting punctuated with amens and hallelujahs in the Squamish vernacular.[29]

Some time later, a Squamish man named Que-yah-chulk or Kwe áh jilk, also known as Dick Isaacs, who then lived at Whoi Whoi, described the first church, built in Gastown at the foot of today's Abbott Street: "I remember old Indian Church over Gastown quite well. Little bit of place on shore … Lots Indians go there from Whoi-Whoi. Big settlement Indians Whoi-Whoi."[30]

Early recollections point up not only the prominence of Aboriginal people around Burrard Inlet, but the physicality of Whoi Whoi and nearby Chaythoos. Charles Tate, an itinerant Methodist missionary, told Major Matthews in 1932: "As a side trip, I frequently took a rowboat or canoe to the First Narrows to visit a small band living in Stanley Park where the Lumberman's Arch now stands. Chief Thomas, of the Squamish tribe, lived there … The Indians did not live in separate homes, but in one long community house."[31]

Men from Whoi Whoi and Chaythoos worked at Hastings Mill alongside other Aboriginal men, some of whom established a "rancherie" adjacent to the mill, only to discover that they were not wanted there when the new manager arrived at the beginning of 1869. According to Major Matthews, "they feared squatters, the establishment of rights, and would not tolerate occupancy for scarcely a day."[32] Under English common law, occupants of land acquired ownership rights over title holders if those occupants were not removed within specified periods of time. The concept of adverse possession, also termed squatters' rights, put the onus on owners to keep others off their property.

Whoi Whoi or Chaythoos was one alternative for dispossessed Aboriginal workers and their families; another was Ustlawn, a short canoe trip away on the north shore of Burrard Inlet. Aboriginal people had long used the site on a seasonal basis and, increasingly, were staying longer. In 1863 Attorney General Crease, on his map of Burrard Inlet, dubbed the north shore settlement "Indian Ranch (Squamish)."[33]

Ustlawn grew in prominence as a Squamish enclave after Hastings Mill refused to allow an Oblate priest, Leon Fouquet, who had been missionizing around Burrard Inlet since 1860, to construct a Catholic church nearby. The mill considered the south shore a Protestant enclave. In the Catholic version of the story, the priest was invited to Ustlawn at the behest of a chief "determined to save his people from annihilation" caused by newcomers' vices of alcohol and prostitution. More likely, the Squamish accepted Christianity in exchange for the Oblates' support in resisting the newcomers, who were increasingly determined to usurp their land and resources. Father Fouquet built a small church at Ustlawn in 1866 and a larger one several years later.

Ustlawn's status was initially unclear. Everyone agreed that Aboriginal people required protection on small reserves of land, which—conveniently—freed up the remainder to newcomers. In 1869 colonial authorities set aside Ustlawn for the Squamish as Mission Indian Reserve Number One. Also surveyed for the Squamish at the same time were the Aboriginal village of Homulcheson at the mouth of the Capilano Creek to the west, which Crease had called "Capilano Ranch," and the Seymour Creek and Burrard reserves farther east.

In 1871 the colony of British Columbia, with which Vancouver Island had been joined in 1866, was enticed into the new Canadian Confederation with the promise of a transcontinental railway. The British North America Act of 1867, to which British Columbia adhered, defined landholding with some specificity. The Act stated in Section 109 that all lands belonging to a province at the time of union should continue to belong to it. According to Section 117, provinces "shall retain all their respective Public Property not otherwise disposed of in this Act, subject to the Right of Canada to assume any Lands or Public Property required for Fortifications or for the Defence of the Country."

In order to determine which properties belonged to the new province, the British Columbia legislature ordered a "Return of Government Reserves," which was compiled in January 1873. The man who had just been appointed commissioner of lands and works did not want to be caught out and so enumerated as many sites as were marked on any of the various maps lying around the Lands Office. He turned up 13 in the Westminster District, including a "military reserve" of 950 acres (380 hectares) "south of First Narrows, Burrard Inlet," about which no other information was given.[34] All of these reserves, military or otherwise, were thereafter treated as Crown land belonging to the province. The understanding was that "as British Columbia had no armories, drill sheds, etc., none of the so-called 'military reserves' had passed to the Dominion" under the terms of Section 117 of the British North America Act.[35] Consistent with this view, a Victoria resident who in 1875 sought "to preempt 160 acres of land" on the peninsula was informed in a private conversation with the commissioner that "several persons had asked for sections of land in this Reserve," and that "if this land was to be disposed of it would be sold at public auction."[36]

Having sorted out "Government Reserves," or so it thought, the province turned its attention to Indian reserves. In 1876, provincial and Dominion authorities established a Joint Indian Reserve Commission to confirm permanent sites for Aboriginal people. Supple Jack, identified as chief of the "Govt Reserve," was one of the people invited to a meeting between the commission and Squamish leaders in November 1876. A commissioner wrote in his diary:

> Monday 13th [November 1876]. Raining all day. Forenoon Mr. [George] Blenkinsop [of the commission] was occupied in collecting the Chiefs of the several [Squamish] villages, using the little steamboat (the "Leonora") for the purpose. Met them in the afternoon. Five of them spoke, after a few words had been addressed to them by the Commissioners—viz:

Joseph of the R.C. Mission village	
Lâ-lâh (son of the late Kapilâno)	Kapilano Creek
Big George	Seymour Creek
Supple-Jack	Govt. Reserve
Slae-Kwul-tuch	Upper [Burrard] Reserve

> After a few re-assuring words, the Inds. were informed that tomorrow the Commrs would visit the several villages in succession, and endeavour to satisfy all reasonable demands ... Her [Queen Victoria's] instructions to us

were that, while doing all in our power to promise the interests of the Inds., the rights of the white settlers should be protected, and the general interest of the Province, in which all must equally participate, be duly regarded.[37]

During their visits, the commissioners counted Aboriginal people. With one exception—Musqueam on the Fraser River—all of the locations around Burrard Inlet were named as Squamish, including Snauq, or Kitsilano. Only the Mission site had a larger population than did the "Govt. Reserve."

Census of Aboriginal people

Taken by British Columbia Reserve Commission, November 1876[38]

	Men	Women	Child	Total	Horses	Cows	Fowl
Musqueam people							
Musqueam Reserve	25	32	39	96	9	31	130
Squamish people							
False Creek [Snauq, Kitsilano]	15	15	12	42	2	0	37
"Govt Reserve"	17	14	19	50	2	7	151
Mission Reserve	41	40	42	123	4	9	100
Capilano Reserve	13	14	14	41	0	4	11
Seymour Creek Reserve	9	8	5	22	0	0	52
Burrard Reserve	13	12	14	39	0	0	105

Everyone was counted, including animals, but only heads of households—virtually all men—were named. Aboriginal surnames were written out as the enumerators heard them, and any Christian first names added. All 50 people living on the peninsula were counted.

Census of Govt Reserve
Taken by British Columbia Reserve Commission, November 1876[39]

Head of Household	Men	Women	Youth	Children	Remarks
Lower Govt Reserve [Chaythoos]					
Kaítluk Supple Jack	1	1	1F	2F	Chief
Govt Reserve Upper [Whoi Whoi]					
Hahlch láh nuk Father old man	1	1			
Ke oólse Peter	1	1		1F	
Skáh luk father	1	1		1M, 1F	
Tum kain Johnny son	1	1			
Tsáh kwilk Charlie	1	1		1F	
sister a widow		1		1M	
Paýlk old man	1				
Se oál chin Charlie	1	1		1M	
Se kwe towts in	1	1	1F		
Kwí oots Thomas	1	1	2M	2M	has for wife widow & 2 children
Chém chuk	1	1		2F	
Kwe áh jilk	1				
Tchén ilthl	1	1		1F	
Se áh milth	1	1		1M, 1F	
Ka náme itch un father	1	1			
Joseph	1				
Kwán itz Thomas	1				
Two brothers of Se kwe towts in working at the Mill					

The census of the future Stanley Park placed Supple Jack, his wife Qwhaywat and three children on the Lower Government Reserve, which his family knew as Chaythoos. Everyone else resided on the Upper Government Reserve, or Whoi Whoi, including Supple Jack's father Hahlch láh nuk, or Khahtsahlano, and his brothers Peter Ke oólse and Skáh luk, with their families. Skáh luk's son Johnny Tum kain headed his own household, probably next door. Chief Khahtsahlano's extended family accounted for almost a third of the households and residents. Also living at Whoi Whoi were siblings Chém chuk and Kwe áh jilk, the second of whom Major Matthews knew by his English name, Dick Isaacs.

The reserve commissioners wanted Aboriginal people to settle down, which is why they assessed housing and counted domesticated animals. The comment on the Government Reserve census ran: "These Indians have squatted on the Govt. Reserve between Coal Harbor and the First Narrows. They have several small cottages but have made little improvement otherwise." Only the Mission Reserve or Ustlawn came in for general approval: "The Mission town as it is called by the tribe is laid out in 2 streets on a patch of open land about 2 acres in extent, the Catholic Church occupying a prominent place in the centre." The houses "have a pleasing appearance when viewed from the sea," being "of the cottage style, white washed and kept cleaner within than is usual with most Indians."

The commission's most important task was to confirm reserves. All of the sites where the Squamish and Musqueam were enumerated were marked out—excepting Supple Jack and the 49 others residing on the peninsula. They posed a dilemma. The Squamish were useful to newcomers' pursuits, so it was strategic to secure permanent residence for them nearby. A commissioner noted in his diary:

> The Indians here are a well behaved industrious tribe. I am told by Mr Nelson of the Moody & Co Mills that the Indians receive annually for labour, Game, Fish &c over 7500 dollars from the two mills and the shipping. That they have become very expert as mill hands loading ships &c &c. that he finds them better than most white men. That it would not only be a great injury to the Indians but a great loss to the white man were they placed on larger reserves [at a distance].[40]

Another commissioner was similarly struck by Aboriginal enterprise:

> At the present time, the Indians of Burrard's Inlet are well clad in the ordinary dress of the whites, and are apparently well fed. Many of them use pocket handkerchiefs … Most of the women whom we saw were comfortably dressed …
>
> Many of the Indians are excellent workmen. They are employed in loading vessels and in general work about the sawmills. Several of them work inside the mills. They receive from 75 cents a day with food and lodging to $1 1/4 or $1 1/2 a day without food or lodging. A ready market exists at the mills for whatever fish and game the Indians bring in. They are evidently a useful portion of the general population. The white settlers say that, with a few exceptions, they are good neighbors … They wished to be permitted to enjoy, in common with the white people, the right of moving about freely and seeking employment or occupation where they pleased … The Indians are a part, and wish to remain a part, of the general population.[41]

The commissioner appointed by the provincial government set out in his diary the dilemma over Whoi Whoi and nearby Chaythoos. He described his discussions with Supple Jack, in which he acknowledged that the commission could not act on its own. No questions existed in his mind, or that of the provincial government, that it had charge of the "Govt. Reserve," as confirmed by its placement on the list of "Public Property" compiled three years earlier. His entries reflect the considerable extent to which the commissioners heard what they wanted to hear.

> Thursday 16 [November 1876]. Steamed up about ___ [blanks are in original] oclock crossed the Inlet to a village headed by Supple Jack ___ Indian name for ___. It appears these Indians took up their abode on this place (a clearing made by Captn Stamp) after the land was laid out as a Govt reserve. I telegraphed to Mr. [Forbes G.] Vernon [provincial commissioner of lands and works] but the line being down could get no answer. My object in sending the Telegram was to ask Mr Vernon if the Prov Government would allow us to lay off a small reserve at this place.
>
> Friday 17 … I lectured Supple Jack. Told him he was wrong in squatting

> on the Govt Reserve knowing it to be such when he did so. He admitted his knowledge of the fact but said White men had done the same thing and he hoped the Prov Govt would allow him the site of his village and enclosures. This would not exceed from six to eight acres. I explained that I telegraphed to Mr Vernon and that owing to the wire being down was unable to obtain an answer consequently that we could not give him papers for that particular place ... We also told him that if Mr Vernon would consent to his having the place he desired we would run in [on the steamboat] before going to Comox [on Vancouver Island] and lay it off for him and give him papers. On this we parted with Supple Jack. He apparently very well satisfied and this closed the business of the Commission on Burrards Inlet.
>
> [I also told Supple Jack] he had a full right to settle with the rest of his tribe on the reserves already made. That if there was any place on the Inlet not taken by whites which he considered a suitable place to let us know and that we would secure it for him. I assured him he would not be made to remove in a hurry. That the Government might allow him to stay there for years but for his own good I recommended him to go on land which he and his family could call their own for ever.[42]

The reserve commissioner's fears were borne out. The commissioner of lands and works responded negatively. The Reserve Commission thereupon "declined to permit Indian reserves on the Government Reserve between Coal Harbour and First Narrows, Burrard's Inlet."[43]

For the time being, under Supple Jack's leadership, the Squamish remained at Chaythoos and also at nearby Whoi Whoi. All the same, by August Jack's birth in about 1880, times were changing. His parents Supple Jack and Qwhaywat took no chances: they had him baptized into the Catholic Church. August Jack's much older sister Louisa was resourceful in another way. A couple of years earlier she had married a white man, John Burns, who built them a small house near Chaythoos. The couple logged for a living and had two daughters: Maggie, born in about 1880, and Addie two years later.

August Jack Khahtsahlano spoke at length with Major Matthews about his childhood.

Our house beside a little creek at Chaythoos … near beach. Close by our house, little garden just beside it, on west side. Oh, little garden, just clear space before whiteman came. I never see, but I think they have it ready like, then when the whitemans came Indians just put in potatoes, turnips. We used ducks, deer, fish, clams, anything that going around that's good to eat for Squamish people; no beef, no pig.

The Royal Engineers, 1859–1863, gave Khaytulk [Supple Jack], my father, for services rendered to them by him [while surveying], a cow, and afterwards he bought a bull. The bull's name was "Chulwalsh." On being called "Chulwalsh, Chulwalsh, Chulwalsh," the bull would come quietly; he came out of the trees to be fed.

We had 12 cows running around, and 8 pigs. [We sold cattle] to the logging camp; dead, not alive. Father used to shoot the steers, then butcher them, and send them to the logging camps. [As for the pigs] the same; kill them and sell the meat, or salt them down and make corned pork. No sheep; had enough trouble with cows and horses.

When we had them cows, we bought our horses; two of them; they had one horse use it for racing New Westminster on Dominion Day. The horses always used to have a big time on Queen's Day; race in Victoria, Westminster; Supple Jack, my father, made lots of money winning race.

We kept the horses and cows in the stable at Chaythoos, and when we wanted to ride to town there was a trail, and we had to ride right around the head of what is now Lost Lagoon; around by Second Beach; there was no bridge; there was a trail through the forest from Chaythoos to Gastown.[44]

In about 1883 Supple Jack was killed in an accident, and, like many Aboriginal people, he was buried above ground.

My mother [Qwhaywat] told me that he, my father, was sick one month and a half and he died. He got hit on the head, kicked by a cow. He had twelve cows and he was milking a cow, and the cow gave him a kick and he bumped on the wall of the stall.

They put his body in a little house of glass with red blankets on top; the way they used to do—they don't do it now—and buried him there at Chaythoos. The house [where we lived] was covered with cedar shake shingles, hand split.

And the grave where my father was buried, it had a cedar shake roof, too. And it was on cedar posts. It was about ten feet long, and about six feet wide, and lots of room inside for a coffin. And there were glass windows all around. The coffin was covered with a red blanket.[45]

August Jack's family supported themselves by gathering food and trading with the newcomers.

One day, when I little boy, with my brother, we been fish-raking in Coal Harbor, got lots herring in canoe, when we go by Brockton Point, tide tip canoe, turn over, lose fish. I hung on canoe hard, we get back again, go back Coal Harbor fish rake more herring, but not so many. My mother dry them, when we get home to Chaythoos my mother dry them on sticks, hot sun, put them in sacks; keep for winter.

Mother milked the six cows in the morning—the other six were dry—and put the milk in big high milk cans—about five gallons—and took it to Hastings Mill in the canoe. [My sister] Agnes milked the cows in the evening when mother was away, and next day it went with the morning's milk to Hastings Mill. Mother took the milk every morning, but I don't know how much she got for it. Louisa, my sister, made the butter.

I had no schooling, cannot read or write. I wish I could but Mother was [left] a widow and I had to look after her.[46]

Nearby Whoi Whoi also remained occupied: August Jack recalled that 11 families lived there in the early 1880s.

You know the Lumberman's Arch [Whoi Whoi] in Stanley Park. Well, the big house was about 200 feet long, and 60 feet wide....That was the "real" pow-wow house. The name of it was Stah-hay; no meaning; just name, and six families lived in it.

Then, to the west of it, was a smaller house, about 30 feet front and 16 feet deep with a sort of little kitchen at the back; I think two families lived in it. Then to the west again was a smaller house, about 24 by 16 feet deep; one family lived in that, and on the extreme west was another pow-wow house—it was measured once—and I think the measurement was 94 feet front by about 40 feet deep; the front was about 20 feet high; the back was

> about 12 feet. Here two families lived. All these houses stood in a row above the beach, facing the water; all were of cedar slabs and big posts; all built by the Indians long ago.[47]

Aboriginal people used other sites around the peninsula as well. August Jack recalled some of them in talking to Major Matthews: "They hold potlatches [gift givings] at Staitwouk [Second Beach]; Qual-kin give that potlatch, and there was another potlatch, a great big one, at A-yul-shun [English Bay beach]. My grandfather, Chief Khahtsahlano, he give one potlatch at Chay-thoos, and after that another one at Whoi-Whoi."[48]

The peninsula was also used as a graveyard. Elizabeth Silvey Walker, a woman born in the mid-1860s to a Portuguese father and Aboriginal mother, remembered practices during her childhood:

Mission Reserve was well established by the time Vancouver came into being in 1886 as the western terminus of the new transcontinental railway.
Norman Caple photo, City of Vancouver Archives, SGN 1460

> There was a lot of Indian graves all along the First Narrows. They did not bury their dead; they put them on the ground, with the blankets, and put a shelter over them; just slabs of wood, no floor, two slabs leaning one against the other to cover the body; ... And some of the little houses had windows of glass in them, but that was only the chiefs, or some "high" Indian, but the others they just laid them on the ground with their blankets and things and put the shelter over them.[49]

The Aboriginal presence on the peninsula was considerable on the eve of the imposition of Stanley Park in 1887. Whatever may have been the land's official status, Aboriginal people still considered it their own. For some, including August Jack and his family, it was a place of residence. For others, it served economic and spiritual purposes. Aboriginal people had been caught up in incredible changes, but the force of colonialism had not squelched their will.

In 1939 August Jack Khahtsahlano drew Whoi Whoi and Chaythoos as they existed, or as he imagined them existing, about the time the Reserve Commission visited there. City of Vancouver Archives, Add. Ms. 54, Stanley Park file

CHAPTER 2

Kanaka Ranch

A young man of 18, William Nahanee posed proudly in about 1890 at the centre of a group of longshoremen on the dock of the Moodyville mill. The photograph reveals the full extent to which longshoring work crossed racial boundaries. Aboriginal men worked alongside Hawaiians and other newcomers in an occupation grounded more in physical strength and camaraderie than in skin colour. Courtesy Laurie Nahanee Cole

August Jack Khahtsahlano's account of his childhood on the peninsula is a story of accommodation to the changes wrought by colonialism. This same ability to respond to circumstances was evident at Kanaka Ranch, a settlement on the south shore of Coal Harbour at the foot of present-day Denman Street, just outside Stanley Park's boundaries.

Kanaka, which was the common term for indigenous Hawaiians, means "person" in the Hawaiian language. The Hawaiians are generally, to adapt Captain James Cook's description of the late 18th century, "well made" with brown eyes, a skin colour varying from light olive to darker shades and wavy, "brownish black" hair.[1] Most of the approximately four hundred Hawaiian men recruited by the Hudson's Bay Company for the fur trade returned home, but others stayed on. Some farmed near their former places of employment or on one of the coastal islands; others headed to the sawmills sprouting up around Burrard Inlet.

Among the men employed at Hastings Mill were Eihu, Nahanee, Keamo and Nahu, who, like most indigenous Hawaiians, each went by a single name. They were illiterate in English, so their names were spoken by others as they were heard and, as with Aboriginal names, got written down in many forms. Some men tacked on a European first name for convenience. Nahanee sometimes styled himself Joe Nahanee, Keamo became James Keamo, and so on.

The mill treated the Hawaiians much as it did Aboriginal workers; hence the second word in Kanaka Ranch. Hawaiians were highly sought after as employees because of their reputation from the fur trade as tough and dependable; it was when the men tried to secure accommodation near the mill that they were not wanted. The granddaughter of one of them described for Major Matthews how "Mr. Eihu, my grandfather, came to Burrard Inlet to work for the Hastings Sawmill." Her "grandfather and grandmother had lots of pigs and chickens, and that was why they had to leave the sawmill because old Capt. Raymur [the manager] did not like the pigs and chickens running all over 'the spit,' you know what I mean, over the sawdust."[2]

The stories that have come down through time—almost wholly oral testimony—speak to the tenacity of the Hawaiians in finding an alternative site when they and the Aboriginal workers were dispossessed in 1869. The Hawaiians did not have the options of Whoi Whoi or the Mission Reserve, but they did have their wits about them.

In searching out a place of residence close enough to Hastings Mill to commute to work, men found that their choices were limited. Governor James Douglas's pre-emption proclamation in 1860 caused a number of Hawaiians to transfer their loyalties in hopes of acquiring land, but property around Burrard Inlet was virtually impossible to get. Colonel Moody had assisted his cronies in acquiring large tracts, and in late 1862 he had arranged, contrary to regulations, for the large parcel located between the peninsula and the town reserve to be treated as a single pre-emption. The land lying between Stanley Park and today's Burrard Street was acquired later that year for purposes of speculation by three young white men: John Morton, Sam Brighouse and William Hailstone.

Eihu may have been the first of the Hawaiians working at Hastings Mill to be attracted to the large Morton, Brighouse and Hailstone tract abutting Coal Harbour. In 1869 he set down on three acres (1.2 hectares). Lying just across the water from the peninsula, the plot extended about 200 feet (60 metres) on each side of today's Denman Street between the water and the future Georgia Street. Coal Harbour's namesake deposits, while not good enough to be mined commercially, offered a useful second income: people made charcoal and sold it to the mill.

Eihu's granddaughter Minnie explained to Major Matthews the circumstances of taking up the parcel: "So they went down to Coal Harbor; down on [the later] Georgia Street, and pre-empted three acres, but the reason they went there to that particular spot, they told me, was because of a little creek there; it certainly was a pretty place with a big beach of pebbles; of course when they started cutting trees, roots and branches drifted in and spoiled it, and the creek dried up, and then my grandfather made charcoal for the blacksmith shop at the Hastings Sawmill; he had great big charcoal pits."[3]

Minnie was particularly proud of Eihu's literacy in Hawaiian, possibly also in English, a feat equalled by few of his contemporaries. She was quite comfortable with Matthews by the time of her fourth visit with him in April 1937, and she brought along a large Bible in the Hawaiian language, printed in 1872, that she claimed had belonged to her grandfather. This volume still resides in the City of Vancouver Archives, sadly lacking its first pages containing genealogy. According to family lore, these leaves were torn out by mischievous great-grandchildren.[4]

Eihu's granddaughter Minnie shared with Major Matthews many of the family stories that had come down to her. She well understood the important legacy that she had acquired by virtue of her childhood and youth on Kanaka Ranch. Courtesy Mabel McPhee

Eihu was keen to settle down with his Squamish wife, Mary See-em-ia, and daughter, Minnie's mother Margaret, born in about 1856. In 1871, two years after lighting on Kanaka Ranch, Eihu took out British naturalization papers in New Westminster, probably because he intended to pre-empt the site where he was living. It seems unlikely Eihu was aware that the land to which he brought his family had already been taken up by Morton and the others. There were very few, if any, signs of possession. What is certain is that Kanaka Ranch suited Eihu's purposes: from there he could go to work at Hastings Mill by water or land.

William Nahanee ensured his family's stories would survive by sharing them with Major Matthews. The two likely came in contact when Nahanee was recognized in 1941 for having been a coal passer on the Hudson's Bay Company steamer Beaver, *wrecked off Prospect Point in 1888.* BC Archives, CM1A1071

Joe Nahanee was another early settler at Kanaka Ranch. Much of what we know about him comes from his son William, who, like Eihu's granddaughter Minnie, took pride in the family stories he picked up during his childhood. He described how, after leaving the fur trade, Nahanee "came up to the Hastings Mill, and went to work firing the boiler room," and "then he took up a place down in Coal Harbour, at what was called the Kanaka Ranch."[5]

Another of the Hawaiians at Kanaka Ranch was James Keamo. According to stories passed down through his son Walter, he was a man of adventure who made his own way to the Pacific Northwest. "He came up here on a sailing ship," Walter told Major Matthews in 1952. "He just came for the trip, and stayed here."[6] Keamo was fishing at New Westminster at the time he got married at the Methodist mission there in 1876. He was in his mid-30s and keen to settle down with his bride, Anne Nelson, the 15-year-old daughter of a Fraser Valley farmer of Scots descent who hailed from New Brunswick. Like her husband, she had a Hawaiian connection: her maternal grandfather was Piopio, a fur-trade employee who in 1824 had helped search out a site for a new fur-trading post on the Fraser River. Piopio was employed at Fort Langley from its beginnings in 1827 through mid-century. Annie Nelson's maternal grandmother was a Kwantlen woman.

Another possible early resident at Kanaka Ranch was a man called Nahu. Like Eihu, he is said to have worked for the Hudson's Bay Company at Fort Langley. In about 1865 he and a woman whom their grandson recalled as "half Hawaiian and half Indian" had a son named Leon.[7] Some time later, some members of the Nahu family made their way to Burrard Inlet and perhaps to Kanaka Ranch. Although Leon's parents disappear from view, a child who spoke to Major Matthews vividly recalled Leon as her classmate in the little school that opened at Hastings Mill in 1873.

> In April 1873 we reached the Hastings Sawmill. I was then a child of nine … Father supervised loading ships.
>
> The first school children I recall included Ada, Carrie and Fred Miller, the constable's children; Dick Alexander, son of H.A. Alexander, mgr. of the mill;

The wedding of James Keamo and Anne Nelson in 1876 was celebrated with all the proprieties of the time, including a formal portrait. Courtesy Keamo family

> Albie, Beckie, Alice (myself) and Addie Patterson; the rest were half breeds or Indians …
>
> On the 10th May 1873 my sister Addie had a birthday party; I was nine. It was held in the school house. All school children, including Kanakas, were invited … The prize [in the first game] was money, which was won by Leon Nahu, a very fine Kanaka boy, the family are still residents of [North] Vancouver. [8]

Kanaka Ranch was located just across the water from Brockton Point, and the Hawaiians made use of its resources. A woman who was a child there during the early 1870s described how "there were a lot of Kanakas about, not just one or two, and they would talk in their language; it was queer to hear them, and they would go out where the lighthouse is at [the tip of] Brockton Point and fish with a line." According to a contemporary, writing in 1876, the Hawaiians worked hard to clear land around Brockton Point, perhaps for a garden. They had done such a good job, he considered that "they should be allowed to purchase their plot out of the reserve ... It would be but justice to let them have the place on favourable terms."[9]

Family life at Kanaka Ranch was complex. Joe Nahanee and Eihu both had children with Mary See-em-ia. Lucy Nahanee may have been born as early as 1866, before the Hawaiians got to Kanaka Ranch; her younger brother William arrived in about 1872. Mary See-em-ia's Nahanee descendants, who have tracked her origins with some precision, say that Mary's mother was a sister of Lâ-lâh, or Lawa, the chief at Capilano Creek whom the Reserve Commission encountered in 1876, making her a granddaughter of Chief Capilano. Mary's mother descended from chiefs at Nicomen in the Fraser Valley and Whidbey Island in the present Washington state. Within this context, the decision to settle at Kanaka Ranch might be viewed as Mary See-em-ia's return to ancestral land belonging to her people. Perhaps it was she who encouraged the Hawaiian fathers of her children to settle there. Fred Alexander, a son of the Hastings Mill manager, recalled that "one man used to come up to the mill store to buy groceries and things for one set of children, and the other came and bought for the other set; just how they arranged it I don't know."[10]

Mary See-em-ia's son William Nahanee described to Major Matthews a quite ordinary childhood, even though his father died not long after his birth.

> When I remember first there were six or seven Kanakas [at Kanaka Ranch on Coal Harbour]; there were two families there. One family was Keamo and the other my mother and father, Nahanee. There was nothing along there except nothing; just rocks and boulders on the beach ... just a little boat wharf on piles; about four piles, usual size; just enough to tie up a row boat.
>
> Coal Harbour is named because of coal; charcoal. My daddy made

charcoal, out of wood, and sold it to the sawmill. They wanted it for the blacksmith instead of ordinary coal; no ordinary coal about some time, so they used charcoal.

[My father] was pure Hawaiian. He had married my mother who came from Capilano (Homulcheson) reserve; my mother's [Indian] name was See-em-ia. Father died about two years after I was born, that is, about 1874, and he is buried on Deadman's Island [located] between Kanaka Ranch and Brockton Point. See-em-ia was the name they gave me when I went to the Hastings Sawmill School; William See-em-ia; Father was, of course, dead.

I had two sisters, Maggie, my sister, that is, half-sister, she is dead now; and the other sister was Lucy; she married, dead now. All older than me. Mary Eihu was my mother. Mother is buried in the Capilano Indian graveyard.[11]

Mary See-em-ia's granddaughter Minnie, born in 1877, spent much of her childhood at Kanaka Ranch. Minnie's mother was Mary's eldest child Margaret Eihu; her father, Benjamin McCord, was a gold miner. Maggie and Benjamin were married at the little Methodist church on the beach in Gastown and settled down at Kanaka Ranch with their three daughters, Minnie, Seraphine and Maud. Maud died as a baby and was buried at Brockton Point. Minnie remembered:

Years ago, when I was a little girl, my sister died, and I afterwards saw her lowered into the ground in that little graveyard [at Brockton Point]. My father made the little coffin.

My father made a small headstone, round at the top, painted white, and put a little picket fence around the grave, and others were nearby; we used to go sometimes and place flowers upon them. We used to go over there in a boat [from Kanaka Ranch]; it was quite a climb up the bank from the beach. Many of the pioneers of Burrard Inlet are buried there.

I can just remember her funeral. I was then about four years old, so it must have been 1881.[12]

Sometime after Maud's death, Maggie Eihu and Benjamin McCord went their separate ways. Maggie found herself a Scots longshoreman named Daniel McPhee, whom she also brought to Kanaka Ranch. She had two more children, first a daughter Irene and then a son Donald, who died young.

Because of Maggie's adventures, her two oldest daughters, Minnie and Seraphine, were raised mostly by their grandmother, Mary See-em-ia. In 1936 Minnie recalled vividly Kanaka Ranch during the late 1870s and early 1880s, particularly her grandmother's determination to create a home there for her extended family.

> Our buildings at Coal Harbor were not much; just a couple of small houses on the beach beside a creek. My grandmother planted apples from seed, and they grew into fine trees bearing such enormous apples; as big as saucers; and we had lots of berries; we certainly did have berries, raspberries, strawberries, blackberries, gooseberries ... I planted a cherry tree down on our property; it's there yet; planted it from seed; it's a beautiful tree now ... No, we were not "on relief"; we had EVERYTHING: lots of fish and game, chickens, and pigs.[13]

However modest the material conditions at Kanaka Ranch, the proprieties held. Minnie's father Ben McCord accustomed her to newcomer ways when she was a young child. Through his influence, she imbibed the colonizing religious experience becoming familiar to Squamish families at Whoi Whoi and on the Mission Reserve.

> I was christened at the little church on what is now Water Street [in Gastown]; I think you know it as the Indian Church, or Wesleyan Methodist church ... My first recollections of the little church are that the Indians used to come to it as well as whites; I was in it many times. It was just a little old building, about as big as these two rooms (16x30'). We entered by a little door from a narrow trail; it was such a little clearing the church stood on; there were stumps all around everywhere; if you went a few feet beyond the church, you were in the thick timbers. Inside the church there were just benches, and, at the front, a bit of a platform on which the minister used to stand, but what minister I don't recall, because I was so small; my father used to carry me into church.
>
> I wore a glengarry, and a kilted skirt; the children used to call me "Scotsy Two Tails." One Sunday, I was sitting there [in church] with father, and Harry Alexander [son of the Hastings Mill manager] pulled my curls. I had on a kilted suit, and a glengarry, I got up and hit him on the head with it. I shall never

forget it; the minister looked at me, and when we came out of church, my father looked sideways at me; he shook his head; oh, he thought it terrible ... They sang the hymns, sometimes in Indian, sometimes in English, sometimes Mr. Tate [the Methodist missionary] would talk; he talked the Indian language well ... He was a great friend of ours. He used to come and see us at Coal Harbor.[14]

Minnie's grandmother Mary See-em-ia was just as concerned as her father that Minnie learn the ways of newcomers. "Grandmother always talked English," Minnie told Major Matthews in 1936. "She had such small feet and always wore boots; and a hat; and she used to tell me to try and do like the whiteman did, copy him, because he knew a lot, and not 'be like a Siwash.' You know how it is. Half breeds either rise or go down; some of them do well; others just go back to Indians."[15] Siwash was the somewhat pejorative word for "Indian" in the Chinook jargon that originated in the fur trade, a simple language virtually everyone spoke and understood.

As times changed, so did life at Kanaka Ranch. It was no longer an isolated enclave, but rather a site from which Mary See-em-ia managed the change going on all around her. Minnie recalled larger events as matters of course, rather than as alien to the everyday world at Coal Harbour.

I went to the Hastings Mill School. Why of course I walked to school from our place [Kanaka Ranch]. How else could I get there? I used to walk along the trail through the woods, and, oh, I was so frightened! I was only a little girl, and runaway sailors had shacks in the bushes; they were hiding there, along by where Cardero Street is now, and I used to hurry by. Sometimes I took the beach, and walked along the beach all the way from Georgia Street to the Hastings Mill School [on Dunlevy Street].

My sister [Seraphine] and I went down to see the [first] train come in; we were just grown up girls. They had a great big arch at the foot of Granville Street (erected by the C.P.R. [Canadian Pacific Railway]), evergreens, and I said to my sister, "Let's get beside this big arch; we'll be safe here in case the engine goes off the track, and they won't run over us." So we got under the big evergreen arch, and peeped through the evergreens at the train coming in.[16]

The arrival of the transcontinental railway in the mid-1880s coincided with fundamental change at Kanaka Ranch. Mary See-em-ia's onetime husband Eihu died in 1886, leaving her without a supplementary income to the foodstuffs she grew for her family and sold to other families, such as those at Brockton Point. Her eldest daughter Maggie had long since had a family of her own. Her younger daughter Lucy Nahanee had also escaped into marriage; her choice was a German man named Lewis Smith, double her 16 years at the time they got together in the early 1880s. Mary See-em-ia's son William Nahanee and her granddaughter Minnie McCord rallied to her support by taking employment: Minnie worked at various odd jobs and William was hired as a longshoreman, to work on the docks, after a stint as a coal passer on the Hudson's Bay steamer *Beaver*, for a dollar a day.

The various Hawaiians who lived at Kanaka Ranch were less of a presence in Minnie's or William's life than was Mary See-em-ia. What comes clear in their testimony is her wisdom and strength. The mother of children by two Hawaiian men, she was very much the matriarch of Kanaka Ranch. She had learned to adapt to a world transformed during her lifetime and was determined that her children and grandchildren would be able to do so as well. Both of her daughters, Maggie and Lucy, had married newcomer men, and she resolved that her granddaughter Minnie would be able to do so as well, by learning their ways. Mary See-em-ia was a survivor, and so was Kanaka Ranch.

CHAPTER 3

The Families of Brockton Point

The south shore of Brockton Point was photographed by Edouard Deville in 1886. Library and Archives Canada, PA-06228

It was not just at Whoi Whoi, nearby Chaythoos and Kanaka Ranch where new, hybrid ways of life were coming into being. A third site, Brockton Point, on the peninsula's eastern tip, was a centre of community for almost a generation before Vancouver was officially founded in 1886. Brockton Point's female originators were mostly Squamish women seeking a comfortable place to settle down; their male companions were among the thousands of newcomers lured to British Columbia by gold during the late 1850s and early 1860s. Such relationships were commonplace during those years, what with the lack of newcomer women and the widespread use of Chinook. Some men and women eventually decided to move on. By the 1870s half of the original arrivals at Brockton Point had been replaced by successors just as eager for a place they could call their own. As the Hawaiians had discovered, it was extremely difficult for men of modest means to pre-empt land around Burrard Inlet.

The precise date of the first arrivals at Brockton Point is impossible to determine. Until the construction of sawmills, the area attracted virtually no attention and almost no records were kept. Apart from the flutter over coal and the mapping of the coastline, the peninsula was left to its own devices. All of the women and many of the men who chose Brockton Point were illiterate, so they left sparse written testimony of their own.

As with Whoi Whoi, Chaythoos and Kanaka Ranch, the best sources of information on the families of Brockton Point are the stories that have come down through children and grandchildren. They can only be partial accounts. Some of the men who opted for Brockton Point had slipped off ships and could be harshly disciplined if they were found. They did not want their pasts or even their birth names to be known.

A handful of names have come through time as the first newcomer men and Aboriginal women to build dwelling places at Brockton Point. Between Joseph Silvey and his wife Khaltinaht, Peter Smith and Kenick and her father Shwuthchalton, Gregorio Fernandez, Joe Mannion and Takood and her father Klah Chaw, Tomkins Brew and his wife, John Baker and Mary Tsiyaliya, it is impossible to know with certainty who got to Brockton Point first and how they did so.

Joe Silvey, Peter Smith and Gregorio Fernandez were adventurous young Portuguese men whose paths must have crossed before they landed on Brockton Point. Others' common use of the adjective "Portuguese" to refer to persons who spoke it as a first language (hence "Portuguese Joe" and "Portuguese Pete") ensured that such individuals would hear of each other's presence.

Silvey and Smith shared common origins in the Azores Islands, a

Portuguese possession in the middle of the Atlantic Ocean. Fernandez hailed from Madeira, a Portuguese island off the coast of Africa. The men's birthplace helps to explain how they got to British Columbia. Men there had fished and whaled on a small scale for generations. These skills were particularly desirable to the Americans, who came to dominate the whaling industry in the 19th century and whose ships sometimes travelled as far as the north Pacific coast. Silvey's daughter Mary shared with Major Matthews the essence of what likely also occurred with the others: "He was about 12 years old when he left the Azores. He got on a ship, and it [was] maybe a whaler, and they got to Victoria, and there he got a canoe, bought it from the Indians, and went up the Fraser River to Kamloops for gold."[1]

All three men sought their fortunes from gold. Whereas Smith and Fernandez mined in the Cariboo, Silvey never made it to the goldfields. His misadventure did, however, have a happy ending, which has survived thanks to his eldest child Elizabeth's conversations with Major Matthews.

> He came down before he got very far up the river because the Indians chased him away ... Then, my father, together with the four or five whitemen who had come down the river with him, went on to the North Arm of the Fraser, in the dug-out canoe, and when they approached the Point Grey [Musqueam] Indian Reserve on the North Arm, they saw a crowd of Indians in front, and they were frightened,

Joe Silvey's daughter Elizabeth was photographed by Major Matthews shortly after she began talking with him in 1938. She had an excellent memory, one that remained consistent over a dozen conversations with Major Matthews across six years.
City of Vancouver Archives, CVA 371-2397

and clasped their hands together before their faces, as in prayer, because they thought they would all be killed, and that the Musqueam Indians were like the Yale Indians. But the Musqueam treated them with kindness, and they sure were *good* to my father and his companions. The big chief, Capilano, from Capilano [on the north shore of Burrard Inlet], happened to be at Musqueam, and he stood in the middle of the crowd of Indians. All the Musqueams had their arrows ready, but Capilano, the chief, stopped them; he put up his two arms over his head, and that motion held the crowd in check.

Father stayed a night with the Musqueam Indians, and was treated so well there, and the next morning, father and his companions went to Victoria in the canoe. He was in Victoria for a while, and then he came back, and he was at Point Roberts ... and my father had a little store there, and that was how he came to propose to my mother [Chief Capilano's granddaughter] down at Musqueam.

Mother and father were out in a canoe, and then afterwards father said by signs, to the old chief, Chief Capilano, that he wanted my mother for his wife, and could he have her; all by signs. Then the old chief said, by signs, that he could; waved his hand and arm with a motion signifying to "take her." He motioned with his right arm, waved, quickly, upward and outward.

She was a pretty girl with dark eyes, and hair down to her middle; large deep soft eyes. Her name was Mary Ann in English; I don't know what it was in Indian, but my aunt's name was Lumtinaht.[2]

Not only was Mary Ann, or Khaltinaht, both Musqueam and Squamish by descent, she had close ties to Whoi Whoi. Her maternal great uncle was Sam Kweeahkult, another of Chief Capilano's sons and, for a time, chief there.

Elizabeth Silvey took particular pride in the fact that her mother was not simply acquired by her father, but that a marriage ceremony took place and that it was respectful of Aboriginal practice.

In those days they were married under Indian law. Well, you know, my father told me how the Indians married; you see, father and mother got married at Musqueam, Point Grey. The old Chief, Chief Capilano, took my father, and the chief of the Musqueams took my mother and the two chiefs

> put them together ... They had canoes and canoes and canoes, all drawn up on the beach, and a great crowd of Indians, and they had a great time. They had a lot of stuff for the festivities, Indian blankets, and all sorts of things, and threw [gave] it all away; they had a great big potlatch. And, then, they put my mother and father in a great big canoe with a lot of blankets; made them sit on top of the blankets, and then brought them over to [Joe Silvey's] home at Point Roberts.[3]

Joe Silvey soon returned to the occupation he knew best, which was fishing. Once he did so, the peninsula became an ideal place to settle down. Not only did his wife have family at Whoi Whoi, but Coal Harbour's waters teemed with herring and other fish. The tiny cove to which he headed on the south shore of Brockton Point had a shallow sandy beach useful for hauling up boats and drying nets. Sawmills needed oil for their machinery, best got from dogfish. A Squamish man named Chillahminst, also known as Jim Franks, remembered:

> Portuguese Joe he first go out Point Grey, out on sandbank, catch dogfish, bring them in Deadman's Island [between Brockton Point and Coal Harbour]; too rough out there. He get oil. Boil them in great big kettle on Deadman's Island, make oil; sell sawmill. That's what Portuguese Joe first do.[4]

Peter Smith, who likely adopted his surname to avoid being caught for ship jumping, headed to Brockton Point for similar reasons: he fished for a living, and he wanted to establish a satisfying personal life. Smith found a Squamish woman named Kenick for a wife, and also a very obliging father-in-law. Thomas Abraham, a Squamish man, explained Smith's family circumstances: "Yes, I knew him. He became the son-in-law of this man [Shwuthchalton]. He [Shwuthchalton] was residing in Stanley Park. He was before up at Squamish River and when his daughter came here he came here ... They were residing there when he took her as his wife ... Shwuthchalton's [other] residence was at Kitsilano."[5]

Another early Brockton Point resident was Gregorio Fernandez, who for convenience sometimes used the first name of Joe. In the early

Joe Silvey was an enterprising and ambitious man with his wits about him.
City of Vancouver Archives, Port P656

1860s he ran a general store at New Westminster, but soon opened a store at Brockton Point, perhaps so he could also fish with his compatriots. Unlike the others, he never married.

In early March 1866, a schooner heading north along the coast was forced by strong tides to anchor in Plumper's Pass, later renamed Active Pass, between Mayne and Galiano islands in the Georgia Strait between Vancouver Island and the mainland. Its crew almost certainly encountered Joe Silvey, perhaps also Peter Smith and Joe Fernandez. The naturalist aboard wrote in his diary:

> March 5th 1866 (Monday). There are some fisher men & one or two other settlers here. One of the former generally known by the generic name of "Portugee Joe" visited us. Joe had just caught lb. 500 of fish—enough for the Westminster & Victoria markets. He sent them up by the "Enterprise." He caught them with double hooked lines but the dog fish (Anarchias Sukleyi) were very troublesome to him biting off the hooks. Joe made by his own

> confession last summer by salting & smoking salmon more than $2000. He had caught a shark, from the liver of which he had extracted 20 gals. of oil. He was thinking of going into whale fishing in the inlet—as they abounded. He was going to use rockets [rocket-driven harpoons].[6]

All three Portuguese men aspired to a better life. In about 1867, Fernandez opened a general store at Gastown that was larger than the one he had been operating at Brockton Point. It was built partly on land, mostly on piles, with a log float that extended out in the water 75 feet (23 metres) at half tide. According to a contemporary, "he used to send off a little scow to the steamers and to the Hastings mill and get his stuff and brought it into his store."[7]

Joe Silvey also wanted to move on. As a necessary preliminary, he became a British subject, and on the very same day that he was naturalized, in March 1867, he signed with his X a request to pre-empt 100 acres (40 hectares) at "Maryanns Point—Galiano Isld."[8] The holding, named for his wife, was used only as a base for fishing. He set his principal sights on Brockton Point and a year later applied for a lease, "a lease of twenty acres on the Government Reserve," promising "to leave at the shortest notice whenever the Government may require the land."[9]

Three years earlier Colonel Moody, acting through Edward Stamp had been given the opportunity to purchase 100 acres (40 hectares) out of the reserve as if it were Crown land, but Joseph Silvey was turned down flat in his request to lease part of the same piece of land. He was informed that "it is not considered advisable at present to grant a lease to any portion of this Reserve."[10] It is tempting to speculate that despite Silvey's naturalization, the men's backgrounds and connections made the difference.

In any case, Joseph Silvey was not deterred in his ambition. He got into whaling, together with Peter Smith and a couple of other seasoned seamen. In Silvey's passing conversation in 1866, he talked about "rockets"—a device so new at the time that Silvey must have had considerable knowledge of the industry to mention it. His daughter

Elizabeth, born in about 1867, recalled in great detail the whaling work that the men did off of Burrard Inlet in her early childhood:

> We saw the schooner coming full sail, and they were towing something white. They were coming fast with all the sails. And they were towing this big thing behind the schooner. Yes. And then they turned it over, it was black, and when they turned it back again, it was white. They had a little wharf, and the schooner docked there; it was piles, small piles, but a pretty good little wharf. And then they had a great big cable as big as my arm; the cable was rope. They lowered the whale boat; they always packed the whale boat on the schooner, and when they saw a whale, they lowered the whale boat. And then had a big line, like a cable, and a harpoon. And then, finally, they had a big shed where they had the iron pots, you know, where they boil the blubber, the fat, and they had the harpoon on the whale's head. And then they hauled it up to the shed. They had a big thing [a windlass] right on the shore; edge of the water, and two men kept going around and around, walking around the big thing. And the rope was coming in, and bringing the whale up; it was a slow job. And then they cut the whale up with a great big knife, ready to boil; all the fat. It was chopped up in squares, and the fat was *that* thick [about 12 inches/30 centimetres]; it was all fat; just excepting the ribs; very fat.[11]

The whaling boom was too good to last, and the industry collapsed in about 1870. Not only were fewer whales turning up, but the price of whale oil fell: a dozen years had passed since ground oil was discovered in the United States. Joe Silvey survived because he was running another business, a saloon just across the street from Fernandez's general store in Gastown. Fernandez had moved to Gastown by this time, and Silvey may also have lived there off and on. The two men became closer friends. Elizabeth recalled:

> My father, Joseph Silvey, put up a saloon; that's what they called it; not a hotel, but a saloon. He built it quite close to the beach; down on Water Street somewhere. I remember all the bottles on the shelf, and there was a counter. It was on the Gastown beach, and the street was just planked over.
>
> The men who came into the bar room used to give me ten cents, or fifty cents, and I used to run over to Joe's store and get candy. Joe Fernandez had

Joe Silvey's saloon, which he called Hole-in-the-Wall, is visible at the far end of Water Street in Gastown. Gregorio Fernandez's store was located just across the street, Gassy Jack Deighton's competing saloon near the big maple.
City of Vancouver Archives, Dist. P11.1

> a great big cordwood stove in the store; I used to stand by it when I went over to get candy from Joe. When I first recall him, he was an old man with a big long beard; all the men wore beards then; even the young men had big beards.[12]

Joe Silvey operated his saloon off and on as economic conditions warranted, his customers being the millworkers. He got a new licence in January 1870, only to shut his doors at mid-year, "owing to the mill being closed." That spring, government surveyors laid out lots in the Town Reserve from Hastings Street north to Burrard Inlet and between Carrall and Cambie streets, but at $100 or more each, they were too pricey for all but a few businessmen. Fernandez bought the property on which his business stood at the original land sale held in April 1870. Silvey did not. Perhaps he was out whaling or, more likely, the business climate was too stagnant for his liking. A year later, on May 9, 1871, Joe Silvey paid $100 for the lot located on the southeastern corner of Water and Abbott streets, probably because he had reopened his saloon.[13]

Silvey's eldest daughter Elizabeth, whose memories paint the most detailed portrait of this time and place, was particularly concerned that Major Matthews understand the dedication with which she was raised by both parents. Her father gave her an understanding of his business ventures, and her mother Khaltinaht, or Mary Ann, shared her Aboriginal heritage. Khaltinaht ensured that Elizabeth got to know her great-grandfather, Chief Capilano, who divided his time between his Squamish and Musqueam allegiances.

> The big chief, Capilano ... was my great grandfather on my mother's side. The old chief lived at Capilano Creek (the village of Homulcheson), but he also had a home at Musqueam, his mother was a Musqueam.
>
> When I was about three years old—it was before my sister Josephine was born—my mother took me over to the Indian houses at Capilano Creek, and there I saw old Chief Capilano; a great big old man with big legs, and loud voice—anyway it seemed so to me; that's how I recall him, of course, I was little and perhaps he looked bigger to me than he actually was—and long white hair hanging down over his shoulders; down to his shoulder blades, and the ends used to curl upwards; he was short sighted.
>
> He was kind, and nice. I was a little girl. He beckoned me to come to him, and I would not go, but afterwards I did, and he took me up on one arm, and held me to his breast. Oh, he was a nice man; everyone liked him.
>
> Great grandfather Chief Capilano used to come and camp at Brockton Point; in a tent in front of our house, and I used to see him resting on his bed in the tent ... and he had a hunch-back slave wife to look after him; I used to visit him constantly in that old tent.[14]

Khaltinaht was especially close to her sister Lumtinaht, also known as Louise. Of the many things they and the young Elizabeth did together, one of those that Elizabeth remembered most vividly in her old age was a large potlatch held in 1870 at Whoi Whoi, where her maternal great-uncle Sam Kweeahkult was then the chief. Because Lumtinaht was related to the chief, she played a special role at the potlatch, in which Supple Jack was a participant. Elizabeth's description of the event captures not just the impressions of a little girl, but also the strength of

No photograph survives of Khaltinaht (Mary Ann), but we can get a sense of her from one that does of her sister Lumtinaht, whom she is said to have closely resembled.
City of Vancouver Archives, Port P392

cultural life at Whoi Whoi.

They gave a great big potlatch in Stanley Park; right where the Lumberman's Arch is. I was little, but I can remember it clearly. My mother took me to it on her back; she "packed" me to it, and when we got near there were "thousands" of Indians: "thousands" of them, from everywhere, Nanaimo, Cowichan, everywhere, and I was frightened. I don't know who gave the potlatch, but I think my grandmother's brother, and I think Supple Jack; yes, that's Khaytulk, that's his Indian name, I think he was in it too.

Sumkwaht was my grandmother, that is, my mother's mother; I don't know what my Indian grandfather's name was, but he was "Old Man" Capilano's son. Sumkwaht had a brother who was chief at Whoi-Whoi in Stanley Park; his name was Sam Kweeahkult; I remember him; he was my grandmother's brother.

They held the potlatch in a great big shed; a huge place; the Indians built it themselves long ago. It was all divided up into sections inside. There was no floor; just earth, and the fires were all burning. A great big high shed, about three fires, but the flames were leaping up high, as high as your chin, and part of the top of the potlatch house was open to let the smoke out.

Before the potlatch started they had a great pile of blankets, and they got a "high" [status] girl to sit on it. That was part of the ceremony. To show that they had the blankets, I suppose. She, the princess, was my aunt; my mother's sister; [grand]daughter of old Chief Capilano. It would be improper to have a common girl sit on the blankets; they had a great pile of them, and a princess sitting on top ...

They even threw all the blankets away from the platform above; throw them down for the people to seize. The platforms were high up, inside, of course, and the chiefs were away up on the platform, and throwing blankets and money down, and those below scrambling for it ...

Mother took me, on her back, but when they began to dance, and throw money about, I got frightened, and ran. I darted through under their legs, in and out of the crowd, and dashed out of the building; I didn't wait for anyone; not even mother; she came after me, and had to take me home; she could not stop at the potlatch because I was so frightened; I was properly frightened.[15]

Khaltinaht died suddenly in about 1871, and Joe Silvey was devastated. So was Elizabeth, who still remembered years later that "her people at Musqueam came for her body and took it in a canoe for burial at Musqueam."[16] It was then, according to Elizabeth, that Silvey sold his Gastown saloon and retreated with her and her baby sister Josephine to live full-time at Brockton Point, where he ran a licensed saloon for a time.

In the early 1870s, Brockton Point's population began to grow. Among the new arrivals joining the Silveys and the Smiths were two young Irish millworkers, Joe Mannion and Tomkins Brew. Mannion recalled:

[I came to Vancouver in] 1865. I was employed at the mill during its construction—the Hastings mill. [It was] being built, yes. The Moodyville mill [was running at that time].

I was about a year here in 1865 and was absent in 1866. [I] came back [and engaged in] mill work. [Then there were large vessels] loading [in the harbour]. Lumber. South American, Australian, and San Francisco. [For] foreign ports. [They loaded] at the mill wharf mostly. The spar ships loaded off the wharf—they loaded in the water, the spars were floated in the water to them.[17]

Joe Mannion got together with a young Squamish woman named Takood, or Long Heels, who lived to the east of Whoi Whoi with her family. Her father was Klah Chaw; newcomers called him "Dr. Johnson" because of his reputation as an Indian medicine man. Young Mannion more or less moved in with Takood's family on the northern shore of Brockton Point, as explained by Emma Gonzales, a Squamish woman born in about 1843, in the third person.

Klah Chaw. He was an Indian Medicine-man. He was there [at Brockton Point] because that was his home. That was his home. She says it was about that [the width of the room] from the high-water mark. It is about 35 [feet]. It was made of shakes. Cedar shakes. She used to come around the place to visit the place with her father—this woman's father. An Indian [called] Marshall [lived in the house on the west side]. Policeman Tom [lived in the next one]. An Indian, too. It is quite a good sized house because the Indians used to use them as an Indian dance-house. They were different buildings.

She says she knows it [when Joe Mannion went to live there]. She remembers when Joe Mannion got there and got together with Dr. Johnson's daughter ... He came there after, when Portuguese Pete was there—Portuguese Pete was there first about four years, after Joseph Mannion came, she says.

Takood [was Klah Chaw's daughter]. She says she doesn't know how many years Joe Mannion was there, but she knows that Joe Mannion had two children when he was living there. Two children were born there. [As to where Joe Mannion lived] it was Klah Chaw's house.[18]

Klah Chaw's son Tesamis, whose English name was Ambrose Johnson, recalled his newcomer brother-in-law. Born in about 1857, he was a child at the time Mannion arrived, but remembered events clearly.

[His father is] Dr. Johnson. Klah Chaw is the Indian name. He says Dr. Johnson used to live there [in Stanley Park]. He says they cleared a little place, where the house was. That was Dr. Johnson's house. He says there was a well

> there [for drinking water]. He says it was on this side of the place where they [Joe Mannion and his older sister Takood] were living. He says, I was a little bit of a boy [when Mannion came]. He says he cleared near to the house, he says—just around it. He says it was made out of lumber. He bought it from the Hastings Mill.
>
> He says the last [most westerly] house belonged to an Indian that we mentioned his name before—but I have forgot—Charlie, the Indian name. [There were] three houses. [Mannion's house was] about 40 feet from this house—from Mannion's house to Charlie's house on the west. [Mannion's house] was in the middle. He says, yes, he could see them fairly well, from the water, when you are out in a canoe. [Mannion's house was] somewhere about near 100 feet [from the present day cut-off road across Brockton Point].[19]

Joe Mannion's countryman Tomkins Brew probably settled at Brockton Point at the beginning of 1869 when he was named customs collector for Burrard Inlet. He probably arrived in British Columbia at the beginning of the gold rush, together with his older brother Chartres and sister Jane. From 1862 he was constable at New Westminster, serving under Chartres, who was chief inspector of police there. Tomkins was living with an Aboriginal woman (whose name has not survived), which may explain why he preferred the relative seclusion of Brockton Point even though his job paid well at $1200 a year. Brew took over Fernandez's house on the south shore after Fernandez moved to Gastown.

Like Joe Silvey, Tomkins Brew sought security of tenure. His family connections made him aware that the peninsula's reputation as a reserve did not necessarily put it off limits. He kept trying, without success, to acquire land there.

> I am afraid my application for the land on Brockton Point as well as the private note accompanying it [sent to the Chief Commissioner of Lands and Works in the spring of 1876] may have miscarried … It would be an immense benefit to me to have the matter settled at once; as I am very poorly off and must find employment for some months. I have been applying for the place since 1869. Some of my applications were taken no notice of, yet others got

> titles to places on the inlet, tho their claims were neither as just or legal as mine. Some queer things about land have been done up here.[20]

Of the six newcomer men who got to Brockton Point first, John Baker is the most elusive with respect to his origins. His grandson was told that he "was an Englishman who used to come on the sailing ships."[21] It may be that Baker was also a ship jumper and did not want his background or whereabouts known. In any case, Baker had a Squamish wife, Mary Tsiyaliya, with whom he lived from about 1871. They made their home at a south shore site that became known as Baker's Point.

John Baker was one of the first sawyers at Hastings Mill and also longshored. He was a versatile man. Eihu's granddaughter Minnie who grew up at nearby Kanaka Ranch remembered how "Baker cured fish there; they had their little place on the point right where the gun is." By the time Minnie spoke with Major Matthews, Baker's Point had been renamed for the Nine O'clock Gun then located there.

Residence at Brockton Point did not necessarily mean retreat. The newcomer men who set themselves down there enjoyed a certain respectability. From 1860 onward, directories were published every few years that listed heads of newcomer households in British Columbia. The directories marked out social boundaries and defined respectability. Persons with non-Anglo surnames were included only where occupational status overrode ethnicity. John Baker, Tomkins Brew, Gregorio Fernandez, Joe Mannion and Joe Silvey all made it into at least one directory during the 1870s. Peter Smith did so in the early 1880s. These men were not on the margin.

For them and their families, Brockton Point became not just a convenient place of residence but a base for family life. John Baker and Mary Tsiyaliya had two sons, Johnny and Willie, and four daughters, Lizzie, Charlotte, Molly and Nora. Tomkins Brew and his wife had a son, Arthur. Joe Mannion and Takood had Margaret and De Vere. Peter Smith and Kenick were, between 1871 and 1891, the parents of Mary, Peter, Thomas, John, Maria, Sarah and a daughter who died

By the time of Joe Silvey's marriage to Kwahama Kwatleematt on September 20, 1872, attitudes had changed since his first wedding, which was conducted according to Aboriginal ways. An Oblate priest married the pair in the Catholic mission church at Sechelt up the coast from Vancouver, whereupon they posed for a formal photograph. Courtesy Jessica Casey

young and was buried at Brockton Point. Joe Silvey and Khaltinaht had two daughters, Elizabeth and Josephine, prior to Khaltinaht's death. Soon after, Joe Silvey married a young Sechelt woman named Kwahama Kwatleematt, or Lucy. They soon started a family of their own at Brockton Point, the two oldest being Domingo and Mary.

In conversations with Major Matthews in the late 1930s, Elizabeth recalled life at Brockton Point. Indicative of the complexities of memory, she said that Tomkins Brew arrived first, followed by her father and then Peter Smith.

> Father's saloon at Brockton Point was where Mr Brew, the Customs officer lived; Nine O'clock Gun. Tomkins Brew was the first to build a house by the Nine O'clock Gun; then we were next; Brew was there when we went there; he was Justice of the Peace. Tomkins Brew was living at Brockton Point when we went there; he had quite a nice little cottage; it was about twenty feet or so—just a little bit—west of the Nine O'clock Gun; on that little bit of clearing

> right on that little point. Then my father was next, then Peter Smith came, and he used to come over and borrow father's tools. Peter Smith had an Indian wife.
>
> Joseph Mannion had an Indian wife; they called her father [Klah Chaw or Dr. Johnson] the "Mowitchman"; everybody was afraid of him; they said he was an Indian doctor. The way he got his name was that when they [white men] wanted a deer, they would tell him to get a deer, and he would say "alright, I get you two," and go off. And he would come back with a deer; perhaps two. Where he got them I don't know, but "mowitch" is the Indian [Chinook] word for deer, and that was how they called him "Mowitch."
>
> I don't know when we left Gastown to go to Brockton Point, but it was before I was old enough to go to school, because I never went to the Hastings Sawmill School ... but I remember Arthur Brew, son of Tomkins Brew; he was a big boy going to [Hastings Mill] school. I got little or no education; only about six months, but I can read a few words.[22]

Elizabeth's younger sister Mary had a less sanguine view of Tomkins Brew: "I did not like him very well, and used to climb up in the boughs of the maple tree, and drop little pebbles on people I did not like who passed underneath; used to climb up there, and stay up in the branches all day when they were looking for me to give me a hiding; used to take a pocket full of pebbles up there with me."[23]

However comfortable Brockton Point might have been, for some of its residents it was only a temporary location. Gregorio Fernandez had been the first to leave, and several other departures marked the 1870s and early 1880s. Tomkins Brew, Joe Mannion and Joe Silvey decided for different reasons that the time had come to move away. They did not necessarily leave by choice: families not only formed at Brockton Point; they came to sad endings. "Tomkins Brew had an Indian wife," Elizabeth told Matthews, "big fine beautiful woman, and he was fond of her. But she got sick, and I can see him yet, with his arm around her neck as she was lying there in her bed; but she did not get better, and she died."[24] Young Arthur Brew was left motherless. According to Fred Alexander, a newcomer child during these years, a couple in nearby

New Westminster wanted to adopt him: "Mr. Cunningham wanted to 'save' Brew's boy." But Tomkins Brew was not about to have his son become a missionary cause.

Tomkins Brew died in New Westminster in 1889, the space for "rank or profession" being left blank on his death certificate. His son Arthur died in 1906 at the age of 40. His death certificate recorded how "Arthur Brew was a prisoner in the Provincial Gaol New Westminster & had Delirium Tremors when brought in, from which he died."

The most socially ambitious of the newcomer men at Brockton Point was undoubtedly Joe Mannion. He wanted more than mill work, which was an acceptable occupation for a young adventurer but not for a gentleman approaching middle age. So in 1874 he bought half interest in a Gastown saloon, and he and two partners transformed it into the Granville Hotel, which he eventually took over as sole proprietor.

About 1879 or 1880, Mannion more or less abandoned his wife in their Brockton Point home, but not before depositing their young daughter with the Sisters of St. Ann in New Westminster. This Catholic religious order ran several boarding schools across the young province that provided a refuge for mixed-race and also Aboriginal and newcomer girls whose families sought their services for one reason or another. Maggie Mannion later described the fundamental change in her young life in a manner very protective of her father's decision:

> At an early age, about three years, I was sent to the convent in New Westminster; scholastic institutions on Burrard Inlet in those days were restricted to the Hastings Sawmill School; and remained there until I was in my teens.
>
> Father took some interest in political and civic matters; he was an alderman of the City Council in 1887–8, but his tastes ran more to literature, reading, etc. … He was a tall handsome man of robust frame … He was, colloquially, known as "The Mayor of Granville," though, of course, no such office existed.[25]

The memories of Minnie McCord of nearby Kanaka Ranch, who like Maggie Mannion was born in 1876, offer a poignant view of events. Her account highlighted the role played by Maggie's grandfather Klah

Chaw in ensuring the transition was as smooth as possible:

> Joe Mannion had a little daughter, she is Mrs. Dr. H.A. Christie now; her name was Maggie, and when her Indian mother died [*sic*]—I think that was the reason—the little thing—she was about five years old—"Mowitch" Jim, her mother's father, brought her to our place, she came to live with us [at Kanaka Ranch] for a few days before they sent her to the convent. She stayed at the convent many years—until she was grown up.
>
> I remember it so well because, when she went, they put her on the stage[coach], she took my little hat, a pretty little hat; how I did love that little hat, and I cried because they put my little hat on her, and there she sat with it until she got on the stage at the foot of about Abbott or Carrall Street; the stage just came so far, as far as it could get, and then turned around. I can see Harry Frieze, the stage driver, up there on the stage with his bugle; he used to put the bugle up to his mouth and blow it—on the stage—and Maggie took my little hat.[26]

In the 1881 census Maggie Mannion was recorded as ensconced at the Sisters of St. Ann in New Westminster, being one of three girls under school age alongside 15 or so students who were there to get an education. Her father had begun anew. He married a woman from the Atlantic provinces with whom he soon produced a second family. As for Maggie, she went on to marry a medical doctor who arrived from Ontario with the railway and made her life on Vancouver's respectable west side. Her brother De Vere became an engineer and moved to Australia, perhaps to escape the effects of his mixed-race origins.

Throughout his life Joseph Mannion remained ambivalent about his Brockton Point interlude. In the public record it was his second wife whom he acknowledged. He took pride in his first-born daughter, but as if she had no mother. In 1912, in his old age, he published in the *Vancouver Province* a reflection that was both a denial and a justification:

> In those days the moral scales were badly unbalanced: the habit of concubinage [with Aboriginal women] was common and growing. It was handed down by the Hudson's Bay Company. The men who fell victims to this

Joe Mannion departed Brockton Point and transformed himself into a respectable businessman. City of Vancouver Archives, Port P143N102

practice can be divided into three classes.

It was common to the small rancher, the shingle-maker, millhand and lone sailor, that is the man who owned a small craft and in himself composed the crew. This class cannot be much blamed, the isolation of their respective callings seeming to compel the practice, but [the second group] the cold utility man who pleaded necessity, convenience, the open door, etc., etc., alleging it was only a tie that could be cast off at any time, found this a woeful mistake. He was more human than he thought. The next was … composed mostly of errant Englishmen, youths without restraint, educated, who had drunk in the romance of the middle ages, husk and all …; and though it may seem paradoxical, quite a few of this class led a blameless life, binding themselves loyally to the duties of husband and parent, virtues which cannot be written

> for the party of the second part. "The old order changeth," thanks to the railroad and the ocean liner, and the decadence of the aborigines, which has swept the practice away for all time.[27]

Joe Silvey also remained ambitious, but for his family rather than despite them. Whereas Mannion denied his wife, Silvey sought to protect his wife and their children from the changing attitudes. Silvey was always on the move, his eldest daughter recalled:

> Father built a sloop; I helped him; he built it at Brockton Point. I was only a little girl, but I could hold the boards, and I could hand him the nails, and could hold something against the other side of the board when he was hammering; put a little pressure on. I held a big hammer on the other side of the board for him when he was hammering the nails. Oh, I was a big girl, about five or six.
>
> Father taught the Indian women how to knit nets at Brockton Point; taught them how to make seine nets, and then he used to stain the nets in vats, and then they went out on the little bit of sandy beach, facing this way [toward Vancouver] from Brockton Point, and used to catch herrings. One would go away out in the boat with one end, and one away out with the other end, and then they would circle around, and two men on one rope end and two men on the other end would pull the net slowly, slowly, into the sandy beach, and they would get, well, I heard them say there was a ton of herrings in the net, you could see the net coming in with the herrings all splashing in it; drawing it up on the beach.
>
> Then they used to put the herrings in barrels, and they used to salt it, and they used to sell the herrings for one dollar a barrel; they used to sell them to the schooners. The schooners used to come in, and get one hundred barrels each, and go away; sometimes as much as one hundred and fifty barrels; *that* one hundred and fifty dollars; they used the herring for bait; used them to catch dog fish up the coast, and they sold the dog fish oil to the [coal] mines at Departure Bay [on Vancouver Island to use for lights in men's helmets underground]. But the oil was so high [in price] those days.
>
> I remember some of the "Gastown" men joking about going to give up storekeeping and lumbering, and go fishing; there was money in fishing; lots of money in it.[28]

From his first years in British Columbia, Joe Silvey was a man with his wits about him. He understood the importance of landholding and realized that having failed to get a lease at Brockton Point, he could never consider it anything more than a temporary respite in his life. He had first considered Galiano Island; in 1872 he set his sights on 160 acres (64 hectares) on Howe Sound but soon discovered that this did not suit either. His next prospect was Reid Island, located northwest of Galiano. On September 9, 1881, he pre-empted 160 acres, to which he soon moved permanently with his family. His eldest son Domingo later acquired the remainder of the island's 225 acres (90 hectares). Joe Silvey successfully supported his wife and 11 children on Reid Island until his death in 1902.[29]

Even as some men left, Brockton Point was being renewed. Joe Silvey did not abandon his house; he passed it on to Joe Gonsalves, who had come from Madeira in the 1870s to run his uncle Gregorio Fernandez's store. Gonsalves later recalled with remarkable precision the character of Brockton Point at the time he came at the age of 17. The account, as did numerous others, wrote Silvey as Silva, which was a much more common surname.

> [When I arrived in July '74] I stopped there [at Brockton Point]. I went there and stopped there. Joe Silva was there and Peter Smith and Joe Fernandez had been living there, he [my uncle] was still in Vancouver at the time. On Water Street. In Gastown running a store. He left there [Brockton Point] before [I came].
>
> There was another party there called Mr. Tomkins Brew, he was living in my uncle's place at the time. He was in the Park in '74. He moved quite a little while after I came there. Probably the last of the year '74, something like that.
>
> [As for Joe Silvey's house] I can't give exactly the right age, must be 15 years old the way it looked. I believe it was built of split cedar at the time I came in. It was rebuilt of boards 1x12 [inches] afterwards. He told me at the time they came in he could not get lumber and he split some cedar to finish the house. About 14x20 [feet], a small house, it was above the high water mark altogether. It was all cleared. A few stumps, not very many; all the tall

timber was taken away. They were forty or fifty feet apart, you can plant all kinds of stuff in between stumps. Small grass, wild grass, no brush at all. He used to have a little garden, I guess, before I came there.

[Peter Smith] was there years before I was. The time I came there it was the same way [as Joe Silvey's house]. The two houses looked pretty old when I came there in '74. It has all been rebuilt before I came there, because it has been there so long and, you see, they couldn't get lumber at first. I believe it was built of split cedar at the time I came in. It was built of boards 1x12 afterwards. He told me at the time they came in they could not get lumber and he split some cedar to finish the house. It has all been rebuilt before I came there.[30]

By the time of Gregorio Fernandez's death a couple of years after his nephew's arrival, the store had gone bankrupt and young Joe Gonsalves turned to fishing for a living. When he was in his mid-20s he married a Squamish woman to whom various names and descents were attributed at different times. The Gonsalves family knew her as Susie Harris, or Harry. Their granddaughter said she was "a Burrard Inlet Indian," and a newspaper account based on conversations with the family described her as "an aunt of Chief Dan George," a Squamish man who later became well known as a movie actor.[31] Gonsalves described her for the 1901 census as a "Siwash" whose first language was "Siwash," but three decades later, when he applied for birth certificates for his children, he said that she was English. The couple's first child Matilda was born in 1884 at Brockton Point, followed at two-year intervals by daughters Elizabeth, Armenia, Virginia and Theresa, and a son named Alfred.

Joe Gonsalves, or Gonzell as his surname was sometimes anglicized and usually pronounced, was not the only new arrival at Brockton Point in the 1870s. Four other men—John Brown, Edward Long, Robert Cole and James Cummings—were attracted to Brockton Point for much the same reasons that their predecessors were. The son of one of them, Tim Cummings, shared with Major Matthews the story that came down through his family:

Father was one of those fellows who got tired of tough living conditions

> in the Scotland of the 'seventies, so he came from the Island of Ankel [in the Orkney Islands] or some name like that, in Scotland, as a sailor on one of the windjammers which loaded lumber at Moodyville Sawmill. There was a whole group of sailors deserted the ship. I know four of the deserters were [Edward] Long, [Robert] Cole, John Brown, and my father, James Cummings. I don't know how they skipped out, but they squatted in Stanley Park, and started fishing for herrings, and all sorts of fish, with drag nets pulled on shore by hand. There was sufficient demand for fish from the ships, mills, and Gastown, so that they could sell their fish. Father continued fishing to the end of his days; he fished out in English Bay, and usually sold his fish to [Charles] Anderson, the fish curer, who used to have a big place at the foot of Abbott Street [Dominion Fish Co.].[32]

If these men did slip off ships, they likely did not do so at the same time. John Brown, or a man by the same name, was a Portuguese fisherman who in 1872 was convicted of manslaughter when his partner fell overboard after fishing for dogfish at Plumper's Pass and sentenced to "ten years penal servitude." Repeated petitions by Brown's "own compatriots" to reopen the case got nowhere, particularly after Brown attempted unsuccessfully to escape custody.[33] Discharged in 1882, Brown made his way to Brockton Point, where he turns up in the 1891 census as a 61-year-old fisherman living by himself immediately west of the Gonsalves family.

Edward Long hailed from Brighton, England. He was, according to his son, "a British seaman—a bucko mate who came up from 'Frisco ... to join a ship and decided to stay."[34] Long, who mostly logged for a living, built himself a house just to the east of where Tomkins Brew had resided.

Robert Cole, considered by his family to be Scots born, settled down west of Brown with a young Squamish woman, Catherine (Kitty) Tom. As did some of the others, he may have moved to the peninsula at his wife's instigation. Kitty's father is said to have been "Policeman Tom," also known as Chief Tom. Two Squamish men with the first name of Thomas are listed in the 1876 reserve census of the Whoi Whoi area.

Robert Cole and Kitty were the parents of David, born in 1878, Thomas three years later, and then a daughter named Mary. Cole worked as a longshoreman.

James Cummings, sometimes spelled "Cumming," was in his 20s when he moved into Joe Mannion's old house on the north shore of Brockton Point. We know quite a lot about him because his son Tim listened to the stories his parents had to tell. He explained that "there were no white women around here ... however Indian girls worked at the cannery," so there his father headed in search of a wife.[35]

> Mother was a Bella Coola Indian who came with her parents in one of those big canoes, paddled all the way from Bella Coola [over 300 miles/500 kilometres up the coast] to work in the salmon cannery at Ladner's on the [mouth of the south arm of the] Fraser [River]. Her Indian name was Spukhpukanum; English name, Lucy. Father met her at the Ladner Cannery and brought her home to Brockton Point. If there was a marriage ceremony, then I never heard of it, but they lived happily together until father died after eighteen years married life.[36]

James Cummings settled down with Lucy in about 1879. They cleared the land and grew fruits, vegetables and flowers. Children soon came along: Tim in 1881, Agnes two years later, then Annie, William and finally Margaret in 1889. As well as caring for her own family, Lucy served as midwife to her neighbours, including Joe Gonsalves's wife Susie.

Brockton Point both remained the same and changed its face between the 1860s and 1880s. At any one time, half a dozen or so families lived there. As some relationships disintegrated, others were developing. More generally, ideas about family life were changing around Burrard Inlet. Eihu's granddaughter Minnie explained how newcomer men with Aboriginal wives were once the accepted order of things.

> A lot of white men had Indian wives. There was Joe Mannion, Tomkins Brew, Navvy Jack [Thomas, who came out with the gold rush, married a half-sister of Joe Silvey's first wife and provided ferry service across Burrard Inlet],

> Gassy Jack [Deighton, a saloon keeper who was the namesake for Gastown], Portuguese Joe [Silvey], John Beatty [an oxen driver at Burrard Inlet logging camps who married a daughter of Chief George of the False Creek Reserve], the Cummings—his family are living in Stanley Park now—and Johnny Baker who had his little house just where the Nine O'clock Gun is, and Capt. [William] Ettershank, the [river] pilot [who married a Squamish woman], and, of course, my own father.[37]

The mixed-race character of Brockton Point and Kanaka Ranch was increasingly called into question. To protect her from scorn, Joe Gonsalves's family obscured Susie's Squamish heritage. The 1882–83 provincial directory put the male newcomer population of Burrard Inlet and vicinity at 297. Calvert Simpson, the storekeeper at Hastings Mill, lamented that the total did not translate into comparable numbers of newcomer children: "Why you could put all the white girls in a big rowboat. When we went off on a picnic, one good big boat would hold all the young ladies there were. [There were] less than [30 children at Hastings Mill School], and many of them half breeds, Kanakas, Indians, all sorts … Of course, after they started to build the C.P.R. everything was different."[38]

Once construction of the promised transcontinental railway got underway, the newcomer population soared, particularly after Burrard Inlet was designated the line's terminus. Not only did more newcomer women arrive, but the lens of public opinion turned what had until recently been ordinary into the exotic, a subject of ridicule. This note appeared in the *Vancouver Weekly Herald* of January 15, 1886: "A dance took place in the Indian camp near the Hastings Mill on New Year's Eve. Several ladies of Vancouver went to see the affair, and looked with great interest at their dusky sisters dancing round the fires in bare feet."

The families of Whoi Whoi, Kanaka Ranch and Brockton Point fared variously into the mid-1880s. Aboriginal people had been the easiest to dispossess. They might still make their home on the tongue of land they considered their own, but so far as newcomers were concerned, they had no claims to it. The process was more subtle for families at Kanaka Ranch and Brockton Point, who were similarly marginalized. Some people, none more so than Joe Mannion, adopted the new thinking, seeing their one-time Aboriginal partners as a deficit to be remedied as expeditiously as possible. Others stood tall, including Joe Silvey and Mary See-em-ia, the proud matriarch of Kanaka Ranch. The departures and arrivals that occurred between the 1870s and mid-1880s at Brockton Point did not fundamentally alter the sense of community that bound families together.

Chapter 4
Imposition of Stanley Park

The first park ranger Henry Avison and his family lived just inside the entrance to Stanley Park. Bailey Bros. photo, City of Vancouver Archives, St Pk P94N53

The imposition of Stanley Park on the peninsula followed fast on Vancouver's creation in 1886 as the western terminus of the new transcontinental railway. The proximity of the two events obscured the fraught circumstances that led up to the peninsula's new status. In the popular imagination, the park rose pristine out of the wilderness.

The government of Britain had, it thought, shed responsibility for British Columbia when the colony joined the Canadian Dominion in 1871. The new provincial government took over Crown land and, apart from the Royal Navy establishment at Esquimalt, the mother country retreated. Nine years later Britain was jerked back into British Columbia's affairs when Canada sought to recover lands that Britain had supposedly acquired for defence purposes during the colonial years. The Dominion government did so first in Ontario, Quebec and the Atlantic provinces and then, in early 1880, turned its attention to British Columbia. Knowing that "a considerable area of lands, sited at important points along the coast line in the province of British Columbia, is held by the Imperial Government as military and naval reserves," the Canadian government requested that everything not still needed "may be transferred to the Dominion."[1] The request was in line with Section 117 of the British North America Act, which stated that all lands "required for Fortifications or for the Defence of the Country" belonged to the Dominion of Canada.

The British government scrambled. Officials in the Colonial Office, which oversaw relations with its Dominions, had no idea what was meant by the request, apart from the Royal Navy facilities at Esquimalt. A diligent search was undertaken through government records in British Columbia on the Colonial Office's behalf. The searchers uncovered correspondence between Govenor Douglas and British officials from December 1859 to January 1860 related to the designation of naval reserves and also "a tracing" on which "certain lands at Burrard Inlet" were "marked" as "Government Reserves," but "as far as I can ascertain these Reserves have not been Gazetted," which was the legal requirement to make them official. That was it. George Walkem, BC chief commissioner of lands and works, reported in November 1880: "No definite record is to be found here as to the Naval or Military Reserves made in the early period of British Columbia's existence. There is no record of the acceptance by the Colonial Office of any lands—even of those at Esquimalt; and the evidence of *acceptance* of the latter would seem to rest solely on their occupation by the Naval authorities … The Colonial Office or the Admiralty may, however, be able to throw some further light on the subject."[2]

A search through government records in Britain proved equally fruitless. Even if lands such as the peninsula had been set aside, they had not been acquired by the mother country.[3]

The official appointed to sort out the mess from the British side concluded woefully that "the whole question is in an unsatisfactory state." It was Joseph Trutch, who had succeeded Colonel Moody as chief commissioner of lands and works and was now acting for the Canadian government, who proposed a face-saving resolution. After having the BC Lands Office compile a list of all possible reserves, he personally attested that they had all been so designated. "I distinctly remember that it was by me, and well understood whilst I was Chief Commissioner of Lands and Works from 1864 to 1871, that several tracts of land were held under reservation—particularly in New Westminster District and at Esquimalt for military and naval purposes." One of these tracts was, he claimed, "at the First Narrows Burrard Inlet." As to the reserves' legitimacy, Trutch pointed to "the sanction and authority of the Governor having under the then system of government full and binding force and effect."[4]

Trutch conveniently overlooked Col. Moody's tendency to act on his own volition, without consulting, much less seeking the approval of, James Douglas as governor or his own willingness as land commissioner in 1865 to sell off part of the peninsula to the English company backed by Moody to build a sawmill there. Then Trutch had acted as if the colony of British Columbia had authority over the peninsula, just as the new province did a few years later in line with Sections 109 and 117 of the British North America Act. Now serving another master, the Dominion of Canada, Trutch made exactly the opposite argument.

It took the Colonial Office another three years to decide what to do. If Britain did not own the supposed reserves, who did? If the then mother country had never formally acquired them, to whom did they rightly belong? At least twice the Colonial Office pondered on paper "whether the lands should be relinquished to the Dominion or Provincial Govt."[5] Given that no record could be found of Britain ever acquiring the reserves, it made eminent good sense to consider them retained by British Columbia as Crown land.

But such an alternative did not win out: the Colonial Office dealt as a matter of course with Dominions, not provincial governments, and it did not want to alienate an important ally. In the summer of 1883 the War Office, likely resorting to Trutch's list, compiled a "Schedule of the Reserved Lands of British Columbia proposed to be surrendered to the Dominion Government." Among 15 pieces loosely enumerated in New Westminster District were "about 3,000" acres (1,200 hectares) "on south shore of Burrard Inlet outside 2nd Narrows" and another 600 acres (240 hectares) on "South Shore of 1st Narrows."[6] Neither corresponded, even roughly, to the peninsula's 1,000 acres.

The Colonial Office's draft memo proposing a way out took Trutch's tack. "Say that Governor Douglas's power to mark reserves in the early days of British Columbia appears to have rested on the 2nd clause of his commission dated 2 Sept. 1858 ['to do and execute all things in due manner.']." It did not matter whether he had formally made reserves, only that he possessed the authority to do so had he chosen to use it. No concern was expressed that the British government was handing over pieces of land it had never knowingly possessed. In 1884, Britain formally turned over to the Dominion of Canada all the lands on the schedule the War Office had compiled. The formal dispatch was carefully crafted to avoid accountability: "As regards the reserves now in question, no formal deed appears to have been made conveying them to the Military or Naval authorities, and I am advised that they may now, in like manner, be surrendered without the formality of a regular deed of conveyance. It appears, therefore, sufficient to state that His Majesty's Government are prepared to surrender the Military reserves specified in the schedule to the War Office."[7]

No sooner did Canada acquire the peninsula, along with the other pieces of property, than private interests began to tug it away. The Canadian Pacific Railway was in the midst of constructing the line that had been promised to British Columbia on its entry into Confederation. The CPR sought to make as much profit as possible by acquiring land all along the way to sell to speculators and settlers. In January 1885 CPR's vice-president requested ownership of the southern half of the peninsula, including Brockton Point, or as much as the government "can spare us," but the Dominion government had not yet decided what to do with its windfall.[8]

Rebuffed in its attempt to secure the peninsula—or at least part of it—for development, the CPR was determined that no one else would do so. The company located the line's western terminus on Burrard Inlet because the spoils to be had there were so great. It snagged a third of the lots that Morton and the others had pre-empted almost a quarter of a century earlier, much of the waterfront along Burrard Inlet and other property as well.

If more land went on the market, such as the peninsula, the price of the CPR's parcels would be driven down, so the company took another tack. The peninsula should become an urban park, an idea newly fashionable across North America. Arthur Wellington Ross, a member of parliament closely aligned to CPR interests, made the pitch in March 1886. He emphasized to the minister of militia and defence how such a park "would be quite an attraction to tourists traveling over our national railway." But the CPR was thwarted for a second time, being informed that the peninsula might become "the site of our barracks and battery."[9]

The CPR tried a third approach. On April 6, 1886, Vancouver formally came into existence with its own governance in the form of a city council. At only the council's second meeting on May 12, it voted to petition the Canadian government "that the whole of that part of Coal Harbour peninsula known as the Government Reserve be conveyed to the City of Vancouver for a Public Park."[10] The motion was made by Alderman Lachlan Alexander Hamilton, land commissioner for the CPR, who had laid out the townsite of Vancouver. Hamilton did not act on his own initiative. The mayor of Vancouver was brother-in-law to MP Ross, who had made the same request on behalf of the CPR just six weeks earlier, and had been turned down.

The land developers, contractors and merchants who composed Vancouver's first city council were just as concerned over the peninsula's fate as was the CPR. They had as much to lose financially if the Canadian government decided the reserve was not needed for military purposes and released it for sale. A parallel, equally important reason was that both rail officials and land speculators sought to depict Vancouver as a desirable place to live, and few amenities were as enticing as a large park adjacent to a city centre. The romanticized association of parks with natural bounty could become a major selling point that would transform the image of Vancouver to be more than just another boomtown.

It took almost a year of manoeuvring behind the scenes to persuade the Dominion government. As Hamilton put it later, Ross used "his influence with the Dominion Government," while he got "the chief officials [of the CPR] at Montreal to use their influence with the government." Permission was finally granted on the condition that the peninsula would revert to the Dominion if it was needed for defence purposes. An Order-in-Council on June 7, 1887, read:

> The Minister reports that he sees no objection to this proposal, provided the Corporation keep the Park in proper order, and the Dominion Government retain the right to resume the property [for military purposes] when required at any time.[11]

The brash young city had got its park. The men in charge could now imprint the peninsula with the image of what they wanted Vancouver to become.

The city began taking control by building a road around the new park. The task was not difficult: the peninsula had been logged repeatedly, numerous private ventures including Hastings Mill having taken advantage of the virgin stands of fir, cedar and spruce. Some of the activity, such as shingle cutting, was informal. Other operators had used teams of oxen on rough roads to skid logs out to the water to be sold to one of the mills. These roads and long-established Aboriginal trails were the foundations for sections of the new road.

Road construction began in earnest as soon as a wooden bridge was laid across the creek that had previously cut off the peninsula at high tide. In this activity, as in so much of the designation and development of the park, the CPR's hand was visible. L.A. Hamilton, the same railroad official who had laid out Vancouver and made the motion at City Council to acquire the peninsula, took the lead. CPR axe men did the actual work.

Road builders had no interest in the families who made their homes on the peninsula. Anything in their way was cast aside or adapted, as with the midden piles used to pave the road. Joe Gonsalves recalled the effects of road construction on the south side of Brockton Point, where his and the Smith, Baker and Cole families lived:

> At the time they started to put the road there, they came through one morning and said they were going to put the road there on this ground, and the surveyors ran the line inside of the fence so I said if they would shift the fence back they could go there. They changed my fence and Peter Smith's fence as well. It was right back to the road, and when they put the road through they shifted it back [toward the water]. The width of the road … No [they never paid me anything, or asked my leave].[12]

Tim Cummings and his family had much the same experience on the north side of Brockton Point:

> The Park road was made around Stanley Park, and ran right through our house; we had to move our house back to let the road go by. Our house was built of sawn lumber, and axe-hewn lumber, and had some kind of a tile chimney, and we got our water from a hole in the ground, and hauled it up with a bucket and a rope.[13]

Squamish families at Whoi Whoi and Chaythoos were hit even harder, in a literal sense. James Clendenning, the man in charge of blazing the trail, recalled the irrelevance of the people his crew encountered:

> My instructions were—I laid the road out according to get the best view of the water as I went around. I was to keep as close to the water as was practicable … On the north side there was a kind of trail along there for a certain distance. There was no house there on the Inlet side until we came up here, where an old Indian woman lived. She was complaining very much

> about her fence being taken down, 'olah,' she said—she talked nothing but Chinook.

One of the road workers later mused how "the Indians were put out of the houses and we were put in." He added with a flourish, "we had an excellent French cook, but the living quarters were not so good."[14]

August Jack explained what happened to his family at Chaythoos.

> When they make Stanley Park road we was eating [breakfast] in our house. Some one make noise outside; chop our house. We was inside this house when the surveyors come along, and they chop the corner of our house when we was eating inside. We all get up go out see what was the matter. My [older] sister Louisa, she was the only one talk a little English; she goes out ask whiteman what he's doing that for. The man says, "We're surveying the road." My sister ask him, "Whose road? Is it whiteman's?" Whiteman says, "Someday you'll find good road around, it's going around." Of course, whiteman did not say park; they did not call it park then.
>
> There were two of them they cut off the corner of our house; just a little bit, so that they could see where to put their survey line ... The man said that when the road goes by here you are going to have lots of money. They said, "Pay to go through your place." But they have not paid yet.
>
> When they cut roadway they go right through our house; my father's, Supple Jack's, grave was about one hundred and forty feet west of house; our house little house in front facing water; big long pow-wow house behind; both made of cedar slabs; been there long, long time, long before my time.[15]

The Vancouver City Council, which had charge of the new park, did acknowledge liability to some extent. In December 1887 it voted "to expend the sum of fifty dollars for the purpose of settling the claims of Indians on the *line* of the Park Road for bushes and fences destroyed." The next July, the council considered "the claims of Mrs. Baker for garden destroyed by Park Road."[16] Mary Tsiyaliya might be a Squamish woman, but she was not about to be deprived of her means of livelihood without compensation. These exceptions did not much affect what occurred.

Once City Council had completed the road, there were two opening ceremonies. Both were held at August Jack's family home at Chaythoos, next to where his father Supple Jack had been laid to rest above ground five years earlier. As soon as his family learned of the plans, they removed the gravesite to protect the remains—an action that only confirmed to city fathers that they were now in control. The families at Brockton Point were similarly put upon. The landing spot for people coming to the ceremonies by water was located virtually next door to the south shore houses.

The first opening was held on September 27, 1888. The official procession of vehicles, headed by the 20-piece city band, left city hall, then located on Powell Street, precisely at 11:00 a.m. for what the local newspaper described as "the open grassy spot near where Supple Jack's grave used to be." Vancouver mayor David Oppenheimer, one of the early land speculators implicated in the city's future, foretold how the park would provide "a place of recreation in the vicinity of a city where its inhabitants can spend some time amid the beauties of nature away from the busy haunts of men." Those inhabitants now numbered 6,000, and that evening the largest ball in the history of the city was held under the mayor's patronage in Vancouver's new opera house.[17]

The second ceremony, a year later, also took place on the "old Indian clearing" which had held Supple Jack's grave. At this event the governor general of Canada, Lord Stanley, formally dedicated the park named in his honour. "To the use and enjoyment of people of all colours, creeds and customs for all time, I name thee Stanley Park." According to one participant, he spoke the words "throwing his arms into the air as though embracing the whole expanse of towering forest before him." Mayor Oppenheimer, in his enthusiastic response, announced that "the citizens … to commemorate the visit … have decided upon raising a cairn in honour of the event."[18] A precedent had been established for the park: that events deemed significant by those in charge were marked. The cairn ended up as a one-ton statue of Lord Stanley.

The final step to taking control, after laying claim and asserting authority, was to establish mechanisms for exercising that authority.

In April 1889 the provincial government amended Vancouver's incorporation act to permit the election of a Board of Park Commissioners with authority to "pass by-laws for the use, regulation, protection, and government of the park or parks."[19]

The new three-man board appointed a park ranger, Henry Avison, to put out fires, prevent logging and generally make sure that everything was in order. Avison had a family, so he had to have a house, which was constructed on the north side of the bridge at the entrance to the park.

Authority within the park was exercised in another way: the use of the land to provide Vancouver with a reliable source of drinking water. A pipe was run from a supply at Capilano on the north shore, under Burrard Inlet, past Supple Jack's home near Prospect Point and through the park along what is known as Pipeline Road. In 1894 Frank Harris, an Englishman, was hired to manage the city's water supply. He built a home in the shadow of Chaythoos; there he and his wife eventually raised 10 children. "Supple Jack was buried close to our cottage," Harris told Major Matthews in 1937, "in a little dead house just where the summer house stands; the little open shelter by the horse trough, just where Lord Stanley dedicated the park. The Indian graves were all along there, by our cottage. The Indians had quite a little place there by our road at the end of the pipe-line road; the old fence was around it for years afterwards."[20]

Supple Jack was not the only person interred on the peninsula, hence the skeletons unearthed during road building. Many early Brockton Point residents had been buried both in the park and on Deadman's Island near Brockton Point, which got its name for this reason. When Eihu's granddaughter Maud died in 1881, she was taken from Kanaka Ranch to Brockton Point to be buried. Her sister Minnie described the setting to Major Matthews years later:

> Father put a little picket fence around her grave and he made a little head board, with a round top; it was painted white, and must have had my sister's name on it because I remember one day when I was at school down at the Hastings Sawmill school, a girl said to me, "I see your name [McCord] on a grave board in Stanley Park."

> There are quite a few buried at Brockton Point; quite a few; Peter Plante's little boy [son of a former fur-trade employee from Quebec, who married a daughter of another former Quebec fur-trade employee, Supplien Guinne, and of Supple Jack's sister Khahmy] is buried there. My father made the little coffin. We used to go over there in a boat, and put flowers on the graves; it was quite a climb up the bank from the beach, because I remember thinking, "what a funny place to put a graveyard; so high up; and all trees." Mother and Mrs Plante went over there the day of the big fire [that burned down much of Vancouver on June 13, 1886] to put flowers on the graves; then we came back to look at the town which had all been burned up. There were quite a few buried on Deadman's Island, too.[21]

Some of the Chinese men who had come from China or San Francisco during the gold rush were also buried there. Elizabeth Silvey recalled Chinese graves on the peninsula from the 1870s or very early 1880s: "There were a lot of Chinamen buried along by Brockton Point, between the Nine O'clock Gun and the lighthouse. We used to walk along there, and in and out among the little mounds; no head boards, it was quite a little burying grounds."[22]

August Jack's observations made clear the extent to which the underground past had been hidden away by the time he spoke with Matthews in the 1930s:

> A lot of Indians were buried right up on the [Brockton] point itself. But the Indians not on the point are under the road now. [There] was a fence around the Indian graves, but the fence all rotted out, and they could not find it; so they can't find it at all now; I've been looking for it myself, but can't find it. You see, the Indians gather the bones and put them in big box; put them all in; bigger box than that, sides about four inches thick.
>
> Indians always bury close to the shore, but the Chinamans are further from the shore than the Indians. I see the Chinamans burning stuff there once—for to feed the dead. The white mans are buried all along that shore too. There are people buried all along there; all along that east shore between the [Nine O'clock] Gun and the [Brockton] point, on the edge of the high bank. Nobody buried on north shore of Brockton point; just east shore.

> No cemetery; no graveyard; just come in boat with the deadmans; climb the bank, dig a hole. They buried whitemans and Chinese; I did see them bury one Chinaman there; after the big fire [in June 1886]. There were a lot of graves—more than twenty; they were burying there all the time before they got Mountain View [Cemetery].[23]

Khahtsahlano was referring to a new civic cemetery, which was cleared and graded in the fall of 1887. With this shift, the peninsula's role as a burial place slipped from view. It was inevitable that the collective memory would be lost, given that no effort was made to maintain fences or provide other markers. To do so would have run counter to the notion of the new park as virginal. The city gloried in how "our city park of nine hundred and fifty acres, in its native grandeur and primitive beauty, will certainly rival if not eclipse any park on the Pacific slope."[24]

Another event at about the same time threatened to erase the living as well as the dead from Stanley Park. Tim Cummings made the connection in talking with Matthews about the last burial he recalled taking place at Brockton Point: "There were about fifty or one hundred graves along the bank above the beach; the [Peter] Smith girl was the last one buried, after the road came, and they started clearing the place for picnics. She died of smallpox during the epidemic."[25]

At this point the causes of the spread of disease were not well understood. Quarantine of people considered infected or otherwise suspect was common practice. Rumours of disease floated about for some time before smallpox was actually detected in Vancouver in April 1888, at which point one of the first actions taken by the authorities was to quarantine the road-building crew. Separated from their foreman, the men continued to work on their own. The families at Brockton Point suddenly became visible by virtue of proximity: fearing that the site was infected, officials forbade everyone in the new park to leave it.

It became imperative to cleanse the park. The new Board of Park Commissioners, at its second meeting on October 20, 1888, requested that the mayor "notify the Squatters on Stanley Park to remove therefrom before the 1st of January, prox, and failing to do so that action be at once taken."[26] By the middle of December the city health inspector had drawn up a list of properties to be destroyed at Brockton Point, giving for each a value, presumably for purposes of compensation:

	Settler value	Estimated value
1. Cummings, dwelling, boat house & wharf		$150.00
2. Cole, small dwelling house		$50.00
3. Joe Sylvia, two small houses, shop & outhouses & fences	$700.00	$200.00
4. Peter Smith, two small houses and out houses & fences (He will take small lot near water & house on it. False Creek preferred)		$150.00
5. John Brown, small house, shop and outhouses	$200.00	$150.00
6. E. Long, dwelling house, outhouses & fences. Will accept same terms as P. Smith.		$125.00

The above are those buildings that have been under strict quarantine and are liable to be still infected.

Other buildings in vicinity & values.

1. Three Siwash houses, present fair valuation	$175.00
2. Small house, built by J. Bruns [Burns]	$40.00
3. Small house on beach near bridge	$100.00
4. A number of Chinese dens of no particular value	

These are all the buildings between the bridge and the pipe line of the water company.

Values concurred in by A.M. Robertson Health Officer (signature)
J. Hartney Inspector (signature)

Vancouver, Dec. 14th 1888[27]

The document is revealing on several accounts. The use of the term "Settler value" indicates that the families were perceived as having legitimate claims to where they lived. Several of the men had been consulted about the value of their "property." Joe Silvey was still considered in possession of the site inhabited by Joe Gonsalves, and had put a value of $700 on his property—considerable for the time. Someone also met with John Brown, Peter Smith and Edward Long, and possibly others. Perhaps because of the death of Peter Smith's young daughter from smallpox, he and Edward Long, who had recently partnered with Smith's eldest daughter Mary, indicated that they were willing to leave if provisions were made for their families at False Creek.

Of the buildings enumerated "in vicinity," the "three Siwash houses" were likely at Whoi Whoi. The "J. Bruns" who built the house valued at just $40 was August Jack's brother-in-law John Burns, who by now had left the park for the Jericho beach area at Point Grey. He logged there, and he planted an orchard to sustain his growing family. His two daughters Maggie and Addie had a younger half-brother David.

The families were not as easy to remove as the men in charge had expected. By December 22, Brockton Point had been declared almost free of the disease, eliminating that rationale for destroying the houses. The families were not without resources. Peter Smith's eldest daughter recalled how they sought the assistance of Theodore Davie, a Victoria lawyer and provincial cabinet minister. By the following March the Parks Board realized its hands were tied. The peninsula was Dominion property and the City of Vancouver had no legal authority to expel the residents. The board contacted the minister of militia and defence in the hope he would instruct the provincial authorities to take action, but others were less agitated than the board over the families' presence, and nothing happened.

The men who lived in "the Chinese dens of no particular value" were not so fortunate. Of the groups making use of the peninsula, the Chinese were the easiest to dislodge, in part because they, like Aboriginal people, counted for so very little in the eyes of the dominant society. Some 15,000 men had come from China to western Canada to build the railway. A considerable number settled in Vancouver, not far from Gastown in what became known as Chinatown, but others preferred to go their own way, and some of them made their way to the new park, settling at what Vancouver City Council minutes repeatedly referred to as the "Chinese Ranches."[28] The use of the term "ranches" suggests a cluster of houses like those of the Aboriginal residents near Hastings Mill and the Hawaiians at Kanaka Ranch.

At the same meeting in March 1889 at which the Parks Board acknowledged that it could not eject the families of Brockton Point, commissioners played the health card in order to go after the Chinese. A motion was passed "to instruct the Health Inspector to take steps towards removing nuisances along the Park Road especially the Chinese." It took a good year for the health inspector to report back, whereupon the board requested him "to take the necessary steps to have the Chinese expelled from the Park." The inspector stated a month later that "the Chinese on the Park were willing to withdraw and allow their buildings to be burnt.[29] The board instructed Henry Avison, the park ranger, to do so. In conversation with Major Matthews in 1958, his daughter Sarah told a somewhat different story.

> [I remember how] the Chinamen in Stanley park established themselves on the point where the Royal Vancouver Yacht Club is now [on the south side of Brockton Point]; it was called Anderson's Point. They had some old shacks; there was more than one, and they were old; I don't know how many Chinamen; there may have been half a dozen or a dozen, I don't know. The shacks were just old cedar shacks, or lumber drifted up on the beach; it was fenced in parts; I don't know where they got their water, perhaps they had a well. I don't recall them having a boat, but they had pigs and a bull. The pigs were in a sty, and the bull was tied up.
>
> The Parks Board ordered the Chinamen to leave the park; they were trespassers; but the Chinamen would not go, so the Park Board told my father to set fire to the buildings. I saw them burn; there were five of us children, and you know what children are when there is a fire. So father set fire to the shacks; what happened to the Chinese I do not know, but the pigs were set loose and the bull untied, and they got lost in the forest of Stanley Park.[30]

The Chinese not only lived in the park, they also used it as a burial site and considered it very important to continue to respect their countrymen's graves through regular visits. The park ranger complained in October 1892 that "Chinese are in the habit of lighting fires in the vicinity of Chinese graves in the Park thereby endangering park property." The chief of police was requested to notify them to "remove the bodies as lighting fires within the Park and limits cannot be permitted," but the practice continued. A child at Brockton Point during the 1920s recalled the Chinese burning whole pigs as an offering to their countrymen interred there.[31] Still, for all intents and purposes the new park had been cleansed of the Chinese presence.

For a time, the families at Whoi Whoi and Chaythoos, Brockton Point and Kanaka Ranch were able to hold on to their dreams. Vancouver began as a small town, so Kanaka Ranch and Whoi Whoi did not come immediately to the attention of real estate developers and others of similar ilk. Once the smallpox scare receded, Brockton Point also slipped from view.

These Chinese men in the late 1800s may have been visiting Stanley Park burial sites. Library and Archives Canada, PA117201

Chapter 5
Generational Transitions

The Brockton Point families' way of life is caught in this image from the 1890s.
City of Vancouver Archives, CVA 371-2196

The families who had managed to stay on the peninsula faced new challenges during the quarter century following the official openings of Stanley Park in 1888–89. No one appreciated that with the passage of time, the families would get on with their lives. The ways in which they did so, as parents aged and died, leaving children in need of care, were unexpected and contradictory. Of the three communities in and around the park, Kanaka Ranch was the most unaffected and the Aboriginal people the least able to maintain a living tie with the place they considered their own.

It is difficult to know how many Aboriginal people still made use of the peninsula at the time Stanley Park was established. The Parks Board referred in passing in 1889 to "the Indian village" and "Indian houses."[1] Some still lived there; others continued to gather resources from its shores and its forest. August Jack Khahtsahlano's family left for Snauq, the False Creek Reserve, after the road was built through their house. It was not an unexpected choice. His great-uncle Chip-kaay-am had gone there at the same time his grandfather Khahtsahlano decided to settle on the peninsula.

Just two Aboriginal families were enumerated on the peninsula in the 1891 census; by 1899 they were gone. Tommy and Jenny Chunth, or Tchén ilthl, were in their mid-30s and their son Thomas was 10. In the 1876 count, the couple had a daughter, who may have left home. Tommy Chunth was employed as a fisherman. Jim and Sally Chamachan were described in 1891 as 55 and 35 years of age. Chamachan worked as a longshoreman, as did many Squamish men during these years, probably because they could fish during the summer as well, if they chose to do so.

Not just the physical presence of Aboriginals, but any reminder of them was obliterated as soon as possible. In December 1899, when the Parks Board was informed that "the Indian buildings on the Narrows were vacant," they decided "to purchase same, at a cost not to exceed $50.00, and immediately on completion of purchase the Park Ranger be instructed to destroy same."[2] There is no indication from whom the dwellings were acquired, but in any case the deed was done, at a cost of just $25, and the structures were set on fire.

For a time it seemed as if Brockton Point would be similarly consumed, if not literally by fire then in practice. The families' backyards became the playground of Vancouver's self-styled elite. No club in the fledgling city was more prestigious than the Vancouver Rowing Club, whose guiding spirit was the very same L.A. Hamilton who had led the effort to acquire the peninsula. As well as surveying the road around the park to ensure it was to his liking, he designed the first bridges to be suitably "rustic" in line with the vision of a pastoral park. The club's first president was Harry B. Abbott, general superintendent of the CPR, and among its membership were leading railway officials, real estate developers, bankers and sawmill owners.

At a meeting attended by the mayor and two aldermen, as well as Vancouver Rowing Club members, Brockton Point was selected as the site for an athletic ground. The men wanted a place to engage in sporting activities in their leisure time. At that time amateur sports were sharply distinguished from professional sports, which were looked down upon because working people were among their audiences. Sporting groups closely aligned to business and civic interests assumed that the park was theirs for the taking, a view with which city authorities heartily agreed. Even as the road was completed around Brockton Point, construction began on the Brockton Point Amateur Athletic Grounds. The city financed both initiatives, at a cost of $30,000. A cut-off road, which still exists, was built across Brockton Point, and a boat landing was constructed virtually at the foot of Joe Gonsalves's house. Thomas H. Boyd, one of the workers, recalled:

> We had our camp there within, I suppose, 800 or 1000 feet of his [Joe Gonsalves's] house. We were looking at it practically every day. In boats—we always had to pass in the rear of his house. We would pass in the rear of it. Well, as I see it now, and as I saw it then, as near as I can recollect, it was close to the water. It was standing high at the back—high next to the water and low on the hillside. Resting on posts or rocks, as I remember it. And there were nets—fishing nets—I can see the nets now—hanging on the beach drying, by the house—and from the house over to our camp—fishing nets, you know. I have talked to him on the road there. I was never in his house. I have seen a woman there as near as I can recollect, and children.[3]

In May 1890, as recorded in the Parks Board minutes, the new sports amenity was handed over "to the Athletic Clubs to be controlled by them, allowing them to charge gate money for matches but on ordinary occasions that the grounds be free to the use of the public."[4] Within a few years of Stanley Park being imposed, the most accessible part of it was privatized in the interests of a few. The lease was granted

The crowds at the Brockton Point Athletic Grounds in 1893 seemed to be a world away from the families living a stone's throw away.
Bailey Bros. photo, City of Vancouver Archives, ST PK P258 N201

for 40 years, and it brought the clubs a steady income.

Brockton Point Amateur Athletic Grounds were officially opened on Dominion Day weekend 1891, admission to the grounds being 25 cents. In the following spring the Union Steamship Company was given use of the Brockton Point wharf on condition that pleasure boats also have access, and that the maximum charge for adults be 10 cents one way, 15 cents return to its downtown wharf.

Uses for the Brockton Point grounds expanded over time. Cricketers and lacrosse supporters built their own pavilions, and from 1894 one could play golf on a nine-hole course that wound around the cricket pitch. Other, less exclusive events included the celebration of public holidays with races and sporting competitions.

The sporting fraternity was not the only interest group with its eye on Brockton Point. The Salvation Army arrived in Vancouver in 1886, and almost as soon as Stanley Park came into being, devotees began rowing over to the Brockton Point cemetery for picnics. One participant recalled:

> The reason we went to the clearing where the Nine O'clock Gun is, now called Hallelujah Point, was that it was about the only place where there was a clearing; we made tea and ate sandwiches, and ran races, and had a lot of singing, and a short service, and my husband used to play the drum, and my son used to stand on top of the drum, and sing a chorus.
>
> There were some grave boards and crosses in the trees close by; there were quite a few little head boards; wood, rounded on the top.[5]

The dapper young and middle-aged gentlemen who idled away their leisure at Brockton Point and the singing Salvation Army picnickers could not have been more different in outlook and aspirations from the families who made their lives just a stone's throw away. The residents' simple accommodations harked back to an earlier

The Salvation Army's picnic shelter at Hallelujah Point, here about 1900, was suitably rustic, in line with keeping Stanley Park "natural."
City of Vancouver Archives, CVA 677-180.13

era in which people fended for themselves, using the natural materials at hand to create dwellings that were intended to suffice, rather than to signal status. Yet these were not just houses; they were maintained places of residence with separate outhouses, fences and gardens. As the 1888 enumeration showed, the Cummings family had a boathouse and wharf, and Gonsalves and Brown both operated shops. The families may have lived modestly, but they were not without pride in their material conditions.

Another couple arrived at Brockton Point. Having taken the railway west from Ontario, 30-year-old Mary Dunbar nursed Peter Smith's wife Kenick through an illness. In appreciation, Smith invited Mary and her husband James to move into Tomkins Brew's vacant house, located between his residence and a home just built by new son-in-law Edward Long. James Dunbar, a Scot eight years Mary's senior, worked as a fisherman, sometimes longshored with Peter Smith, and for a time was a lighthouse keeper. The Dunbars, who had no children, were the sole white couple to live at Brockton Point. They sometimes took in boarders, such as a young piano teacher from Ontario, who shows up in the 1891 census. At some point in the 1890s, the elderly bachelor John Brown either died or left.

The families at Brockton Point and Kanaka Ranch occupied a borderland between two ways of life. To ambitious young Vancouver, they did not matter. The 1893 Vancouver directory included Long and Smith as "fisherman, Water front, res Stanley Park," but the only people listed under "Stanley Park" were the ranger Henry Avison and a couple of other park employees. Subsequent editions of the directory excluded most Brockton Point heads of households. The men and their families did not fit into the neat assumptions about race, racial difference and ways of life that predominated in the new City of Vancouver and, for that matter, the rest of British Columbia and Canada.

So far as the emerging dominant society was concerned, the Darwinian notions of survival of the fittest that grew out of the colonial impulse seemed amply to have been borne out. In this thinking, the whitest people had, during the past centuries, changed the world through their racial superiority, and the basis upon which they did so—the usurpation of indigenous land and resources—was a necessary step along the way. Canada may no longer have been a colonial possession, but the attitudes that grounded the phenomenon around the world were alive and well.

In general, no one knew what to do with mixed-heritage persons, as were the second and subsequent generations at Brockton Point, Kanaka Ranch and to some extent at Chaythoos. Almost all newcomers preferred not to associate with them, convinced that they were contaminated by their inheritance. The time was gone when unions between newcomer men and Aboriginal women were tolerated for lack of alternatives. Their legacy in the form of mixed-race children was for the dominant society an unwanted reminder of an unfortunate past, when some men were so morally weak as to cohabit unwisely. Overall, hybridity was more despised as an inheritance than was Aboriginality, because of the widespread belief that Aboriginal people would disappear in the near future, in the face of newcomers' superiority in every facet of life. Missionaries such as Father Fouquet and Charles Tate were lauded for doing what they could in the interim.

The double irony was that the very same society that rejected mixed-race people decreed that they could not adhere to their maternal inheritance, either. The British North America Act of 1867, which legitimized Canada as a nation, made Native people wards of the Dominion government, overseen by a Department of Indian Affairs. Questions over rights were resolved by the concept of status: only those whose fathers were Aboriginal were "real Indians."

Any cracks to be found in this wall of exclusion came through missionary zeal. Across Canada the churches had gotten to Aboriginal populations early on, as at Burrard Inlet, and they continued to be full partners with the Canadian government in the process by which Aboriginal peoples stripped of their land were to be made malleable and docile. The Mission Reserve was repeatedly held up as exemplar of what could be accomplished for status Indians, who were the only persons legally permitted on reserves. The British Columbia directory of 1882 lauded "the white cottages and simple church of the Indian (Catholic) mission."[6]

The uneasy relationship that existed between the Oblates' ambition for the Mission Reserve and the limitations imposed by the concept of status came to the fore with the Bakers, who were the first of the Brockton Point families to be caught up in a difficult generational transition. John Baker died in 1888 and was buried on nearby Deadman's Island. His Squamish wife Mary Tsiyaliya, who was left to care for half a dozen children on her own, moved to the Mission Reserve, where her relatives lived. The Oblates were strategic in managing the edict that only people with status could live on reserve. Mary Tsiyaliya's grandson Simon recalled, "My grandmother and her teen-aged daughters were told they all had to marry Indians from around there. Those days, the church didn't want to have a half-breed marrying a half-breed, so they all married Indians from the reserve."[7]

The condition that Baker's widow and daughters marry Indians was a way to ensure they would acquire status. A historian who did research on the Mission Reserve in the early 1950s heard repeatedly how the Oblates "arranged a number of marriages between the Squamish and people of mixed descent of both sexes," noting that "the present day Bakers and a number of others are offspring of these marriages."[8] Mary Tsiyaliya soon wed Chief Squamish Jacob, a descendant of Chief Capilano, as was Joe Silvey's first wife Khaltinaht and perhaps Mary See-em-ia.

The Baker daughters likely considered they were exercising free will in their choices of partners. In subordinating their newcomer to their Aboriginal inheritance, they were also bowing to the wishes of the Catholic Church and the Canadian government. Their nephew Simon Baker recorded how all four daughters wed men with status.[9]

The Baker sons followed suit by finding Aboriginal partners. Willie married Mary Ann Kenakelut and settled down on the Mission Reserve. His older brother Johnny took Chief Joe Capilano's daughter Susan of the nearby Capilano Reserve as his second wife. Their son Simon recalled his mother as a strong woman who essentially completed the process by which the Baker family recovered their Squamish inheritance. "My mother knew everything about our ways, our culture. She knew how to prepare our food, dried salmon, everything. She also made baskets of all kinds."[10]

For the Parks Board, the Baker family's departure from Brockton Point was providential. They quickly co-opted the site where their house stood. Steamship service with Asia had commenced shortly after the railway arrived, placing more pressure on governments to provide secure navigation in and out of Burrard Inlet. A lighthouse was constructed on the tip of Brockton Point in 1890, and one of the keeper's jobs was to set off a dynamite charge every night at 9:00 so ships in the harbour would have the correct time and be able to measure tides accurately. The practice was dangerous, so in 1894 a muzzle-loading cannon was erected near the Bakers' former home in a wooden shed. Its charge was set off by a telegraph operator typing a

In 1900 a shed was built around the Nine O'clock Gun, erected six years earlier near John Baker's former home. The Vancouver photographer Leonard Frank took this image sometime before the shed was demolished in 1936.
Leonard Frank photo, City of Vancouver Archives, P121N164

key to close the circuit at precisely 9:00 each evening. What had once been Baker's Point became known as the Time Gun, or Nine O'clock Gun, which it remains to the present day.

Other members of the second and third families from Brockton Point, Kanaka Ranch and Chaythoos were also caught up by missionary zeal, but in a very different way. The Oblates and other missionaries hoped that when their charges moved onto reserves, as did the Baker family, they would perforce pursue the sedentary lifestyle newcomers associated with being "civilized." Aboriginal people did not always agree, and their resistance led to the establishment of segregated residential schools intended to educate Indian children into newcomer ways during their impressionable years so they would apply their new cultural practices when they returned to their home reserves. The Department of Indian Affairs co-operated with religious groups to build schools, which were for that reason meant to be restricted to status children. The difficulty was that many Indian parents saw no reason to give up their sons and daughters.

The Department of Indian Affairs intended Coqualeetza to provide older children with industrial education. Not only was such training at the apex of the residential school system, the imposing three-storey brick building made Coqualeetza the largest school in British Columbia, which was at the forefront of Canadian provinces in promoting industrial education. BC Archives, H-07253

The intermediary to hybrid children from Brockton Point, Kanaka Ranch and Chaythoos filling in for them was the Methodist missionary Charles Tate, who got to know the families while preaching at Gastown during the 1870s. Posted to the Fraser Valley, 100 kilometres east of Vancouver, he first took some local children into his home and then convinced the Methodists to construct a residential school, with the financial assistance of the Department of Indian Affairs. The budget for the new Coqualeetza Industrial School, completed in 1894 and intended to enroll 100 children, depended on a per-student subsidy from Indian Affairs, but it could not attract enough students.

So Tate began to recruit non-Methodist and mixed-race students to fill the spaces. Three children with origins at Chaythoos, 11 from Brockton Point and six whose families had lived at Kanaka Ranch were rounded up to sustain Coqualeetza during its first decade of operation. All of their fathers were newcomers, which meant that despite their Aboriginal mothers, none of the children had status.

August Jack's sister Louisa Burns enrolled her children Addie and David in Coqualeetza when it opened in 1894. She felt she had little choice after her husband died and she was left to fend for herself. Clearly conscious that the school was closely monitored by the Department of Indian Affairs, Coqualeetza's administrators, in the official ledger recording "Admission and Discharges," fudged the records.[11] Addie and Dave were shown as Squamish in spite of their white father. Four weeks later their sister Maggie, two years younger, joined them at Coqualeetza. Their mother Louisa moved to Snauq, or Kitsilano, where her family had gone from Stanley Park. The fact that her great-uncle Chip-kaay-am, or George, was the long-time chief there may have facilitated her being slipped onto the reserve.

Death also gave the nudge to the Peter Smith family from Brockton Point. Kenick died not long after their eldest daughter Mary settled down with Edward Long. The three youngest children needed care. Their Catholic father also considered he had little choice. The matron sympathetically recorded their arrival at the school's opening: "The Smith family—Johnnie, nine; Maria, five; and Rita [Sarah], three,—

were accompanied by their father, who seemed almost heart-broken to part with his children, but the mother was dead, and he had to be from home most of the time, for he was a fisherman."[12]

Soon after, they were joined there by their older brothers Thomas and Peter. The column in the official school register for "tribal origin" listed the Smiths as "Squamish" with a father named only as Peter and an "unknown" mother.

The Smiths' neighbour, 13-year-old Tommy Cole, was also among the first pupils enrolled at the school's opening in 1894. Following his father's death, his mother Catherine found herself a new partner in an Italian fisherman who styled himself variously John Marianna and Mariano Caros. Legally wed in October 1891, they lived at Brockton Point and had two daughters, Rosa and Kitty. Whatever happened to the marriage, authorities soon decreed that Catherine was an unfit mother. According to family memory, Tommy was dispatched to Coqualeetza and the two little girls whipped up into an orphanage, from which they were fostered out to white families, to be brought up as if they were white.[13] Their older brother David was, at age 16, old enough to fend for himself, and so escaped the fate that beset Tommy and the others.

Kanaka Ranch children were also recruited. Seraphine McCord was enrolled, possibly because of religious affinity. Her mother Maggie, Mary See-em-ia's daughter by Eihu, had recently brought her second husband, Daniel McPhee, to Kanaka Ranch, and his Baptist orientation was not that different from the Methodism underpinning Coqualeetza. Seraphine's older sister Minnie, who later became Major Matthews' informant, had left school at age 10 to work as household help and then, at age 18, had married a bookkeeper born in Montreal, William Smith. The Coqualeetza ledger conveniently described Seraphine as Musqueam. Maggie McPhee also arranged for three of her nieces and nephews, the children of her younger half-sister Lucy Nahanee Smith, to enroll at the school. None of the Kanaka Ranch children was more than one-quarter Aboriginal.

Sparse Aboriginal descent also proved no barrier to two children of James Keamo, who had briefly lived at Kanaka Ranch, ending up at Coqualeetza, even though they were only one-eighth Aboriginal and Catholic to boot. At the time they were enrolled, Emma, age 14, had already completed the third standard and Josephine, 12, had finished the second at the Port Hammond public school near their Fraser Valley home, which raises even more questions about how their presence was justified.

Other Brockton Point children soon followed. James Cummings died in March 1897. Having fallen ill, he had time to make out his will, leaving his property in trust for the support of his family and also "for the education of my children." The witnesses were his Brockton Point neighbours, James and Mary Dunbar. Just two weeks later, three of his children joined their Smith and Cole neighbours at Coqualeetza—Tim, aged 16, Agnes, 13, and William, nine. Annie, aged 12, followed in August, and Maggie, just seven, in November. Annie's daughter explained how "they were all taken from the mother" on the grounds that "she had no way of supporting them, there was no welfare, she had berries in her garden and she went fishing in the inlet, caught the odd fish but that's all the income she had, and she had those five kids. So the government came along and said, 'well, we'd better take them to the residential school,' and that's what they did. They all went."[14]

The identity of the Cummings children was even more obscured in the Coqualeetza register than were those of the other families. They were admitted without a surname, recorded in the ledger with "father's name unknown" and no information as to whether he was living or dead. Their mother was identified as Lucy in the case of four of the children and as Spokl-wo-hannum on Annie's record, a variant of her Bella Coola name, indicating that the children knew her by both names. The children's "tribal origin" was, not surprisingly, given as Bella Coola. While Tim, William and Maggie were described as without previous schooling, Agnes had attended "Vancouver Public School, 2 years & 3 months," Annie for three years.

Despite a diversity of inheritances and upbringings, children were all treated at Coqualeetza as if they were stereotypically Aboriginal.

Agnes and Maggie Cummings pose formally with their mother Lucy shortly before being sent to Coqualeetza in 1894. As with the others, the Cummings children in no way conformed to the stereotypes that Coqualeetza and the other residential schools publicly evoked to justify their existence.
Courtesy Keamo family

The records are filled with examples of this outlook, such as a matron's reference, shortly after the school opened, to the "squalor and filth unutterable" of the homes whence students came. A visitor came away overwhelmed, after hearing from staff about "the native Indian character impregnated, as it necessarily is, with heathenism."[15] For the school to fulfill its mandate, its students had to be constructed as "wild and wandering," to quote from a Methodist promotional pamphlet, prior to their being taught the newcomer's ways with which they may well have entered the school in the first place. In effect, they were taught that they were inferior to the newcomer descent that they embodied alongside their Aboriginal heritage. The irony of their circumstances verges on the unbelievable.

It took some time for Coqualeetza to jell, and at the beginning a certain improvisational character prevailed, as the head who succeeded Tate in charge of the school, Rev. Ebenezer Robson, made clear in his diary, in reporting on Seraphine McCord from Kanaka Ranch.

> Sat. Sep. 22 [1894]: Miss S. [Smith, a teacher] & Mrs. B. [Burpee, sewing teacher] report case of violation of rules against 3 of the big girls Lizzie [Jim], Martha [Thompson] & Seraphine [McCord]. Lying in both senses of the word (3 in a bed telling falsehoods) & in one case swearing are charged.
>
> Mon. Sept. 24: After prayers & breakfast had an interview with the 3 girls before their teachers. They had nothing to say for themselves, but declined to ask forgiveness, saying they would rather be punished. They are to have bread & water only during the pleasure of the faculty. At noon they ate nothing at all.
>
> Wed. Sept. 26: Found all of the rebellious girls had submitted saying they had been whipped & locked up on previous occasions of misbehavior [when Rev. Tate was in charge] but had always had plenty to eat. They had never been starved. Glad we have found a new trail to their wills.
>
> Thurs. Sept. 27: Had an interesting prayer meeting at night. Elizabeth [Madden], Martha, Seraphine & Maggie [Cooper] spoke & quite a number held up their hands [to indicate their willingness to be saved].[16]

This incident points up the importance of right action and right belief consistent with Methodism, and more generally Christianity, whose precepts children might well not have known until they transgressed them. Fifteen-year-old Seraphine, for one, quickly learned that the appearance of religiosity gave a certain freedom of action not otherwise allowed students in the school. Robson noted approvingly the next February that "Seraphine made a wonderful prayer for a 3 months convert."[17]

Other students, including 18-year-old Thomas Smith from Brockton Point, were not given an opportunity to repent. The enormity of his crime was simply too great, although his brother Peter, also likely involved, was spared the punishment of expulsion meted out to Thomas. Robson noted:

> Thur. Dec. 13 [1894]: After [prayer] meeting Mrs. H [Hensel, assistant matron] told me P.S. [Peter Smith?] had confessed to being one of the boys who had visited the girls in their dormitories at night for immoral purposes. It was a terrible revelation.
>
> Frid. Dec. 14: Got up at 4:30. Asked P.S. about the bad business & received the names of 16 boys & 7 girls who have been in the affair. The boys would get out of their dormitory window (4th story) & climb into the eve trough & then walk along to the girls' window & get in—the girls would reverse the process … I placed the whole matter in [matron] Miss Clark's hands but she said it would take all of us to manage so grave an affair. I then at her request got all the boys whose names were on my black list to come in the reading room & got every one of them to confess to having been in the girls' dormitory at night—16 of them in all. Then I took the girls & got them all (7) to confess having been in the boys' dormitories & 3 having lain with the boys. The two accounts again same in smaller details. At 2 pm we held a meeting of the advisory (informal) & advised that Jos. Sewell, Thomas Smith & Geo. Matheson be dismissed from the Institute. Also that Lizzie [Jim] be dismissed and others suitably punished. Martha [Thompson] was to be kept awhile to see if we can find a place for her & Maggie [Cooper] till her mother could be written respecting her. Miss Clark & I then prescribed a week on bread & water & cancellation of 1/2 holidays for a month for all who had been in bed with the girls, or girls with boys. For those who had only been in the girls' dormitories we prescribed cancellation of 1/2 holidays for a month. It was grim to do that with the exception of P.S. who seemed to have no realization of the enormity of the sin or repentance.
>
> Sat. Dec. 15: Woke up the young fellows & Harry [assistant] drove them to the landing along with Mr. Tate [former Coqualeetza head]. In the afternoon I drove Lizzie home to her father taking along a sack of flour for her father & giving her a plain, earnest, kind talk as we journeyed on.[18]

Even though Thomas Smith left Coqualeetza under a cloud, he did not escape oversight. Rev. Robson rejoiced to learn a couple of months later that "Thomas attends church & class regularly" back home at Brockton Point.[19]

Sometime after Seraphine's mother Maggie decided to remove her from Coqualeetza in early 1895, she was pressured to go back. At first, as Robson wrote, she was doubly cherished as the returned prodigal:

> Wed. Feb. 13 [1895]: I was sorry to see Seraphine [McCord] go but perhaps it is for the best. At any rate her mother has the right to take her away.
>
> Thur. Mch 28: Then on to Coal Harbor [Kanaka Ranch] where I had a talk with Mrs. McPhee re Seraphine going to canneries, protesting against it. Then on to Robinsons, Homer St., where Seraphine works.
>
> Sun. [Nov.] 10: Went on to Coal Harbor & had a talk & devotions with Mr & Mrs McPhee.
>
> Wed. 15: Came over to Westminster by 10 a.m. train, bringing the children two boys & Seraphine.
>
> Sun. 17: [At the religious service] Seraphine came seeking restoration.
>
> Sun. Dec. 1: Campground service at 2.30, taking wife, Martha [Thompson] & Seraphine with me.
>
> Sun. Jan. 19: Eliza Marwick & Seraphine McCord stood up as volunteers for mission work at any time & place and in any capacity in which the Lord may call them.[20]

Seraphine could keep up the charade only so long. Her desire for friendship with the other girls, including Addie Burns from Chaythoos, won out over her subordination of self to the school's wishes.

> Sat. [Feb.] 21 [1896]: A sad day! ... Stated the [unspecified] case against each of them separately to Nellie [Taffendale], Seraphine [McCord], Mary Ann [Thomas], Catherine [Naho], Lou [Forest] & Addie [Burns]. They each admitted in substance the charges. Had meeting of teachers at noon. Miss Alston, Miss Smith, Miss Burpee & Mr. Pearson favored whipping. Mrs Nicholas did not. After school I administered the punishment to the first 3 and admonished the others accepting their expressions of regret & promise not to offend again.[21]

The administration at Coqualeetza became increasingly rigid. By the time the school claimed the Keamo and Cummings children in 1896 and 1897, it was determined to prevent mothers like Maggie McPhee from removing their children at will. Fifteen-year-old Maggie Burns, the eldest daughter of August Jack's sister Louisa, had slipped away in January 1895, after just 10 months there. The Methodists appealed to Dominion officials, saying that "in order to obtain the best results," children should be compelled to "remain until grown up, say till the age of eighteen years." Determined to ensure that Louisa's two younger children, Aggie and Dave, would not follow Maggie's example, Rev. Robson made a special trip, likely to Snauq, to get Louisa's signature: "Called in at cabin en route to North Arm [of Fraser River] & got papers for Addie & David for 18 yrs."[22] Before his daughters would be admitted, James Keamo had to agree that they belonged to Coqualeetza until they reached age 18.

From the Dominion government's perspective, Coqualeetza's principal defect lay in its acceptance of hybrid children. The Department of Indian Affairs became aware of the practice when the school summarily turfed out a "half-breed Simsean [Tsimshian]" and three others from the BC north coast in January 1895. Their misdeeds as they made their way home hit the Victoria press, causing chagrin all around. Possibly as an object lesson to other institutions, Indian Affairs' annual published report of 1896–97 quite unusually distinguished Coqualeetza's "Indian boys and girls" from its "half-breeds."[23]

As a consequence, Coqualeetza took even greater pains to treat all of its students as if they were wholly Aboriginal: "We are helping them to break their 'birth's invidious bar,' and to rise in the scale of being to a position religiously, socially and educationally nearer to that of our own more favored race."[24] These easy assumptions about racial difference were not lost on outsiders, including Mary Dunbar. She accompanied her neighbour Peter Smith and his eldest daughter Mary on a visit to his children. As Robson reported defensively in his diary, she understood well what was happening at the school.

Thur. [Sept.] 5 [1895]: Mr Barraclough brought Mr. Smith up from the

> steamer & his daughter [Mary] & Mrs. Dunbar were with him (S.). The last was drunk & demonstrative, had talked in a very unbecoming manner to Mr. B en route & on arrival was full of faultfinding. The visiting party were served with tea in the reading room; but this woman was indignant & paced the hall calling out her dissatisfaction. Hearing her enquire for me I stepped out when she swept out of the front door saying to me over her shoulder "I am not a Siwash, I'm Mrs. Dunbar," so I said "goodbye Mrs. Dunbar" & closed the door. She went to Mr. Pearson & asked him to take her to the best hotel in town. She then boarded a passing wagon & left, Mr. Smith going with her. He too had been drinking & I had spoken to him about doing that & bringing the woman here in such a state. Led the prayer meeting Peter's sister being present.[25]

The expectation that children would remain until they reached adulthood, so that their characters could be fully formed along the intended lines, could be thwarted by three means.

The first was through death, as occurred with three, or fully a quarter, of the Brockton Point children sent there during the 1890s. The first parent to suffer such a loss was Peter Smith, whose 11-year-old son John "died Feb 2, 1895, of scrofula [tubercular infection of lymph glands in throat] having been delicate when entering the school." By falling back on religious belief, school officials denied any culpability for his death. The annual report of the Methodist Women's Missionary Society explained how "he was one of the nine who came the day the Institute was opened, and we are glad to have been allowed the privilege of showing one of these little ones the way to Jesus."[26]

Maria Smith suffered a similar fate to her brother John. In the midst of being trained in "housekeeping, sewing," Maria fell ill and was sent home in 1903. Coqualeetza, like the other residential schools, had by this time learned that it was not good for their public image for children to be seen to be dying there. It was not the school's fault when students became ill, nor should it be so perceived; "serious illness will occur, betraying the presence of hereditary traits."[27] It was the children's genes, not just their minds, that were inferior. Maria, who had been admitted to Coqualeetza at age six, succumbed to tuberculosis 18 months after being returned home. The Cummings family also gave a son to Coqualeetza. Less than a year there, 10-year-old William Murphy "died Jan. 12, 1898, of pleurisy," as the register tersely summarized a life and a death.

The second means to escape Coqualeetza before adulthood was to run away. Tommy Cole tried at least once, unsuccessfully, and was returned in humiliation.

> Sun. [Oct.] 27 [1895]: Was informed after service that three boys had skipped before service began. Tommy [Cole], George Kipp & Isaac Charley. Could not get any information from the boys as to their going, though several knew of it.
>
> Mon. 28: Got up at 4 a.m., woke Harry, & we drove to Sumas Landing & woke up the two Indian families there, but could hear nothing of the runaways. Then drove to Ch[illiwac]k Landing & enquired of the Indians but found no tidings of the lads. We then came home & got breakfast. I then went through Skowkale & Encacuse [Indian reserves] with similar result. I heard, however, that Chief Joseph of Squi is Isaac's uncle & after dinner I started with wife to visit that place. Calling at Mr Barraclough & was informed that he had found the 3 boys a mile this side of Knight's Mill Popcum & brought them back. They had walked all night. They were now at dinner. Gave wife a short drive & returned home bringing the boys with me. It being recess most of the school boys stared at them as they came into the yard.
>
> Tues, Oct. 29: According to decision of teachers meeting held last night, I whipped Geo. Kipp, Tommy Cole & Isadore Charley giving Geo. the largest dose. I gave the boys a talk about it & tried to impress upon them how foolish & wrong it was to do as they had done.[28]

Two and a half years later, in the spring of 1898, 17-year-old Tommy Cole tried again and this time made it home to Brockton Point, where his mother was now living on her own. By then he was fed up with his training in "farming," which in practice meant a lot of hard work taking care of animals and crops around Coqualeetza. The school usually went to great lengths to track down errant students and return

Tommy Cole, likely shortly after he escaped Coqualeetza in 1898, aged 17.
Courtesy Laurie Nahanee Cole

them, by force if necessary, but in Tommy Cole's case there was only a cryptic note in the register: "His return was not desired."

The third means of early escape was to be asked to leave. By 1897 the school was being scrutinized for both hybrid and Catholic students. The Oblates, who ran a competing institution at nearby Mission, demanded Catholic children be transferred there or at the least removed. In the spring of 1899, after three years at Coqualeetza, Emma and Josephine Keamo were "discharged as Roman Catholics by order of the Department" of Indian Affairs, as were the three young Smiths whose mother Lucy grew up at Kanaka Ranch. The notation at the end of the Smith family entries in the school register is curt: "Non-Indian."

For the other members of the second and third generations, no escape was possible until they reached at least 18 years. Like the once flourishing villages of Whoi Whoi and Chaythoos, Brockton Point and Kanaka Ranch had in their absences become shadows of their former selves. A handful of the middle-aged and elderly were left to cope as best they could. Only Joe and Susie Gonsalves had withstood their family's dismemberment, their children taking advantage of local public schools. All three sites predating the imposition of Stanley Park seemed about to fade away, thanks to the unprecedented reach of missionary zeal and of the Indian residential school.

Of the Brockton Point families, only the Gonsalves children escaped residential school. The formal portrait of Matilda and Elizabeth at ages 16 and 14 was taken in 1900 at Imperial Studies, located at the corner of Carrall and Cordova streets. It may have been intended to emphasize their Portuguese inheritance.
Courtesy Llewella Duncan

Chapter 6

Life Goes On

Sisters Annie, Aggie and Maggie Cummings, part of the second generation at Brockton Point, pose with Annie's two oldest children, Mona and Olive, in the garden of the Cummings's home in Stanley Park in the summer of 1912.
Courtesy Keamo family

The members of the second and third generations from Chaythoos, Kanaka Ranch and Brockton Point who gave their childhoods and youths to the residential school both did and did not return to the lives they had left behind. They were eventually freed from the institution, but their experiences had changed them in ways beyond their control, even as the settings in which they had been born altered during their absences. The most remarkable aspect of these transitions was the younger generation's commitment to life going on as it had prior to their departures. Brockton Point in particular was renewed. The young people who had been born on the borderlands between two societies made that middle way concrete on their return to the only home they knew.

Being outside of Stanley Park's boundaries, Kanaka Ranch was subject to its own set of pressures. Just as the City of Vancouver claimed the peninsula, so others competed to put the rest of Burrard Inlet in their own names. John Morton and his two partners, who had pre-empted the area abutting the peninsula in the early 1860s, gave part of their holdings to the Canadian Pacific Railway, which in exchange agreed to locate the terminus nearby. The rest they divided between themselves. Morton's share contained the three acres of Kanaka Ranch.

Quite remarkably, the matriarch of Kanaka Ranch, Mary See-em-ia, stood up to John Morton. Because the legal records have not survived, it is impossible to determine precisely what happened, but it is almost certain that she proved adverse possession, or squatters' rights, to at least part of the land. To do so in accordance with the law in Vancouver, she would have had to show 20 years of unbroken occupation. Almost four decades later, John Morton's widow Ruth was still indignant about it when she talked with Major Matthews:

> When we [my husband John Morton and I] went to England, they, Brighouse and Hailstone, did not look after the property, and there was a woman, her name started with "M," and she squatted on the land, and it seems if they stay long enough you cannot get them off, and Mr. Morton tried and tried, but he could not get her off; the Indian woman just stayed. And Mr. Morton had an agent, the Rands [Vancouver real estate, insurance and financial brokers], and they were supposed to look after it, but they never could get the woman out. It was down by the "Arena" [corner of Georgia and Denman streets]; expensive water lots, too, weren't they?[1]

The outline of the story can be pieced together from oral recollections, land records and the remarkable document that Mary See-em-ia sent to the Vancouver mayor and city council in 1899.

Vancouver, B.C.
October 1st 1899

To the Mayor
and City Council

Gentlemen:

Me and my husband squatted on a piece of land fronting on Coal Harbor in the year 1869.

My husband took out his naturalisation papers out in New Westminster on the 4th day of August in the year 1871, and resided on the land until the time of his death. We had a boy and a girl born on the land, who are now married, and living with their familyes [*sic*] on said land and have been living on the land continuously since the time of their birth.

The land is situated on Georgia street with about 400 feet of frontage on said street, thence running north to the waterfront on Coal Harbor, Denman street continued to Coal Harbor would go through the center of the property. About four years ago a real estate dealer tried to dispossess me and my family off the said estate, and took the matter to the courts, whereas the judge of the Supreme Court held in this city on the 23rd day of July 1899, sustained our squatter's rights.

Notwithstanding the fact of the verdict of the high court guaranteeing our title to said land said real estate dealer has broken down our fences, destroyed portions of our orchard, and taken possession of five sixths of our land, and on September the 23rd last Monday, they destroyed and burned 3 of our dwelling houses, and consequently has left some of the family in destitute circumstances.

Said real estate dealers have erected a board fence round the property, and are advertising the land for sale, and we ask as common citizens from the City Officials to grant us their protections [*sic*].

MARY EHIU + [her mark][2]

Mary's son William Nahanee confirmed to Major Matthews that it was indeed his mother who had written the letter.

> Mary Eihu was my mother; it is my mother's letter dated October 1st, 1899, re the Kanaka Ranch at the foot of Denman ... I am the son mentioned there, that is William, and the girl mentioned is my sister Margaret, or Maggie. I was a plaintiff in the Court case, I suppose, as it says, 23rd July, 1899, and spent a lot of money trying to keep that property ... I had no claim; it was my mother, Mary Eihu. I was just helping her, but it was no good to us; we could not sell it; we had no deed nor anything, but this McPhee [married to my sister Maggie] and others must have worked something; otherwise how could they have sold it, or else my sister got the property.
>
> After we won the case in the courts, Dan McPhee started a little store on our property, the little store was on the [northeast] corner of Denman and Georgia.[3]

John Morton's land agent began harassing Mary See-em-ia to abandon Kanaka Ranch in the mid-1890s. When she refused to do so, he took her to court. In a letter written to his wife in mid-May 1895, Morton referred to "the squatter on the beach" and "the trial which will come off in two or three weeks." Mary See-em-ia must have proven adverse possession in a lower court then or subsequently, for land records attest that on February 23, 1899, Morton agreed to transfer Lot 14 of District Lot 185 to Mary's daughter "Maggie Eihu otherwise known as Margaret MacPhee."[4] Maggie was illiterate and signed with her X, just as her mother had done. Lot 14, which comprised a sixth of Kanaka Ranch, lay at the northeast corner of Georgia and Denman streets, extending 66 feet (20 metres) along Georgia and 180 feet (54 metres) along Denman to the Coal Harbour waterfront. According to Mary See-em-ia's letter, her rights were sustained in a higher court on July 23, 1899, which is consistent with Lot 14 being registered in her daughter's name on September 27.

Mary See-em-ia's letter indicates that she believed she had proven squatters' rights to the entire three acres. Her plea to the mayor and city council protested that five-sixths of Kanaka Ranch was being forcibly removed from the family's possession to be sold to others. The fence was torn down, the orchard destroyed, houses burned. Whether she was kept in the dark by her daughter and son-in-law, or the situation was more complex, Mary's daughter Maggie had already accepted ownership of one-sixth of the three acres. Some descendants consider that Kanaka Ranch was meant to be divided into six parts between various family members, who were then prevented by force from taking up their portions of the property. No land transactions for the remainder of the three acres that had been Kanaka Ranch occurred until 1913; it remained in Morton's name. Mary's granddaughter Minnie suggests that her mother Maggie and stepfather Daniel McPhee may have made a deal with the lawyers to ensure that at least a part of Kanaka Ranch remained in the family's hands, very conveniently their own. "Mother had to give the lawyer some money, and that was how she got the land; but it was a pre-emption. It was in 1895 that mother gave the lawyer the money. The Mortons never bothered us."[5]

Whatever the particulars, Mary See-em-ia's daughter Maggie came out the winner. Her daughter Minnie recalled the address of the parcel that survived in the family as 1789 Georgia Street West. There Maggie and her husband ran what her grandson Norman recalled all his life as "grandmother's store."[6]

Mary See-em-ia went to live with her son William. In the early 1890s he had married Cecilia Johnny, a Squamish chief's daughter from the Mission Reserve. Sometime thereafter, they moved to Moodyville, where William worked on the waterfront as a fireman, oiler and longshoreman. At the time of the 1901 census, he recorded making a very respectable $600 over the past year. No one remembers when Mary See-em-ia died. She was buried in the Capilano Indian cemetery, and Joe Nahanee's bones were later moved there from Deadman's Island.

The Nahanee family re-created at Moodyville the sense of community they had known at Kanaka Ranch. Their neighbours and good friends were the Nahus. William Nahanee and Leon Nahu, a few years apart in age, were likely friends from childhood. As with so many of his counterparts, Leon Nahu turned to longshoring as a way to get ahead through hard work and determination. In about 1890 he settled down in Moodyville with Mary Haley, whose father was an indigenous Hawaiian and mother an Aboriginal woman. Mary brought two young

The sense of community originating at Kanaka Ranch comes through in this photo, taken in 1906 to celebrate the ninth birthday of William Nahanee's son Edward, who sits in the middle of the front row. The story told in the family has his mother dressing him up in anticipation of the party, whereupon he snuck off fishing. Proudly packing home a large fish that he caught, young Ed was spanked for spoiling his new clothes, even though the fish became the centrepiece of the party food. Nahanees, Eihus and Nahus were among the party guests. William Nahanee stands on the left in the back row. Sitting in front of him is his wife Cecilia, holding their son William. Their son Ben is immediately left of his brother Ed, their daughter Maude sits on a lap above and to the right of Edward. William Nahanee's sister Lucy Smith stands next to him. His half-sister Maggie McPhee is four persons to the right. holding her young son Donald. Maggie's daughter Irene stands in front of her aunt Lucy. Maggie's daughter Minnie McCord Smith is not in the photo, but her son Albert is on the right in the front row, her daughter Edith behind Edward on the left. Leon Nahu's family is represented by his daughter Agnes, third from the left in the front row, and son Jimmy, second from the right in the top row. The others in the photo were part of Mary Nahu's extended family. Photo and information courtesy James Nahanee

sons to the union. Frederick Halliday West's father was said to be a passing sailor come to load lumber at Moodyville, Joe Harmon's father an equally obscure newcomer. In 1894, perhaps to get the two young boys out of the house while caring for her young family by Nahu, Mary handed them over to Coqualeetza. The school register is once again skilfully written: 10-year-old Freddy, who had already attended public school for several years, and his seven-year-old half-brother Joseph were described by tribal origin as "Tswassen [Tsawwassen]." They remained only a year before returning home. Leon Nahu was a good provider to his five children and two stepsons. He valued respectability and, by the turn of the century, was a longshoring foreman earning $1,000 a year.

Before long the Nahanee family moved from Moodyville to the Mission Reserve. Maude Nahanee, born in 1901, explained how her parents circumvented the usual prohibition against women who had "married out" returning home.

> Anyone, including in-laws, who wants to move on to the reserve has to get permission, so my father got permission from the old chief and, in return for the old chief accepting us to live there, my father promised the chief that he would finish building the [St. Paul's] church. That's the church that is still standing today [1957], down below 3rd in North Vancouver.
>
> My father built those two spires. It took him a long time, nearly two years. He sold his two lots he had in North Van, that's how he was able to finish building it.[7]

The two other trade-offs for the Nahanee family were to downplay their Hawaiian descent and to embrace Catholicism. James Nahanee recalled from his childhood how his grandfather "did not mention his Hawaiian ancestry."[8] The day after Christmas 1910, the Oblate priest baptized William Nahanee and his seven children, ranging in age from 11 years to four months.[9]

The Nahanee children also became caught up in the residential school phenomenon. Just beyond the Mission Reserve church, "on the hillside is seen the school where ten sisters strive to instill some idea of

Catholicism's encouragement of social proprieties is evident in the formal portrait taken at the baptism of Maude, Edward, Ben and William Nahanee at St. Paul's Church in 1910. Courtesy Laurie Nahanee Cole

the arts of civilization in the minds of the little Indians," the *Vancouver Province* intoned in 1909. Despite its location on the reserve, then home to about 400 Squamish, St. Paul's was emphatically a residential school. "The children live at the school, and are under surveillance all the time."[10]

As with their counterparts at Coqualeetza, the young Nahanees were taught to be Indians—to internalize inferiority and to defer to the dominant society, which no one wanted them to join. "There is no other fate for them here than to follow in the footsteps of their ancestors," Oblate Father Ermund Peytavin told the *Province*. "The boys become fishermen, idle and shiftless as their elders, and the girls become wives of fishermen, and household slatterns. What else can they do, poor things?"[11]

Maude Nahanee Thomas remembered: "Sometimes the sisters would tell us that we were 'dirty Indians' and that they had made a great sacrifice in coming out from France to teach us. They gave us a terrible inferiority complex and some of us never really got over feeling how inferior the white people think we are."[12]

Young men and women were far more industrious than the stereotypes would have them be. As with so many others with similar origins, young Nahanees turned to longshoring, one of the few reasonably paid occupations where skin colour did not act as a bar. On leaving residential school in about 1912, William and Cecilia's eldest son Ed headed to the docks. "In those days you lined up at the dockside, and they said, you and you and you … Four men aside on a sailing ship, two wire pullers, a donkey [engine] driver, and four men on the dock, they would have to make up the loads, maybe fifteen men for a whole ship. Ten hours a day, no overtime, forty-five cents an hour, and a donkey driver got an hour extra for getting up steam. Six days a week, you made sixty hours a week. The job [of loading a ship] would usually last six weeks."[13]

The Nahanee family, together with the Bakers, became mainstays of the Mission Reserve. Cecilia, who died in 1918 of tuberculosis, is said to have "dedicated her time to the up-keep of St. Paul's Indian

Church, for example, scrubbing floors, replacing the flowers, etc." Women in the church recalled to her granddaughter Laurie in 1970 how, so very long ago, Cecilia "had taught the ladies in the community to bake cakes and crochet." William and Cecilia's daughter Maude used the skills she acquired at residential school to act as a secretary for her father. She recalled "how depressed he was over the whole condition of the Indians, how down-trodden they were, how pushed aside, how ignored." William Nahanee turned to political activism, as did other family members, including Maude, over the years.[14]

A researcher who talked with eighty persons on the Mission Reserve in the 1950s concluded that the three principal families were "Baker, Paull, and Nahanee." A list compiled by the Oblate priest Thomas Lascelles in the early 1980s of "Squamish people [who] were prominently committed to the church from the beginning and on down the years" similarly included numerous members of these two families—the Bakers and Nahanees—originating at Brockton Point and Kanaka Ranch.[15]

William Nahanee was not alone in drawing on his Squamish heritage. On being widowed, his older sister Lucy Smith also did so, moving to the nearby Capilano Reserve. A man who made his home there recalled her vividly: "Lucy Smith lived across from us, she was also living by a slough, her house. She was Hawaiian and they call them Kanakas."[16]

At the much diminished Kanaka Ranch, life went on. Maggie's grandson Norman McPhee, born to her daughter Irene, retained all his life very warm memories of his childhood there amidst his extended family. The ties between Kanaka Ranch and Brockton Point remained strong.

> I was born on Kanaka Rancherrie on the 18th of August 1915, the last person to be born there. I don't know who my father was, maybe that's why I was named McPhee after my grandfather. He was a Scotchman from Glasgow who worked on the docks as a longshoreman. My grandfather died when I was just a year old. I don't remember him, but I remember my grandmother very well. I was with her more than with my mother. When I was about two,

my mother Irene got together with a fireman who worked for the CPR, Tommy Armstrong, and they had two sons before they split up.

We all lived at Kanaka Ranch, but I spent more time with my grandmother than with my mother. My grandmother Maggie raised me. I remember the boat we had. We would row over to Deadman's Island to play and build forts.

My grandmother used to take me with her when she went visiting. She was friends with Agnes and Margaret Cummings, who lived in Stanley Park not far from Kanaka Ranch. We used to visit my aunt Maud's grave by the Nine O'clock Gun. My grandmother's half-sister Lucy [Nahanee Smith] lived on the Capilano reserve in North Vancouver. Grandmother would take me on the ferry and then on the train to go to Capilano to visit Aunt Lucy.

The first school I went to was when we were still living at Kanaka Ranch. It was on Denman Street in the West End [a middle-class residential area adjacent to downtown Vancouver].[17]

Among the second and third generation at Kanaka Ranch, no one came to a sadder end than Mary See-em-ia's granddaughter Seraphine

Kanaka Ranch was still a lively place when Norman, born in 1915, was a child there. Here he sits on his mother Irene's lap at his birthday party, enjoying an ice cream cone like the others. Courtesy Mabel McPhee

McCord. When she was 18 years old, at about the time when the dispute over Kanaka Ranch was in full force, the once rambunctious and then outwardly devout young woman was discharged from Coqualeetza. Her five years there had been intended to give her expertise in "Housekeeping, Sewing," but not life coping skills. Seraphine went to live with her older sister Minnie, Major Matthews' informant, likely to help care for her three young children. Shortly after the turn of the century, Seraphine, now in her early 20s, decided the time had come to get on with her life. It was unacceptable for unmarried young women to live on their own, but they could hold jobs and board with respectable families, which is precisely what Seraphine did.

Five years in residential school gave Seraphine McCord domestic skills, perhaps the confidence to sew her own clothes, but not the attributes necessary to survive emotionally in adulthood.
Courtesy Mabel McPhee

In 1907 Seraphine followed her sister's example by finding herself a newcomer husband, Jens Marstrand, a Dane whose family manufactured roofing. The couple settled down in the New York Block Apartments at 658–660 Granville Street, downtown. Their neighbours in the 23 other flats were teachers, artists, salespeople and businessmen.

Whether or not it was the legacy

of her years in residential school, Seraphine proved unable to adapt to her changing circumstances. Less than a year into the marriage, she died "by taking a dose of bichloride of mercury, self-administered." At the time, bichloride of mercury tablets were widely used as an antiseptic and also in a douching solution to prevent conception. The substance was part of many households but was highly poisonous and was known, almost celebrated, as a means for women in particular to commit suicide, or to threaten to do so. So it is not surprising that the *Vancouver Province* headlined on page one, "Woman Took Heavy Dose of Poison." The feature article explained how Seraphine had taken "four or five antiseptic tablets," whereas "a single one of these tablets is said to be sufficient to cause the death of thirty persons."[18] Seraphine either suffered a terrible accident or successfully took her own life. As the inquest on her death reveals, it was not the first time she had cried out for attention, or perhaps had need to.

A neighbour living above the Marstrands' flat testified:

> It was very late Saturday night May 9th we heard music downstairs in Mr Marstrand's rooms which was usual so we did not take any notice of it. I then went to bed and had a sleep. I wakened about ten minutes after two o'clock in the morning hearing a woman sobbing. She was crying as though she were in great pain. I wakened [my husband] Mr. Fowler and we listened to it for a long time and heard very often a woman's voice saying, "don't." Sometimes she was very hysterical sometimes the cry was very hysterical and sobbing very violently. This continued for a long while. Mr Fowler wanted to go and see about it but I did not want him to interfere thinking it might be a quarrel … The trouble lasted two or three hours.[19]

Seraphine's husband gave her raw egg white, a recognized antidote to bichloride of mercury. Otherwise he did not take the matter seriously at first, perhaps because, as Seraphine's friend put it, "she was subject to these spells." But her condition deteriorated and she was finally admitted to St. Paul's Hospital, where she died a week after ingesting the tablets. Times had changed: her younger sister Maud had been buried at Brockton Point in 1881, but Seraphine was laid to rest at the still new Mountain View Cemetery. Her headstone reads:

In fond memory of Seraphine
Wife of J.L. Marstrand
Died May 16, 1908
Aged 27 years[20]

It is more difficult to follow the Burns children, whose mother Louisa grew up at Chaythoos. The Coqualeetza register contains a single line for recording each student's time at school but a full quarter-page to monitor their subsequent life. The entries had little good to say about August Jack Khahtsahlano's older niece Maggie, who left after just 10 months there: "Returned to her people, her subsequent history unsatisfactory." Maggie was living at "Squamish" in 1901. Half a dozen years later she paid the school a visit with her three children, and by 1912 she was "living at Capilano." Perhaps because she had few options, Addie Burns remained at Coqualeetza into her early 20s, likely helping out around the school. Her training in "Housework sewing music good in all" prepared her for the housekeeping job she then held in Vancouver and, in February 1909, for her marriage to a florist born in Derbyshire, England. Edgar Evans was 27, a year older than Maggie. Her uncle August Jack explained how Addie "lives over by Magee Road" in the middle-class Kerrisdale area of Vancouver.[21]

By the time of his departure from the school in 1901, at the age of 18 or 19, Maggie and Addie's younger half-brother Dave had only got to the second level. The fault almost certainly lay with the institution rather than with Dave: it was usual for residential schools to pay very little attention to children's actual schooling. For unknown reasons he was given no specialized training intended to help him earn a living. All the same, he fulfilled the school's expectations for its former pupils: "Living near Vancouver leading a regular life 1908." A subsequent undated entry suggests by its length high interest in his voyage of self-discovery: "Name changed. Living on Musqueam Reserve near Vancouver. Discovered after leaving school his father's name was Locke—and is now known as David Lock. Kerrisdale P.O. (Musqueam

Reserve)." August Jack was similarly intrigued, recalling in the late 1930s: "Dave Lock; used to be city policeman, but he's half Indian."[22]

The members of the second generation at Brockton Point proved to be the most resilient in retrieving a space they considered their own. Tommy Cole escaped from Coqualeetza after four years. Thomas and Peter Smith spent just 10 months there before, respectively, being expelled and departing voluntarily. Their young brother John died at Coqualeetza a week short of a year there, and Maria attended for 10 years before being sent home to die in the care of her sister Rita, also there 10 years. Tim Cummings spent three and a half years at Coqualeetza, and his sisters Agnes, Annie and Maggie seven and a half, eight and 11 years respectively. William Cummings died at Coqualeetza 10 months after his arrival. Together, the second generation at Brockton Point contributed 56 years of their lives to Coqualeetza. They had all essentially been filler, permitting the school to maintain its public face as a successful residential school for Aboriginal children.

Every one of the eight who survived the residential school returned to the only home they knew, and by so doing consolidated their families' hold on Brockton Point. Departing students were charged to erect "houses copied from those occupied by white people" that were "painted, heated by stoves, and comfortably furnished," and they did precisely that.[23] Brockton Point was, both literally and figuratively, the reserve to which the lessons of residential school commanded their return. The second generation went to work, they married and they became ordinary, embodying in that ordinariness their strong commitment to the place where they were born and where they were more than ever convinced they belonged.

When the second generation returned, they found their families' backyards even more cluttered with sporting facilities. Cricket, golf, rugby, hockey, lacrosse, polo, bicycle racing, lawn tennis, field sports—they were all there.

In 1895, the same year the Vancouver Rowing Club built a clubhouse next door to the Brockton Point families, the Royal Vancouver Yacht Club got permission to build on the site from which the Chinese had

In 1905 the Vancouver Rowing Club established a clubhouse on piles on the foreshore of Brockton Point. This photo is from about 1920.
City of Vancouver Archives, 99-1481

been removed some years earlier. By then virtually every Vancouver sports club—all restricted to men, and to respectable men at that—had a presence at Brockton Point. Vancouver was hit by recession in 1912, whereupon the Brockton Point Athletic Association proposed to allow a professional team onto the grounds. It was a practice still considered unacceptable even in hard times, and to avoid such a development the Parks Board took over the lease and the grounds management.

The assumptions about social and racial superiority held by the Parks Board, and more generally the City of Vancouver, caused the families at Brockton Point to continue to be overlooked. They were essentially invisible, a situation that worked to their advantage as members of the second generation regrouped, determined that life would go on. They had serious obstacles to overcome: they had been triply shortchanged in their education. Their schooling at Coqualeetza was mediocre at best. They had been deprived of the opportunity to attend public school alongside their peers, which would have familiarized them

Maggie, the youngest of the Cummings daughters, may have had a special reason to erase her years at Coqualeetza. A list of students made while she was still there counted eight "halfbreed children for whom the Government allows no Grant," but she was not among them, indicating she was classed as an "Indian."[25]
Courtesy Keamo family

with life in Vancouver outside of Brockton Point. They had also been deprived of the lessons in practical living that their parents could have given them.

The second generation made sense of their years at residential school in different ways. A woman who married into a later generation of the Smith family commented, "when the Smith children left Coqualeetza the one thing they knew was that they didn't want to be Indians." Despite the three decades the Cummings children collectively spent at Coqualeetza, according to Annie's daughter, they "never talked about the experience afterwards to the family."[24]

Each person coped differently. Like the Bakers, Tommy Cole increasingly identified more with his Squamish than his newcomer inheritance. Acording to the Coqualeetza register, he was "living with his mother still at Brockton Point, Vancouver, & doing well—June 1901," and then "still making his home at Brockton Point 1910." For a time, his grandson Robert recalled, Tommy worked on seagoing

Dave Cole with his Squamish wife Agnes Jack and their two young children, Edward and Mamie, in about 1905. Courtesy Laurie Nahanee Cole

vessels. He picked up enough Chinese to be able to speak with the vegetable sellers from China who were a familiar sight around Vancouver neighbourhoods. Like his father before him, Tommy Cole was a versatile man who fished and longshored with his older brother Dave.

By 1901 Dave and his Squamish wife Agnes Jack had moved on to the Mission Reserve. Still living at Brockton Point, Tommy Cole developed close relationships with both Squamish and Musqueam families. At some point he got together with Matilda Peter, who had several children by an earlier marriage at Musqueam. Tommy and Matilda's daughter Rose, born in about 1913, recalled Brockton Point as "a beautiful place to grow up."[26] She skated with her brothers Tommy and Robert, rowed across to Deadman's Island and even caught rides with park visitors in horse-drawn sleighs. Robert, who was born in 1915, attended Lord Roberts School in the West End, walking or cycling there each morning and afternoon.

In sharp contrast, Dave and Tommy Cole's half-sisters Rosa and Kitty, who as young children had been removed by authorities, were

Tom and Dave Cole's half sister Rosa (centre back) worked as a live-in companion and housekeeper for a North Vancouver family. Courtesy Elsie Kerr

lost to the family. On Rosa's marriage to a steamfitter from Ontario in Vancouver in 1915, she knew her father's name and that she had been born in Stanley Park, but had no idea who her mother was. Her daughter Elsie made clear just how complete the forced separation had been.

> My mother Rosa and her younger sister Kitty were taken away from their mother and put in an orphanage in Vancouver, around Broughton Street. Aunt Kitty became "Miss Kitty Lee." She lived in Seattle and never married. Mother went to a white family in Capilano, she was a companion or houseworker,

> she married dad who was white. Mother didn't really know she had Indian heritage. She went from an orphanage to a white family to a white husband. She never said she was Indian, she never told any of us.[27]

The Cummings siblings were particularly strategic in making use of their time at Coqualeetza to find marriage partners. Tim in 1900, Agnes in 1904 and then Maggie in 1909 returned to their mother

The Cummings family home was nestled between the road around the park and the shoreline of Burrard Inlet. Courtesy Keamo family

Spukhpukanum, who in the interim scraped out a living as best she could at Brockton Point. "She had a rowboat there, and they'd go out in the inlet, and they could sell the fish to people in Vancouver."[28]

Tim and Agnes Cummings found jobs, which eased their mother's circumstances. Tim worked on the docks, but his farming training at Coqualeetza was not entirely wasted: all his life he remained an enthusiastic and devoted gardener and orchardist. About a year after Agnes had arrived at Coqualeetza, a dressmaking department opened up to earn money for the school by making garments "for the white people in the neighborhood, as well as for the teachers."[29] Agnes became a dressmaker after she left the school.

The two oldest Cummings offspring remained single. Asked by a reporter later in life why he never married, Tim harked back to his time at Coqualeetza: "I had a chance to get married when I was at the Indian school in Chilliwack, but she grabbed somebody else. Didn't want to come to Vancouver, I guess."[30] Tim and Agnes's younger sister Maggie worked in a Vancouver laundry before marrying a fellow student from Coqualeetza with links to Kanaka Ranch.

Lucy (right) socializing with a friend, likely on the verandah of the Cummings's Brockton Point home. Courtesy Keamo family

As for Leon Nahu's stepson Frederick Halliday West, the school register proudly noted under his record, "Married Maggie Cummings Dec 1909." The newlyweds settled at Brockton Point in a house Tim helped them to build just next door. It was from there that Fred and his brother-in-law Tim set off each day to longshore in the pattern of so many Brockton Point and Kanaka Ranch men.

The fourth Cummings sibling at Coqualeetza became its stellar student. In July 1904 Annie gained high-school admission and attended at Chilliwack for a couple of years while still living at Coqualeetza. The matron made a special request that, after taking "a sort of Practical Normal Course under our teachers here for three or four months," Annie "be permitted to teach an Indian school under the Methodist Missionary society." As to the reason, "she is very virtuous and though timid has a strong will and impresses every one with a sense of dignity which defies undue familiarity."[31]

Coqualeetza's annual reports to the Dominion government repeatedly put Annie front and centre:

> 1906: One of our pupils has been in the high school all the year with the object of preparing herself to be a teacher. She hopes to secure a position where she may help her own people as mission teacher.
>
> 1907: One of the pupils from the school left last November to take charge of an Indian school, and is doing excellent work. She has obtained a teacher's certificate. This gives one an idea of the possibilities of the Indian children.[32]

Annie Cummings went to teach at a Methodist Indian day school at Cowichan Bay on Vancouver Island, but her heart was not in the Cowichan Valley. For all of the rhetoric to the contrary, she was not an Indian, nor were the pupils "her own people." Annie returned home after a year to prepare for her wedding to the older brother of her Coqualeetza schoolmates Emma and Josephine Keamo. James Grant Keamo, whose father had lived at Kanaka Ranch for a time, was the eldest in a family of nine. To help support his younger siblings, he had entered the world of work in about 1885 at the very young age of eight. One of his first responsibilities was carrying 100-pound sacks of flour from the riverboats that stopped near his family's home in New Westminster, where they had moved from Port Hammond. The difficulty of others' understanding his surname caused him to change it to Campbell for purposes of work. Major Matthews' informant, Minnie McCord Smith, recalled: "Well, I guess they couldn't pronounce his

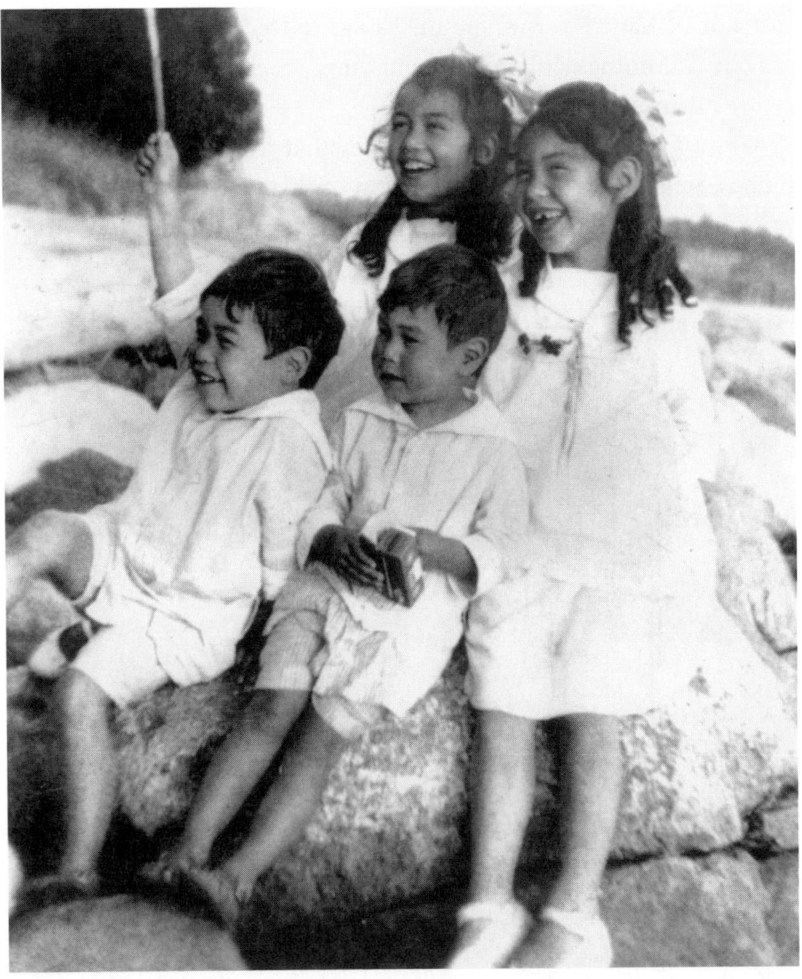

Sunday visits to the Cummings's home in Stanley Park were a welcome respite from Annie's everyday life in east Vancouver. Olive and Mona Keamo were joined in the family by Elmer and Jimmy, who looked forward to visits to the nearby beach as much as their sisters did. Courtesy Keamo family

name properly, or couldn't spell it if they could, so one day they said, just offhand and as though they were irritated, to him, 'Oh, we'll just call you Campbell'."[33]

James Grant Keamo/Campbell and Annie Cummings were married on the last day of December 1908 in a Methodist ceremony at the Cummings family home at Brockton Point. They settled down on the east side of Vancouver, where they soon started a family. For Annie, the one Cummings sibling who left home, Brockton Point remained a centre of family conviviality.

Grant Campbell, as he became known at work, was a foreman at Empire Stevedoring, a flourishing local company founded in 1907. He was responsible for hiring gangs of workers and organizing the load within a ship.

Photographs like this one with James Grant Keamo/Campbell at the centre of his gang with his arms crossed, testify to the pride taken in hard work well done. Courtesy Keamo family

Men tended to become identified with particular foremen, and thereby companies and types of work, the affiliations being to some extent based in race. Grant Campbell and his fellow foreman Leon Nahu were most likely to hire gangs combining Squamish men with members of families originating at Brockton Point, Kanaka Ranch, Whoi Whoi and Chaythoos. In a tradition harking back to the first sawmills on Burrard Inlet, their gangs tended to load lumber.

James Grant Keamo/Campbell was able to hold the foreman's position by virtue of his wife Annie helping him figure out how to distribute the goods between the three or four holds in a ship. Their daughter Olive explained how Annie's years at Coqualeetza and teaching at Cowichan Bay came to good effect.

> As my Dad progressed in his job, the Empire Stevedoring Company made him foreman. The men gathered at the longshoremen's hall and waited for jobs. He hired men from the Union Hall for each ship that came into the harbor.
>
> My mother helped him to load the ship because you can't have it lopsided, you must have the same amount of cargo in the holds. My mother used to figure it all out for him because she was a school teacher. She would figure it out, and he would sort out how many people he needed by using matches, she would help him to place matches to make up two or three gangs of sixteen men each.
>
> The Company, Empire Stevedore, would call him at home and he would go down to the hall with little bundles of matches and, when he chose a man for work, he gave him one of the matches and when each bundle was gone, he knew he had a gang. It was his job to know how many gangs he would need to load the ship. He also had to know how much of these huge logs to fill the hold of a ship.
>
> They worked that ship until it was loaded or unloaded. The time spent did not matter, however long it would take from a few days to weeks. It sometimes took a couple of weeks to load a ship.[34]

In contrast to the other families, only one of the three children of Peter Smith and Kenick to survive residential school made his adult life at Brockton Point. Thomas was almost 17 when his father enrolled him in 1894. He was trained as a "Blacksmith, General Domestic," but went back to being a fisherman after leaving the school. By the summer of 1900 Thomas Smith was, according to the register, employed as a sailor on a deep-sea vessel, the *Empress of India*. The final sad entry noted that "he drowned at sea near Cape Flattery, 1904."

It was not easy for male newcomers to find white wives at this time, as there were still not as many newcomer women as men in British Columbia. It was therefore almost acceptable to marry a woman of mixed heritage, particularly if she had been suitably brought up to assume a submissive domestic role, as with girls who attended residential school. August Jack's sister Louisa wed John Burns. At Brockton Point, Peter Smith's eldest daughter Mary had caught Edward Long. Maggie Eihu of Kanaka Ranch twice found a newcomer husband, as did her half-sister Lucy and her daughters Minnie and Seraphine. Rita Smith followed in this tradition. She disappeared from both the school's and her family's view after marrying a newcomer man and moving to Saskatchewan.

Young Peter Smith was the most closely watched over of any of the Chaythoos, Brockton Point or Kanaka Ranch students, because he married a favoured fellow student. Despite being 18 at the time he was enrolled, and despite being implicated in the morals scandal that caused his brother Thomas to be expelled, Peter remained at Coqualeetza into the next year, reaching the third standard. Like his future wife, he was a school favourite, and Rev. Robson noted sadly three days after his departure: "We miss the earnest face & words of Peter. May God keep him safe from harm."[35] According to the register, he "returned to his home at Vancouver where he pursues his occupation as fisherman, & conducting himself in a most exemplary manner."

The practice of encouraging departing students to marry each other was common in the residential school system: the administration believed that the students would monitor each other and therefore would be less likely to fall back into their Indian lifestyles. Peter Smith's interest in his fellow student Martha Thompson was, however, no ordinary matter. More than any other individual, she had caused the people in charge of Coqualeetza both joy and anxiety during the school's first years.

Martha was the first child taken into Charles Tate's home in April 1888 at the age of nine. Her mother Jeannie was an Ohamil woman from the Fraser Valley; her father was a bit of a mystery, as was the surname sometimes given her of Thompson. When the new school opened in early 1894, Martha was registered as student "#1." This status she quickly abused. Martha was one of the girls caught in bed with Seraphine "telling falsehoods" and also one of those most complicit in the nighttime visits between dormitories that got Thomas Smith expelled in December 1895. Martha was spared, only to get into far more serious trouble a month later. At first Robson sought to downplay her role, but to no avail, as he wrote in his diary:

> Frid. [Jan.] 4 [1895]. Was awakened about one o'clock by [matron] Miss Smith who informed me that Jos. Wilson was in the big girls' dormitory ... We kept him locked in a small room till Mrs. Ashworth & Mr. Wells, accompanied by Constable Lay, came & making out a warrant, upon information laid by myself, had him before them for trial. Miss Smith, Martha [Thompson], myself & Pearson were the witnesses ... [Joseph got] into Martha's dormitory & had just got into bed with her when disturbed by Miss Smith's lamp.
>
> Mon. [Jan.] 28: Joseph Wilson was put on trial, witnesses myself, Miss Smith & Martha. Martha was led by Morrison, counsel for J.W. to admit having been in Wilson's dormitory & in bed with him before 4th Jan & that she had no objection to his visit to her on Jan 4th save that Miss S. might find them out & that she had written a love letter to him—letter being produced & read by counsel to Judge Spinks. As we could not prove that Martha was under 15 & a virtuous girl the case fell through & the prisoner was dismissed.[36]

Rev. Robson's charge against the 19-year-old Tsimshian man, Joseph Wilson, of "burglariously breaking into and entering the girls' dormitory ... with intent to know carnally one of the female pupils" fell flat given Martha's clear provocation for him to do so.[37] Coqualeetza itself ended up on trial in the press. The salacious details, including Martha's letter filled with sweet nothings, became public knowledge.

Coqualeetza Institute

My dearly beloved,

I received your kind and welcome letter and was much pleased but one thing I am sorry about is that you think I don't like you. If I did not like you I would not have given you my hair. You are the first and will be the last. I am sorry that I cannot have a chance to play with you ... I am always wishing to go with you to your home. I love you very very much. I have not much to say tonight. Good night dear love.

Your really friend,

MISS M. T.[38]

Since Martha was by now aged 16, the easiest solution would have been to marry her off to the fellow student with whom she was implicated or to some other suitable young man. Coqualeetza found itself in a double bind. On the one hand, Martha was having none of them. On the other, her family was determined, if she was sent home, to find her a husband within the Aboriginal community, which would lose her to the school's ministrations.

A two-prong approach was taken. The first was to find Martha a work situation nearby, in the pattern used by residential schools to maintain surveillance while accustoming older female students to the menial way of life deemed to be their destiny. The second was to hustle the prodigal to salvation. Each step along the way was carefully monitored in Robson's diary, indicating the special place she still held in the school.

By the autumn of 1895, not only was Martha back in favour, she was being courted by Peter Smith—with the school's full approval. She was repeatedly paraded as the model of what residential education could accomplish. She and a young Squamish girl, Mary Ann Thomas, were given the honour of waiting on Governor General and Lady Aberdeen's table when they came to lunch at Coqualeetza, and she was front and centre at the farewell activities surrounding Rev. Robson's departure from the school. Martha was maintained as a student until the very day she and Peter Smith were wed.

The capstone rehabilitating the irascible Martha was her marriage. The school matron described it for the Methodist Women's Missionary Society: "September 24th [1896] she left us for a home of her own. She was married on that day to Peter Smith, an earnest Christian young man. He spent one year with us … Their home is in Vancouver city, where they will attend the Princess Street Methodist Church. It meant so much to us to have our first wedding such a one."[39]

It was of utmost importance that the young women who attended the residential schools demonstrate the good results of their training in the neat and orderly arrangements of their homes. Almost as if Martha were reciting by rote, she reported back to the school her pleasure in "the quietness of a little home of my own." In fact the couple lived, together with his widowed father until his death in 1905, in the house in which Peter had grown up. Determined to impress Indian Affairs officials with the success of Coqualeetza, its principal was effusive about Martha Smith's circumstances: "She and her husband reside in Vancouver. Their home is a model of neatness and taste, and furnishes

Moodyville longshoremen belonging to the "Star Gang" in about 1920 included Peter Smith and Tommy Cole, standing on the far right; Peter Smith's son Tom, sitting in the centre, and Leon Nahu's son Norman, sitting three persons to the right. Courtesy Laurie Nahanee Cole

in itself and its occupants a striking illustration of the good work which is being done for those in the school."[40] Shortly after her marriage, Martha Smith is said to have planted the lilac that still blooms at Brockton Point.

Peter and Martha Smith long continued to be treated as if they were school property, the model Indians that legitimized the residential school enterprise. In due course they faced up to the expectation that their children would follow them to Coqualeetza, which by now enrolled children only from about age 10, consistent with its emphasis on occupational training. The Smiths had two sons and five daughters born between 1897 and 1908. The three oldest, Edith, aged 12, Mamie, 11, and Thomas, 10, had already attended Vancouver public schools for three or four years at the time they were handed over to Coqualeetza in the fall of 1909. Their parents surrendered them until the age of 18, demonstrating the tremendous hold that the residential school maintained over men and women who had spent their childhood and

All of Peter and Martha Smith's surviving children were surrendered to Coqualeetza from the age of about 10 until 18. This undated photo of Peter and Martha Smith's children with others was taken at Brockton Point.
Courtesy Marlene Smith

youth there. Three of Peter and Martha Smith's four younger children succumbed to illness, leaving Adelaide, or Ada, to join her siblings at Coqualeetza in 1914.

Initially the Smith children's cousins, the Longs, who lived nearby at Brockton Point, had childhoods much like those of other children across Vancouver. Their oldest son Ed recalled:

> I used to go across [to Dawson school] on a boat with Joe Gonsalves's family … We used to land and had to walk up a hill. We'd get up on the sidewalk and walk up to the school … It got so we couldn't tie up there and had to tie up somewhere else and our boat would be missing sometimes and we had to wait for it to be found … It would take us an hour and a quarter from Stanley Park, the Nine O'clock Gun. I used to live right alongside it.[41]

Then came family disruption: Edward Long died in 1900. According to his namesake son, "he got hurt, he was logging or something, he got jammed up."[42] Three consequences ensued. The first was that Ed left school and went to work sooner than he would otherwise have done. He followed his uncle Peter, who rose to be a foreman, and the others to the docks in a transition that was not easy, but was assisted by the camaraderie that went with longshoring. Ed Long explained:

> I started working on the waterfront in 1904. I was a skinny and light and scared kid going on 13 and wearing short pants.
>
> My uncle [Peter Smith] got me the job of wirepuller on an old schooner at Hastings Mill. What a frightened young fellow I was when I got down there! I looked at the ship and I looked at the porthole and a guy said, "Here's your wire." And he passed it out from the donkey [engine] that was alongside the ship. They passed the wire out through the porthole to me, and from there I dragged it out to the dock. The guy gives me the order. He said, "I want a 20x20 forty feet long," or a 12x12 certain length, and I had to give him the lengths and I didn't dare make a mistake and I was really scared for the first couple of days.
>
> The fourth day I was down there, I was going along. "12x12!" I was trying to push it, I was frightened anyway, and I must have hit something on the dock and it tipped over and just touched my toe. I was jumping around

> and Mr. [Leon] Nahu, the "gentleman" on the waterfront at that time, he said, "You sit down there for a while." He was the foreman, superintendent, everything. "I'll get a bucket of cold water and put on your toe, it's swelled up. So he bandaged it up for me and cut this shoe for me. And he says, "Can you manage it?" I said, "I don't know, I'm kind of scared about it." And he says, "We'll shift around, we got a bell boy down below"—the man who's supposed to look after the bell, who gives the signals—so I was given the poor little whistle.[43]

The second consequence of Edward Long's death was that his widow Mary found herself a new partner: Joseph De Costa. He was a logical choice, being Portuguese, Catholic and a longshoreman. De Costa had arrived in British Columbia from Portugal in 1904 and was just approaching 30 years of age, a time of life when men were prone to think of settling down. He moved in with Mary in 1907. Three children—Joseph, Adelaide (or Lila) and Henry—followed over the next half dozen years.

Mary Smith Long De Costa had her hands full and perhaps for that reason acquiesced to the third consequence, her two younger Long sons' dispatch to Coqualeetza in 1910, a year after their Smith cousins had been enrolled. They were accepted there despite being only one-quarter Aboriginal and Catholic at a time when the school was being closely monitored. William and John's younger sister Josepha was enrolled in December 1914, the same time as her cousin Addie Smith.

Once again, Coqualeetza played a double hand. In the hopes of obtaining Indian Affairs funding, the administration attempted to portray both the Smith and Long children as status Indians and as Methodists. Government officials were not impressed, particularly with the addition of Josepha and Addie at the end of 1914. Their memo made clear that while missionaries may be operating residential schools, the Department of Indian Affairs maintained a very close watch over them: "Adelaide Smith's parents are both half-breeds living in Stanley Park near Vancouver; they never lived on an Indian reserve nor are they following the Indian mode of life. Josepha Long's father was a white man and her mother a half-breed. She has lived at Stanley Park all her life. Her father is now dead and at present her mother is living with a man named Cole [*sic*—Costa]."[44]

The stability at Brockton Point was strengthened by the Gonsalves family, which lived on the south shore between the Coles and the Smiths. Joe Gonsalves headed the only family on the peninsula unaffected by the residential school. In 1904 he bought out the general store at Irvines Landing near Pender Harbour, up the coast from Vancouver. Having fished for a living since arriving at Brockton Point in the early 1870s, he was familiar with the area and saw this as an opportunity to improve his family's circumstances. Gonsalves named the area Madeira Park after his birthplace. He did not, however, abandon the

Alfred and Lena Gonsalves celebrated their wedding in 1912 with a formal portrait. Courtesy Willard Gonsalves

Brockton Point property he got from Joe Silvey, but rather maintained both residences.

Joe Gonsalves's son Alfred, born in 1891, continued to make his home full-time at Brockton Point. In 1912, at the Gonsalves Hotel in Pender Harbour, he married a young Aboriginal woman named Lena Victor.

Their son Willard described the quiet everyday world of this, yet another second-generation family making their home at Brockton Point.

> My father, Alfred Gonsalves, had a gasoline engine certification. He worked for forestry taking people around in his boat.
>
> My mother was Lena, Angelina Victor. She was born around Calgary somewhere. Her father worked around Boston Bar on the railroad. She was at a convent in Kamloops [in the BC interior], then to Vancouver, first working for some family. She worked for my grandfather, which is how she met my dad. Or maybe she was working for a family and met my father there. She was all Native, but she didn't ever admit she was Native.
>
> Our property [on the south shore of Brockton Point] was right down at the end of the short cut [road] as it went down to the water. We were five—Margaret, Albert (Sonny), Isabel, Myrtle, Willard. I was the youngest. We had an orchard down there. We had quite an orchard on our property—apples and pears and plums. I remember my oldest sister Margaret looked after me. She used to tie me up so I wouldn't run away. My oldest sister tied me up outside in the orchard so I wouldn't run away.[45]

Life for the Gonsalves family was not just about themselves, it was also about neighbourhood and community. Young Willard recalled his childhood:

> We had a lilac tree on our property that's still there. Martha Smith lived next to the De Costas. She was a very nice person as far as I was concerned. Aunt Martha, as we called her, claimed it was her tree.
>
> Smith and De Costa and Tommy Cole and Long were our neighbours. On the other side of the point were Tim Cummings and his two sisters. You could easily walk between them. It was just a short little walk [along today's short cut road].

The De Costa children spent much of the time on the beach outside their home just west of the Nine O'clock Gun. Joseph sits on a rock with his sister Lila in about 1918, with Deadman's Island in the background.
Courtesy Amber Stubbins and Debra De Costa Stubbins Smith

> There was cricket at Brockton Point. They'd come sometimes on Sunday for the cricket match, but not to our place.[46]

The second generation took charge not just at Brockton Point but also in the workplace. Longshoring, in which most of the men engaged, was a tough occupation. Individual and group survival depended on manoeuvring between employers' need for dependable labour

Family members sustained each other in the workplace, as with Dave (left) and Tommy Cole at Rivers Inlet in 1932. Courtesy Laurie Nahanee Cole

and the desire to improve conditions of work. As early as 1906, men loading lumber, many of them Squamish but also including members of families originating at Brockton Point and Kanaka Ranch, formed their own trades union, nicknamed Bow and Arrows. James Grant Campbell/Keamo, William Nahanee and Peter Smith were all active in the new union, which voted half a dozen years later to become a local of a more successful counterpart. Ed Long was one of two lumber handlers appointed to the union's executive. The local's president was William Nahanee, and Leon Nahu's son Herbert, or "Jumbo," was also very involved. After the longshoremen's union was smashed by employers in 1923, men with origins at Kanaka Ranch and Brockton Point, together with workers who identified themselves as Squamish, took the lead in forming a new iteration of Bow and Arrows. As recalled by William Nahanee's son Ed: "We belonged to the Bow and Arrows. I was secretary-treasurer the same time as Andy Paull was business agent. I was only there as secretary for about six months and then I went bossing. This was around 1923 or 1924."[47]

Generational transitions for families originating at Kanaka Ranch and Brockton Point resulted not in the disintegration seemingly unavoidable at a time when so many children were being scooped up into residential school, but in life going on. Even though most early residents of Kanaka Ranch had gone their separate ways, a sense of community continued in the workplace. Kanaka Ranch itself persisted in part. The second generation at Brockton Point regrouped on site, partly because their homes survived relatively intact during their absences. Residential school became a stage in their lives rather than an obstacle to their moving ahead. Their marriages and, more generally, their behaviour drew on their long years away, during which they had been virtually commanded to return home and to retreat into obscurity so as not to threaten the dominant society coming into being across Vancouver, British Columbia and Canada.

CHAPTER 7
Changing Times

Brockton Point in 1915 had an established look about it.
J. Wood Laing photo, City of Vancouver Archives, CVA 677-228

When Martha Smith planted the lilac at Brockton Point shortly after her marriage, it was a way of affirming to herself, her family and her teachers at the residential school that she now had a home of her own. She and the others from Chaythoos, Brockton Point and Kanaka Ranch had followed Coqualeetza's admonitions by settling down in one place. Men's hard labour on the docks supported their families and also contributed to the economic well-being of the growing city of Vancouver. Brockton Point families had every reason to be optimistic about their future. Or so they thought.

The Parks Board, and more generally the people of Vancouver, became ever more ambitious for their park. The city was expanding: a population of just over 25,000 at the turn of the century quadrupled over the next decade. Stanley Park was perceived as the critical counterpoint to the dramatic changes occurring in the city. The park functioned as its original promoters had foretold: "Ten minutes after leaving the city one can be so secluded as to believe civilization miles and miles away."[1]

From its inception the board was eager to be in step with the broad-based urban parks movement across North America and Europe. No longer was it just a matter of catering to interest groups, as with athletics at Brockton Point. The Parks Board and its supporters sought to improve on nature. Park Ranger Henry Avison took the lead with animals: his family began accumulating pets—not cats and dogs, but raccoons, deer and bears. The collection took on the appearance of a zoo, whose tentacles moved out across the park. Black swans and kangaroos were imported from Australia and grey squirrels from New York, on the assumption that they would be a lively attraction for visitors. In contrast, lowly crows were unwanted, so in 1902 the Vancouver Gun Club was given permission to shoot them on designated days each month, a practice that continued for years. Later, owls and hawks were targeted because they might be killing ducks, which were deemed proper park denizens.

The natural contours of the park were reformed. The mud flats at the park's entrance were considered unseemly, and so turned into an artificial lake, named Lost Lagoon. But this was not enough. In 1911 a Parks Board member returned from a tour of American urban parks to declare, the Vancouver press trumpeted: "City is Behind in Park Affairs." The next year the board engaged a well-known English landscape architect, Thomas Mawson, to beautify nature. A public uproar followed the board's acceptance of his proposal for a sports stadium and natural history museum, and the plan was abandoned.[2] Other changes went ahead. Through the initiative of the park superintendent, as the park ranger was now called, construction began

The once flourishing Squamish village of Whoi Whoi had by 1912 become Lumberman's Arch. Within the year it was a popular summer playground.
City of Vancouver Archives, Arch P40

in 1917 on a seawall around Stanley Park, starting at Second Beach, to counter erosion during winter storms. Financial support came from a variety of bodies, including the Canadian government, the city and some private agencies. The seawall was finally completed in 1980.

Greater interest in Stanley Park drew attention to Deadman's Island, lying about a hundred yards off Brockton Point. The young city had taken for granted that the 7 acre (2.8 hectare) island was part of the park. After all, it was an island only at high tide, otherwise approached by foot from Brockton Point. Something else was happening. During the 1890s a number of people had set themselves down on the shores of the island in an echo of what had happened three decades earlier at Brockton Point and Kanaka Ranch. According to a contemporary account, "rows of more or less primitive shacks, most of them built on log floats, lined the western side of the island."[3]

Typical of residents was Angelo Sarcia, a lifelong bachelor who,

The City of Vancouver was so convinced that Deadman's Island was part of Stanley Park, it had a footbridge built to there from Brockton Point shortly after acquiring the peninsula. For others the island was a home, as indicated by this view from Brockton Point at the turn of the century.
City of Vancouver Archives, M-3-16.1

having jumped ship in about 1895 when he was in his late 20s, used Deadman's Island as a breathing spot from which to fish and bide his time. Four years later the young Italian, who longshored alongside his Brockton Point neighbours, got himself naturalized as a British subject.[4] Angelo was befriended by the Smith family after he and young Peter met in a pub and discovered they could understand each other between Angelo's Sicilian and Peter's Portuguese learned from his father. When Peter's young son Tom decided "to find out what would happen if he filled his pockets with rocks and jumped into the water, Angelo rescued him and became part of the family."[5]

Even as city officials determined to get rid of such people, the situation on Deadman's Island grew more complex. A Seattle lumberman, Theodore Ludgate, visited Vancouver in 1898 on the lookout for a sawmill site. He heard about Deadman's Island and got in touch with the Canadian government, which without consultation

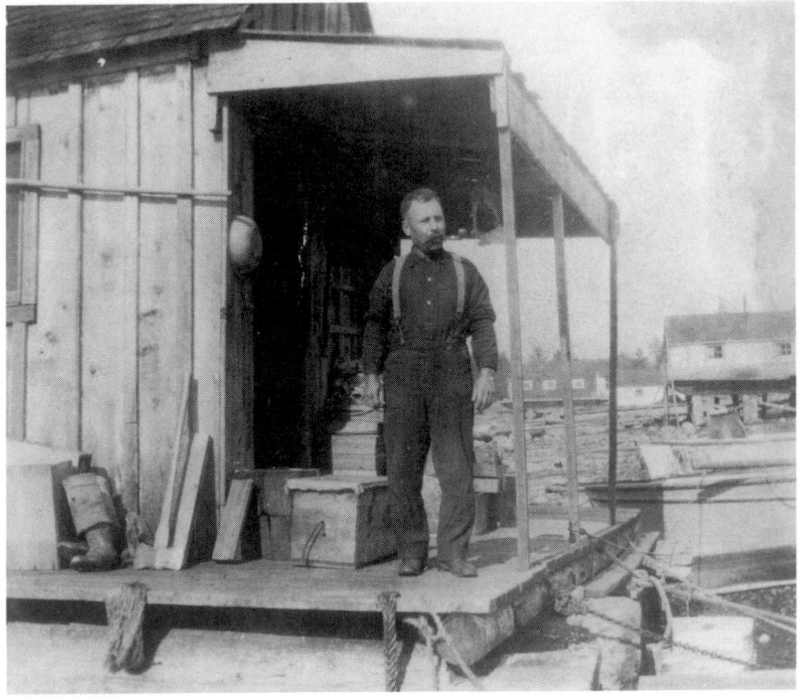

Angelo Sarcia took pride in his Deadman's Island floating home, here in 1905.
Courtesy Rennie Smith

granted him a 25-year lease with an option to renew. Vancouver City Council was furious, despite the new lessee promising to employ upwards of a thousand men. Vancouver residents were sharply divided over the issue, and protests were held when loggers arrived to cut the trees.

In 1899, British Columbia took the Dominion government to court. British Columbia argued that Deadman's Island belonged to the province. The island did so either because it had never been reserved or, if it had, because it had remained with the province at entry into Confederation, just as the province had considered the peninsula to do prior to its handover by Britain to the Dominion of Canada in 1884. Much as in the early 1880s, a frantic search ensued through colonial records, once again with no satisfactory result. Provincial

Librarian E.O. Scholefield testified that a thorough search of books and documents turned up no information relating to reserves. In December 1901 the judge of the BC Supreme Court who tried the case ruled for the province on the grounds that the surviving lands records were too confused and the term "reserve" applied too loosely to admit to any single conclusion. No "'valid reserve,' whatever that expression may mean, in favour of the Imperial Government has been shewn to exist."[6] In September 1904 the Dominion government successfully appealed the decision to the full BC Supreme Court, whereupon the province appealed to the Privy Council in England.

In a decision that applied equally to the peninsula, the Privy Council affirmed in August 1906 the Dominion's right to enter into the lease. "Their Lordships think that it is impossible to consider the history of the island except in conjunction with the history of the land [peninsula] of which it truly forms a part." Unlike the lower-court decisions, the Privy Council did not cite legal precedent, but rather constructed the past to its liking. Much as the Colonial Office had done in 1884, the Privy Council used Douglas's far-reaching mandate as its basis to uphold the status quo. When laying out New Westminster, Moody "specially discussed the case of protecting the rear of the position by means of fortifying Burrard Inlet" with the Colonial Office. It followed logically "that thereafter portions of land were set aside as military reserves ... Governor Douglas, acting through Colonel Moody, had the power to reserve what he chose, and it needed no adhesion on the part of the Admiralty or the War Office to make the reservation effectual.

The peninsula was, the Privy Council ruled, intended to be a military reserve and thereby to belong to the Dominion. It was so indicated by Royal Engineer Lance Corporal Turner in 1863 and on the provincial enumeration of reserves of 1873, and confirmed by Britain by virtue of its agreeing to transfer the peninsula to Canada in 1884. From the Privy Council's perspective, "it is certain" Britain would not have done so unless there had been "communication made long before by Colonel Moody."[7]

Confirmed in his possession of Deadman's Island, Ludgate set about evicting the 150 people living there. Some of them, including Angelo Sarcia, got legal counsel, and the fight that ensued eventually involved sheriffs and fisticuffs. The *Vancouver Province* reported in the spring of 1912 that a group of men from the sheriff's office, together with Ludgate, "carried the firebrand to Deadman's Island in Coal Harbor today and burned to the ground many of the squatters' shacks upon the island."[8] However, it proved so difficult for Ludgate to overcome strong local opposition and to secure financing that in the end no development resulted.

The Deadman's Island situation drew attention to nearby Brockton Point. The Parks Board's earlier attempts to take charge had been stymied. Shortly after the original Order-in-Council of 1887 granting the peninsula's use as a park, the City of Vancouver had asked the Canadian government how title to the lands would be conveyed to the municipal government. The city pointed out that it would be difficult to keep out trespassers without a concrete proof of ownership. However, the Dominion refused to provide any further documentation. A decade later, in 1897, the Vancouver City Council tried again, using the Brockton Point families as an example of the trespassers they needed to keep out of the park. The resolution said, in part:

> Whereas the corporation of the city of Vancouver have no powers vested in it further than the right to use the said reserve as a park.
>
> And whereas there are a number of small dwellings of a very undesirable character existing on the foreshore and other parts of the said park harbouring squatters, undesirable characters, such being detrimental to the interests of the public and unsightly.
>
> And whereas there is now no power vested in the corporation [of the city of Vancouver] to prevent the continuance of the nuisances that exist and usefulness to the public of the park is seriously affected thereby, and in consequence thereof the citizens cannot use the park to the same advantage as they could if such nuisances were repressed, and there always exists a great danger of fire destroying the trees and beauty of the park unless control is vested in the city.
>
> Be it therefore resolved that it is in the interests of the city and the public

> generally that power be vested in the city that would enable the corporation to put an end to the nuisances that do now exist, and to prevent the occurrence of them in the future.[9]

It was not until 1908 that the city was finally given a reneweable lease for 99 years. By this time virtually all of the Squamish who had once made the peninsula their home had departed. Drawing from their extensive research into Squamish history, Randy Bouchard and Dorothy Kennedy have traced a number of them. Joe Mannion's father-in-law Klah Chaw, or Doctor Johnson, moved north to Howe Sound. Kwe áh jilk, known as Dick Isaacs, had several residences before settling on the Mission Reserve. August Jack Khahtsahlano's cousin Johnny Tum kain, who lived at Whoi Whoi at the time of the 1876 enumeration, also eventually moved there with his family. Tommy Chunth was given in 1901 as "Old Tommy" living on the Capilano Reserve, where he died in 1928. Se áh milth, also counted in 1876, migrated between several Squamish enclaves before settling in New Westminster. Jim Chamachan, enumerated in Stanley Park in 1901, moved shortly thereafter to the False Creek Reserve or Snauq, whose residents were pressured to sell it off to the federal government for a small part of its resale value in 1913.

The only Aboriginal person apparently still living in Stanley Park was a Squamish woman known as Aunt Sally, who was the sister of Chém chuk and Kwe áh jilk, both of whom were enumerated there in 1876. From the early 20th century, Aunt Sally was mentioned in Parks Board minutes, usually as an aside, as in the reference to "the cost of clearing & macadamizing proposed to road way from New Pavilion to a point on Main Road near Aunt Sallie's." Another time, "the wharf on the Narrows side, near Aunt Sallie's," was damaged. In July 1909 the Parks Board sent a letter to the provincial fruit inspector complaining about the "bad condition of fruit trees in Indian Aunt Sally's orchard in the park."[10]

The largest number of people living in Stanley Park was at Brockton Point. The Cole, Gonsalves, Smith, De Costa, Dunbar and Long families were on the south side. On the north side, just across the shortcut road, were Tim and Agnes Cummings, who lived with their mother, and next door their sister Maggie and her husband Freddy West.

It was the second generation's determination to make lives for themselves there, much as they had been instructed to do at residential school, which made them increasingly visible.

Aware of ongoing negotiations intended to give Vancouver greater control over the peninsula, in 1904 Peter Smith and Joe Gonsalves requested title to their properties, on the grounds that they "took up their abodes there many years ago, thinking the land was open for occupation." The city's lawyer responded that "the squatters who have occupied more or less dilapidated shacks in Stanley Park ever since that tract was thrown open for a Park have no legal rights there." The easy assumption was that their arrival followed rather than preceded the park's imposition on the peninsula. He added that, should the city evict them, "any claims for compensation for value of buildings or improvement should be settled by the provincial Government."[11]

In 1909, after learning that new structures were going up at Brockton Point, the Parks Board again sought advice from the city's lawyer, who responded that it was within its rights to tear down any buildings that were under construction. Nothing was said about buildings already existing—implying, it would seem, their right to be there. In that same year, the board consulted their lawyer about the "fence of half-breed Mr Cummings encroaching on road." The city solicitor recommended sending him a letter "asking that fence be moved [back 10 feet] and [requesting] that he [Tim Cummings] would [do] so [himself] so that it was carried out legally."[12] Again, there was an implication of possession.

Four years later, these families, who had until now lived in the shadows, came full force into public view. Early in 1913, after the Parks Board accepted the Mawson plan to redesign the park, the Dominion minister with responsibility for Stanley Park suggested "that the Board deal with the squatters before proceeding."[13] The *Vancouver Province* sent a reporter to check out these hitherto unknown persons, and the result was a large, somewhat garbled news feature published on May 10.

> Before Vancouver was born, when the population of the shores fringing Burrard Inlet consisted for the most part of the native Indian tribes ... sailing ships, manned for the most part by Mexicans and Portuguese sailors, were wont to come to anchor in the Inlet and stay for a month or two, while the vessels were loaded with lumber from the camp and mills. Finally, a few ventured ashore to begin life anew, settling in what is now known as Stanley Park ... It is estimated beyond doubt that it was before the year 1870.
>
> As time went on, the first squatter was joined by others, notably by "Portugee Joe," and "Portugee Smith" and the descendants of these early squatters still inhabit the original squatting ground. Whether Smith is still living is a matter of doubt but there is no doubt about "Portugee Joe's" existence. The old gentleman, whose proper name is Joseph Gonsalves, is still alive and well. He lives in Pender Harbor, where he has a hotel and post office, and his family, or some of them, live in "the old homestead" which their father staked out in 1874.
>
> Crossing over the bridge of Coal Harbor and turning to the right, where the road takes a curve just past the horse exercising ground and Deadman's Island—which obtained its name through being used as a burying ground for the squatters and Indians, the last interment being that of Johnny Baker, who was buried there about twenty-five years ago—the wayfarer comes upon a group of about a dozen unpainted, tumble-down shacks and sheds, with one or two cottages in a better state of preservation.
>
> On the shore in the vicinity is a jumble of logs and other flotsam and jetsam of the harbor, interspersed with the remains of boats and canoes, fallen into decay with the exception of one or two which are still in use. These shacks are surrounded by a rude fence of palings, and present, just now, an uncouth picture, with their mossgrown, ill-made roofs, some roughly shingled, some merely boarded, open in places to the sky, with rusted stove pipes thrust through gaps in the roof, in the midst of the flowering fruit trees which the early squatters planted around their humble dwellings.
>
> In these weird structures dwell the descendants of the hardy pioneers who sailed the stormy seas to find at last a refuge amid the calm and hush of the primeval forest, and to watch the growth of a modern miracle—the hewing

> of the city of Vancouver out of the jungle and the wilderness just across the harbor.
>
> Not all the inhabitants of the tiny reserve are white men, for some of the Indians still stayed near their alien neighbors and have dwelt there in peace and contentment with their lighter-skinned brethren. As far as can be ascertained the history of the little community is a history of peace, unbroken by such untoward happenings as feuds between the different races. …
>
> Between Brockton Point and Prospect Point, but much nearer the former, close by the Lumberman's arch is the home of "Old Sally," a famous old Klootchman [Chinook for "Indian woman"], whose house used to be a stomping ground for the Indians, where many a Potlatch was held in the days gone by, while in the vicinity also lives Mrs. Cummin[g]s, a fullblooded Indian, whose husband was a white man whose name she still bears. Mrs. Cummins is scarcely able to speak a word of the English tongue, in spite of her long acquaintance with it.

The families were romanticized, but not quite. They were made just a bit too real for the Parks Board's liking, and the board was forced into action. At its very next meeting, the chairman was instructed to consult the city solicitor about the families with a view to laying the matter before the provincial McKenna–McBride Commission, which was reassessing the reserves set aside for Aboriginal people. If the families could be fitted into this mould, then any worries about adverse possession would be gone, since status Indians had no such rights. Not surprisingly, the commission responded that the issue was outside their scope. The request makes clear that the board still had no real idea of who lived in the park, and probably did not much care.

After 1913 it became a waiting game or perhaps, more accurately, a game of cat and mouse. So long as the families did not embarrass the Parks Board for not having dealt with them, they might be allowed to remain. Any assertion of autonomy caused the board to tense its muscles. In 1915, Tim Cummings's brother-in-law Frederick West requested permission to erect four poles along the road at Brockton Point in order to bring telephone and light service to his house. His wife

Maggie worked as a dressmaker at home and would like to do so in the evenings, as well as during the day using natural light. In response the board passed a motion "that this Board does not recognize the right of Mr. West to reside in Stanley Park, and therefore does not grant the said request." Sadly, West died just a month later on a fishing trip, from exposure to the "icy waters of Capilano" River.[14] He jumped in to save Maggie, who had fallen overboard. She was subsequently rescued, but was left without children, husband or electricity at the age of 25. An everyday amenity increasingly available to Vancouver families was denied her.

Two years later, Ed Long hired a lawyer to try to get permission from the board "to erect a house for additional family accommodation in Stanley Park." He was by now a longshoring foreman, bossing his own gang, and wanted to settle down, to marry and start a family. Refused permission, he went ahead quietly and built a home of his own between the Dunbars' and his mother and stepfather's dwellings.

Another request, from Tim Cummings, was fairly straightforward. Explaining that sewer construction in the park had drained the well supplying his family with fresh water, he asked in early 1918 for a service connection to the water pipe that ran past his house. The Parks Board was convinced that to grant this request would be a step toward recognition of the families' rights, but they eventually agreed to a compromise initiated by Vancouver City Council to install "a public service tap near the Indian House on Stanley Park Road."[15]

No question exists but that ideas about race affected the Parks Board's attitude to the families of Stanley Park. The board routinely referred to the families as "either Indians or halfbreeds," with the exception of "one white family," by which was meant the Dunbars.[16] James died suddenly in 1913, leaving Mary a widow, but no less determined to make Brockton Point her home.

The families were thereby placed outside of the boundaries of acceptability. While persons of all inheritances were permitted within the park, care was taken to justify multiple presences by appealing to a sense of the voyeur, a desire to encounter the exotic. A newspaper feature on Stanley Park in 1909 reported how "prosperous families rub shoulders with tall swarthy Sikhs, alert Japanese, chattering Chinese and stolid siwashes," noting how "the vivid-patterned shawls of the klootchmen compete with the gorgeous turbans of the Hindu for prominence in the color scheme." When it came to persons under their oversight, the Parks Board took care that they were white. A lease made in 1912 with a company renting canoes and rowboats stipulated that "White labor only shall be employed." The next year the board contracted for ice cream at the park's new pavilion with a company that, the local Trades and Labour Council charged, "employed Asiatic labor." The board had already checked out "the class of labor employed," and did so again to discover "two Japanese working, washing milk bottles," at the dairy next door. It was only after the manager swore an affidavit that the pair had nothing to do with his ice cream company that the board was satisfied and let it keep its contract.[17]

No aspect of the changing times was more ironic than the Parks Board's encouragement of a different kind of Aboriginal presence in the park at the very time it was struggling with the resident families. In April 1919 a delegation from the Art, Historical and Scientific Society, self-proclaimed keepers of Vancouver's history and heritage, appeared before the board on "the subject of instituting in Stanley Park a model Indian Village, and to suitably house and preserve historical relics and curios relating to the Indians." The board gave its vigorous support to what was termed an "old-time Indian village."[18]

As a first step toward the Indian village, the society secured two totem poles, more accurately interior house posts, carved by the well-known Kwakiutl (Kwakwa̱ka̱'wakw) artist Charlie James for a house at Kingcome Inlet on the BC coast. The Parks Board wanted them to be painted and approached "Indian Chief Harry," who "quoted the sum of $61.00 for painting, after the cracks had been filled with putty at the Board's expense." The board decided that instead of Chief Harry, "such poles [would] be painted by the Board's own employees," demonstrating that the painting was done for reasons of decoration rather than authenticity.[19] Soon the board had three more poles in its possession. This was an age when anthropologists and archaeologists, notably Franz Boas on the BC coast, were making the province's Aboriginal heritage fashionable in forms safely sanitized from the realities of their everyday life. The passion to rehabilitate the imaginary Indian who existed prior to the arrival of newcomers was very different from coexisting with real people.

As well as depicting a time long past, the Indian village and its totem poles would represent the BC north coast rather than Squamish or Musqueam ways of life. This, the *Vancouver Province* pronounced, was because the Kwakiutl and Haida were "the most advanced of all British Columbia Aboriginal tribes in culture." They were distinguished by "strong physique and higher mental capacity" and a "far higher degree of courage and intelligence than their more easy-going and pusillanimous cousins of the south." A popular guide to Stanley Park similarly explained how "the Haidas were the most outstanding and intelligent of the tribes on the Coast."[20]

Even as the push for romanticized Aboriginality steamed ahead, the uneasy truce between the Parks Board and the families at Brockton Point fractured. In 1918 Maggie Cummings West rented out her house for the summer—overstepping her boundaries, as far as the Parks Board was concerned. The vivid recollection of Mary Ashby, who was a child of the visiting family, emphasizes the great extent to which the Cummingses and their neighbours had become stigmatized and stereotyped.

> In 1918 my father brought our family from New York State to Vancouver. We arrived on the CPR in company with many returning soldiers who kept us—my sister, brother and myself wide eyed with stories of the Wild Pacific West, mostly exaggerated. While still in the east, a visitor from Vancouver had told us about a house in Stanley Park that could be rented from an Indian lady, a Mrs. West I think her name was—a very handsome woman. There were two houses side by side on about the spot where the totem poles now are, and facing the inlet …
>
> That was a wonderful summer for us … The house we rented had a garden full of old fashioned flowers and the biggest, best raspberries in the whole

world. I don't remember playing far from our immediate surroundings, too often—there was plenty to explore in the woods and on the beach in front of our house. Occasionally a dugout canoe would come paddling over from the Indian reserve in North Vancouver, with women selling or trading their woven baskets, at that time quite common but today considered treasures. In place of money they accepted used clothing, preferably men's suits …

Perhaps our favorite game we three children, ages five, seven and ten, liked was to wait for the sight-seeing bus—the "rubber neck wagon"—to pass by. The driver would stop in front of the house and through his megaphone would tell his passengers that "here lived the last natives of the area." At this point the three of us would jump out of the bushes, dancing and yelping like true Indians—we thought. We were suntanned enough to look the part. My brother claims we were thrown shiny pennies for our efforts but I don't remember that …

When school opened in September my sister and I left each morning with our jam sandwiches to walk the long way to Lord Roberts School, a distinct shock after our summer's freedom. In October we moved to a house in the city.[21]

Having endorsed the Indian village proposal, the Parks Board wanted more than ever to remove the real thing. The city's 1908 lease to Stanley Park was "subject until their determination to any existing leases of portions of said land," so although the park commissioners considered that they had "an absolute right under their lease to evict the Indians," the city solicitor was not so sure. In his view, "the Indians remain on sufferance to the Crown, and cannot be interfered with by the City of Vancouver."[22]

Joe Mathias, chief of the Capilano Reserve, got wind of the board's intention and took the initiative. On his behalf a letter was sent to the Canadian government in June 1919, seeking to "ascertain what title the status Indians in Stanley Park possessed."[23] The letter forced the Canadian government to sort out its position with respect to the families. In October 1921 the chief inspector of Indian agencies for British Columbia advised the Department of Indian Affairs to limit its responsibility to Aunt Sally and her extended family, the only "pure" Indians in the park.

> While there are at least eight families living on the park property, there is only one of pure Indian blood, the balance being either half-breeds or whites, therefore the Department has no particular interest in the other seven families, whose homes are on the beach at Coal Harbour [Brockton Point].
>
> The Indian family are in the park proper close to the first narrows entering Vancouver Harbour. They claim they have lived there all their lives, though they are of the Kapilano stock, having originally come from Howe Sound where there are a number of reserves belonging to the Squamish Band. This family are:–
>
> Howe Sound Jack aged about 90 years,
>
> Sally, his wife, aged about 80 years,
>
> Mariah, the daughter, widow, aged 48 years,
>
> Margaret, grand-daughter, child of Maria, aged 14 years.
>
> These Indians, through long and uninterrupted occupation of about two acres of land, have under squatters' rights acquired a valuable holding, and I fail to see how they can be removed unless they are compensated for give [*sic*] any claim to the same. They inform me they would be willing to move away if they are fairly dealt by. They have their holding fenced in and under cultivation with fruit trees and berry bushes. The house, however, is dirty and untidy.
>
> If the Park Commission were given absolute rights, under the lease, to eject the Indians, such lease must have been given to them in ignorance of the fact that this family at least has been living on the property long before the Imperial Government conveyed it to the Dominion Government for military purposes [in 1884], and I therefore think it would be well for you to make such representations to the Department of Militia and Defence as will prevent the Vancouver Park Commission from removing the Indians mentioned unless they are duly compensated for any claims they may have.[24]

Then came another provocation. In October 1921 the Parks Board contacted the city solicitor "in regard to a certain squatter in Stanley Park" who "had purchased lumber for making an extension to the building."[25] The alleged transgressor was Alfred Gonsalves, whose father now spent most of his time at Pender Harbour. The board requested that the city solicitor begin a test case that might lead to a larger one for the eviction of all the families.

The press coverage illuminates the chasm that divided the families from the dominant society. They considered that they belonged just as much as did everyone else, but others wanted none of them. A front-page article in the *Vancouver World* newspaper dismissed Alfred Gonsalves as "an Indian living in Stanley Park," whereupon Alfred's father penned an indignant letter to the editor. "I cannot let pass the absurdity of calling him an Indian, and request that you make the necessary correction. I was born of Portuguese parents at Madeira and leaving my former country when a boy, came to this province as a young man, settling at what is now Brockton Point in 1874. My son, Alfred, was born and brought up at this place, and educated at Dawson school in the West End. He is an expert engineer … He is in every way a 100 per cent Canadian citizen."[26]

Thirty-year-old Alfred Gonsalves was charged in Vancouver Police Court with violating the city's building bylaw by not obtaining a permit. His lawyer argued the bylaw was ultra vires because Stanley Park was "a military reserve" under the authority of the Dominion government. In other words, the city bylaw did not apply. The magistrate hearing the case called an adjournment to give the defence lawyer time to refer the matter to the attorney general of Canada, who decided not to get involved, and Alfred Gonsalves was fined $25.[27] The Gonsalves challenge to the city's authority spurred the Vancouver city solicitor into action. In October 1921 he advised the Parks Board to begin "an action for ejectment against all people squatting in the Park, who should then have to prove their adverse possession of over sixty years."[28] The reference was to the Dominion statute. The proposal had enormous appeal, but three considerations needed tending.

The first related to the status of the Aboriginal family living near the old village site of Whoi Whoi. The Department of Indian Affairs had by now determined that "Aunt Sally had been the wife of Chief Kulkalem, the original squatter on the property, and Mariah her daughter" by him. Howe Sound Jim at some point "simply came to live with her" and so had no claim. The situation became more urgent when Aunt Sally, who had been "very aged and frail," died on April 19, 1923.[29] Her daughter Mariah immediately hired a lawyer to look after her interests. No one quite knew what her decision portended.

The second and much more critical consideration had to do with the length of time necessary for people to acquire ownership based on occupation. The City of Vancouver required only 20 years' residence to claim adverse possession, whereas the Dominion government demanded 60 years. Whether or not the precedent was in anyone's mind, the outcome at Kanaka Ranch could not have given assurance. The Eihu family had proven squatters' rights, based on the city's measure. The land at the corner of Denman and Georgia streets became more and more valuable with the passage of time.

Now, even the longer time period was running out. The board used a visit to Vancouver by the Dominion solicitor general to take him "upon an inspection of the squatters' property."[30] The tour, together with the realization that action had to be taken now or not at all, caused the Canadian government to change direction.

In early April 1923, the Department of Justice instructed the City of Vancouver's legal department "to take all necessary steps in the name of the Dominion Government and the City of Vancouver to institute proceedings in the Courts for the ejectment of the squatters," and stated that the Dominion government would cover all costs. The Department of Defence almost immediately threw its support behind the Department of Justice. It too had been convinced that "the houses and other buildings did not add to the general appearance of the Park."[31]

The Dominion government's decision to join the case and pick up court costs left a third consideration. The families had repeatedly asserted that "they do not intend to move unless they are given what they consider will be adequate compensation for their 'squatters' rights.'"[32] Compensation had followed the road-building debacles at the time of Stanley Park's imposition and had been behind the 1888 enumeration during the smallpox scare. The principle grounded the city solicitor's opinion, in 1904, on getting rid of the houses and the language in the 1908 agreement to do with "existing leases."

The City of Vancouver decided on an end run. Rather than seek eviction and be liable for compensation, it would ask the courts for "a declaration of title to determine what right, if any, the squatters have against the Crown and the City." By this means, compensation would have to be paid only if the defendants "established a good statutory title providing possession for more than the statutory period" of 60 years and so had to be "dealt with either through expropriation proceedings" or "through private negotiation by way of purchase."[33]

The city launched its dispossession cases on April 21, 1923. Two months later the Dominion of Canada formally joined it as a co-plaintiff. The defendants were nine in number, comprising Mariah Kulkalem and eight heads of families at Brockton Point.

Defendants in suit launched by City of Vancouver on April 21, 1923

Name	**Basis of suit**
Mariah Kulkalem	Daughter of 'Aunt Sally'
Alfred Gonzalves [*sic*]	Son of Joe Gonsalves
Peter Smith	Son of Peter Smith
Ed Long	Grandson of Peter Smith, son of Edward Long
Mary Smith DeKosta [*sic*]	Daughter of Peter Smith
Edward [*sic*—Thomas] Cole	Son of Robert Cole
Mary Dunbar	Widow of James Dunbar
Agnes Cummings	Daughter of James Cummings
Mary [*sic*—Margaret] Cummings [West]	Daughter of James Cummings

The cases for dispossession were handled for the plaintiff by George E. McCrossan, who was Vancouver city corporate counsel. The defendants had no choice but to hire lawyers. The cases against the five mixed-race families living on the south shore of Brockton

Point—Gonsalves, Smith, Long, De Costa, Cole—were to be tried together. Tommy Cole's son, who was a child at the time, recalled Alfred Gonsalves paying a substantial portion of their lawyer's fees.[34] Gonsalves chose Roy Long, known for his willingness to take on a wide range of defendants. Acting for Mary Dunbar was Cecil Killam, a bit more of an establishment figure. The Cummings sisters, who were tried together, hired N. Rigby Fisher.

The nature and extent of public reaction to the lawsuit is difficult to gauge. The protest that did jangle a nerve came in a letter written to Prime Minister Mackenzie King and to the member of parliament for Vancouver immediately after the lawsuit was launched in April 1923. Both men forwarded their copies to the Department of Indian Affairs. In the letter, an elderly Vancouver woman named Margaret Perceval waxed indignant over "steps to evict the Indians from Stanley Park."[35] Referring to Mary Smith Long De Costa, she wrote in very sympathetic terms that were, at the same time, grounded in the assumptions of the day linking skin colour to capacity.

> She is a very estimable woman, but quite an Indian you know, & incapable of living as we do—so I am terribly worried over it. She is so patient & gentle & yet she shows the strain she is under. She came to see me about it.—I have written to the Premier & told him I am writing you.
>
> She has a small shack, you may remember, close to the road, & her sons have built a small four-roomed cottage where they live with their sister. These children were brought up at the Chilliwack school [Coqualeetza]. Their name is Long, as their mother had been a long time a widow when she married De Costa. Two of her sons enlisted [in the First World War], though they were very young, & one is not very strong on account of an illness he had while away.
>
> All her associations are bound up in the very little bit of land on the beach of Brockton Point where she lives. I have known her for many years, & have a deep feeling of friendship for her. She is such a simple child of nature. I am quite sure that if she is turned out of her humble home she will not survive it long. Her sons built a small neat cottage close to her little place, & her daughter keeps house for them, while they work at fishing or what not—very

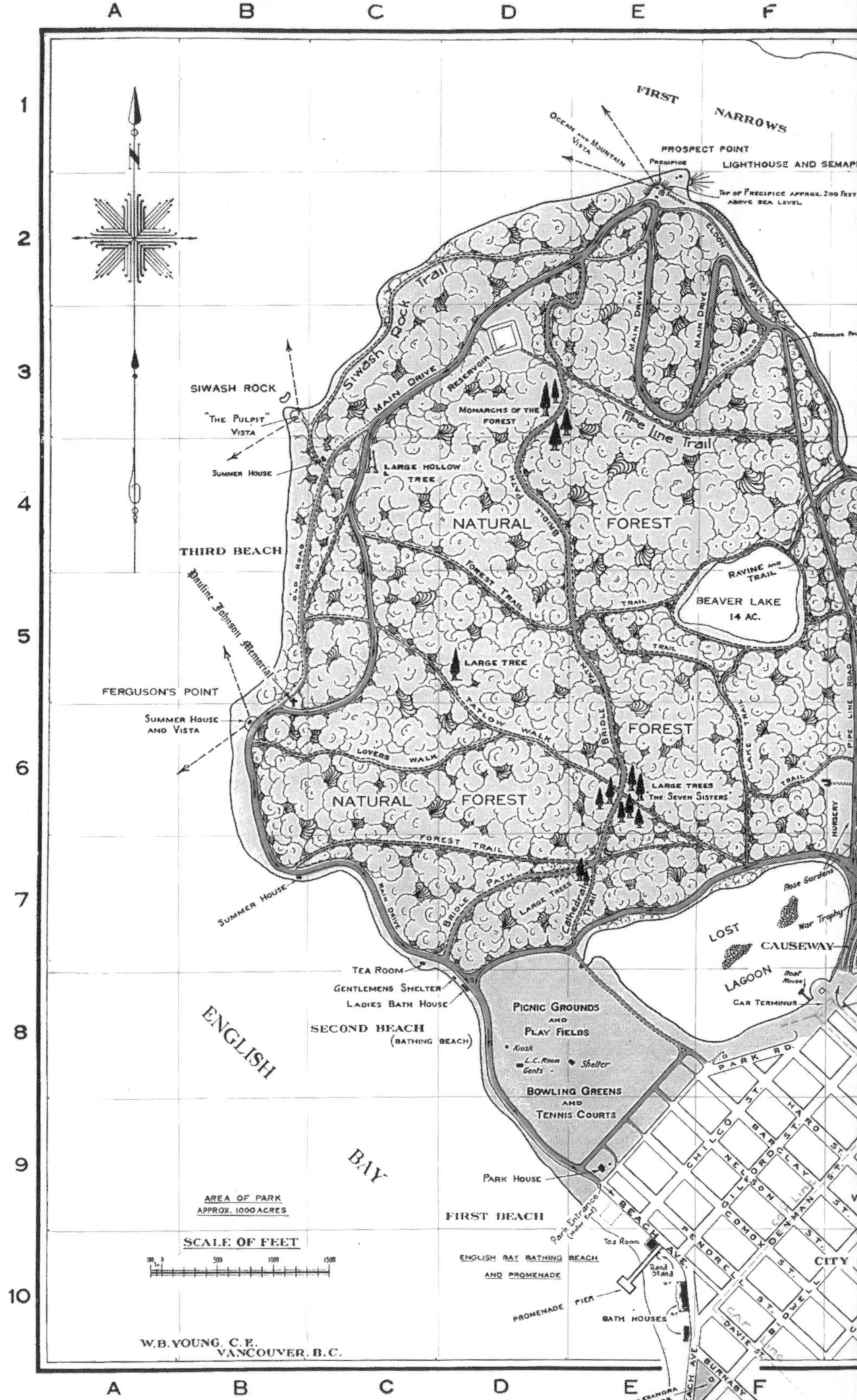
A B C D E F
1 2 3 4 5 6 7 8 9 10
N
FIRST NARROWS
OCEAN AND MOUNTAIN VISTA
PROSPECT POINT
PRECIPICE
LIGHTHOUSE AND SEMAPH
TOP OF PRECIPICE APPROX. 200 FEET ABOVE SEA LEVEL
SIWASH ROCK
"THE PULPIT" VISTA
SUMMER HOUSE
Siwash Rock Trail
MAIN DRIVE
RESERVOIR
MONARCHS OF THE FOREST
Pipe Line Trail
ELDON TRAIL
LARGE HOLLOW TREE
NATURAL FOREST
THIRD BEACH
OLD ROAD
FOREST TRAIL
BRIDLE PATH
Pauline Johnson Memorial
RAVINE AND TRAIL
BEAVER LAKE
14 AC.
TRAIL
LARGE TREE
FERGUSON'S POINT
SUMMER HOUSE AND VISTA
TATLOW WALK
FOREST
LAKE TRAIL
PIPE LINE ROAD
LOVERS WALK
LARGE TREES
"THE SEVEN SISTERS"
NATURAL FOREST
NURSERY
FOREST TRAIL
SUMMER HOUSE
Rose Gardens
War Trophy
LARGE TREES
Cathedral Trail
LOST LAGOON
CAUSEWAY
Boat House
CAR TERMINUS
TEA ROOM
GENTLEMENS SHELTER
LADIES BATH HOUSE
PICNIC GROUNDS AND PLAY FIELDS
Kiosk
L.C. Room Gents
Shelter
BOWLING GREENS AND TENNIS COURTS
ENGLISH
SECOND BEACH (BATHING BEACH)
PARK RD.
CHILCO ST.
HARO ST.
BARCLAY ST.
NELSON ST.
GILFORD ST.
COMOX ST.
DENMAN ST.
BAY
PARK HOUSE
AREA OF PARK APPROX. 1000 ACRES
FIRST BEACH
Park Entrance
BEACH AVE.
PENDREL ST.
SCALE OF FEET
500 1000 1500
ENGLISH BAY BATHING BEACH AND PROMENADE
Tea Room
Band Stand
CITY
PROMENADE PIER
BATH HOUSES
DAVIE ST.
W.B. YOUNG, C.E.
VANCOUVER, B.C.
ALEXANDRA PARK
BEACH AVE.
BURNABY

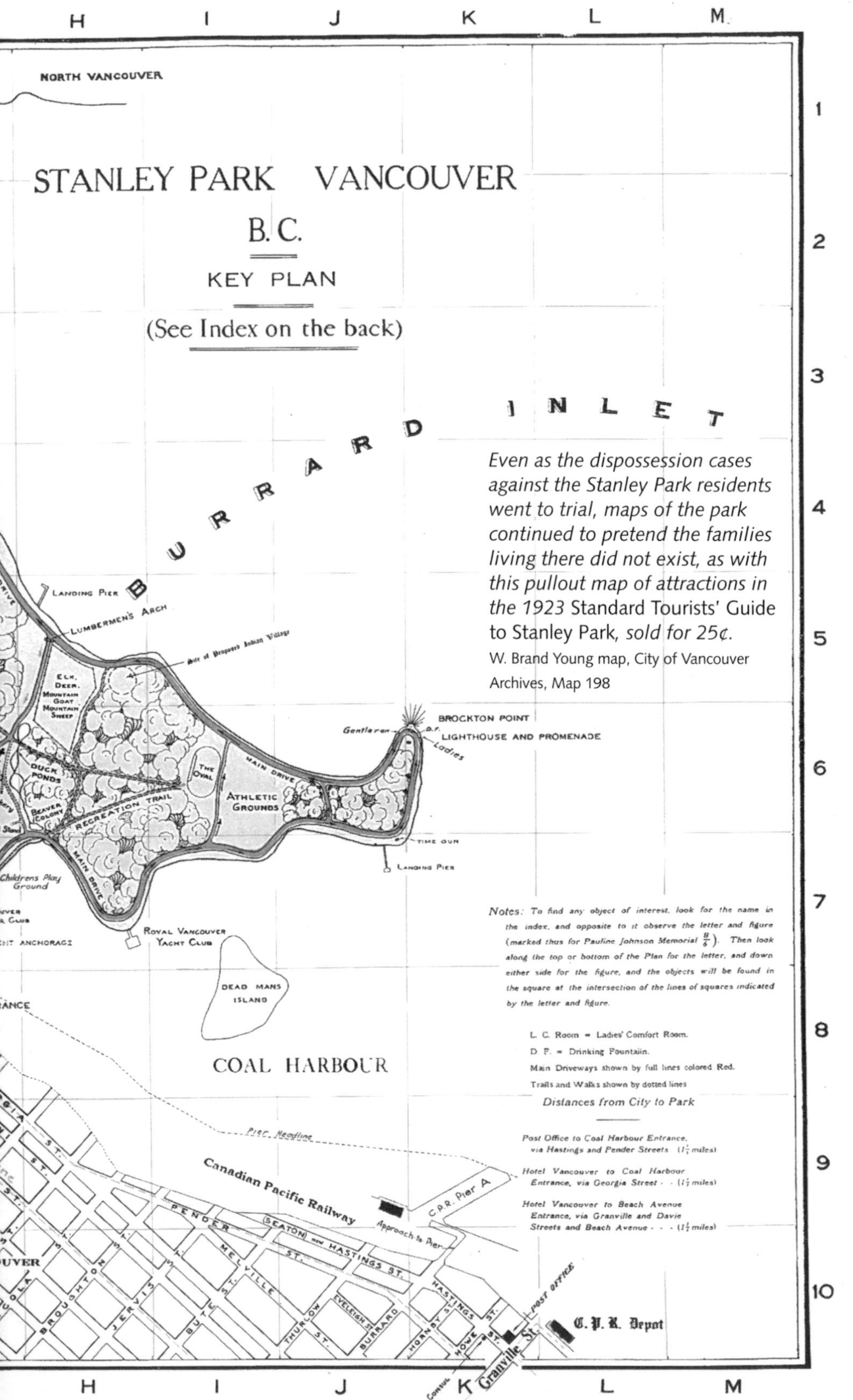

Even as the dispossession cases against the Stanley Park residents went to trial, maps of the park continued to pretend the families living there did not exist, as with this pullout map of attractions in the 1923 Standard Tourists' Guide to Stanley Park, *sold for 25¢.*

W. Brand Young map, City of Vancouver Archives, Map 198

respectable boys they are too & quiet. She has two other children with her & her husband who is a white man but who is not very steady. Her little place is not in anyone's way & is not an eyesore by any means, quite the contrary.

Surely the Dominion of Canada can afford to let this poor innocent creature, whose forefathers were here long before we were, spend the rest of her days where she is. Her mother & grand-parents who were all Indians lived there before her.

They move heaven & earth to put an Indian village & totem poles to make a pretence of helping our poor Indians & yet this eviction will take place unless you will prevent it.[36]

A letter writer to the *Vancouver Province* a couple of months later was even more blunt than Margaret Perceval in his comparison of attitudes toward real and imagined Aboriginality:

While the park authorities are doing their best to drive the Indian squatters out of Stanley Park, the Art and Historical Society is doing its best to get an imitation of an ancient Indian village erected on the very spot where some of the squatters now live.

It is true these Indians no longer live in wigwams or dress in skins and blankets—yet they are the genuine relics of the aborigines and though the influence of the white man has robbed them of much of their picturesqueness they are still interesting. Many of us felt a pang of pity for the old squaw [Aunt Sally] who died after being told that the Christian white man was going to turn her and the remains of her tribe out of their homes. To be sure, she was very old and the news may, or may not, have hastened her end, who knows? but I think many will agree with me in thinking that if the society would lend its energies to preserving what we have left of the natives and their little homes in the park that the addition of a totem pole or two and a collection of Indian relics and basket work, housed in a wigwam that might [be] erected in or near the present village, would have added interest and attraction because of the tang of reality that would prevail in the presence of the squaws and papooses, to say nothing of the noble red man himself when he happened to be at home.

A number of us would be very sorry to miss them in the primeval forest

> of Stanley Park, where they seem to belong and to fill in the picture with the wanted touch of natural life.[37]

The fundamental difficulty was that no one, apart from a few letter writers, had any interest in supporting people who were biologically neither one thing nor the other. Aboriginal people with status did have a protector of sorts in the Department of Indian Affairs, but not people of mixed race living in between Aboriginality and the dominant culture.

For a good quarter century from the imposition of Stanley Park, the families who made it their home existed, but they did not exist. They occupied an intermediate position in a province and a city that increasingly did not acknowledge the mix of attributes that they embodied. In that middle location, they made their homes. The commitments made by Mary See-em-ia in 1871, when she planted apple and cherry seeds at Kanaka Ranch, and by Peter Smith's bride Martha a quarter of a century later, when she signified possession by setting out a lilac beside her new home at Brockton Point, were about to be tested as never before.

Chapter 8

To the Courts

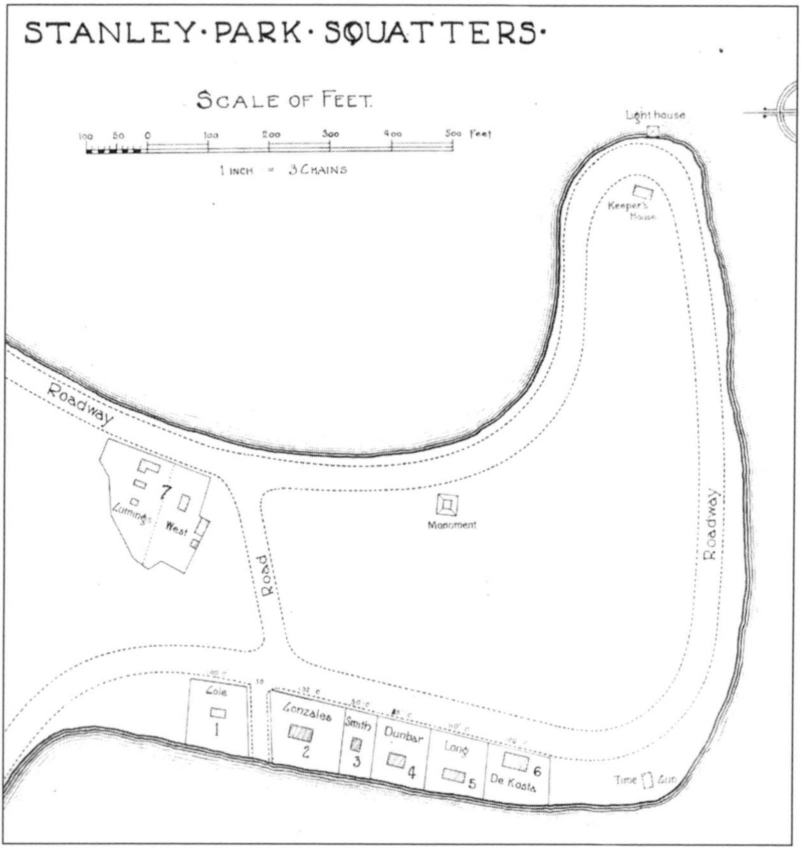

The plans of Brockton Point prepared by the Vancouver city engineering office showed clear divisions between the families' houses, in line with assumptions in the dominant society about the primacy of private property.
City of Vancouver Archives, Map 649

The dispossession cases that the City of Vancouver and the Government of Canada launched against the families of Brockton Point in April 1923 took two and a half years to work through the courts. Their fundamental first step was the four trials held in November 1923 in the BC Supreme Court.

Chronology of cases against families of Stanley Park

Case against Alfred Gonzalves [*sic*], Peter Smith, Ed Long, Mary Smith DeKosta [*sic*] and Thomas Cole	BC Supreme Court trial	November 5–8, 1923
	Decision against defendants	November 16, 1923
	Appeal decision for defendants	October 7, 1924
	Supreme Court decision against defendants	May 6, 1925
Case against Mary Dunbar	BC Supreme Court trial	November 9, 1923
	Decision against defendant	November 16, 1923
	Appeal decision for defendant	November 11, 1924
	Supreme Court decision against defendant	October 6, 1925
Case against Mariah Kulkalem	Adjourned	November 12, 1923
Case against Agnes Cummings and Mary West [*sic*]	BC Supreme Court trial	November 15, 1923
	Decision against defendants	November 16, 1923
	Appeal decision for defendants	October 7, 1924
	Supreme Court decision against defendants	October 20, 1925

The four cases are best considered as a group. They all had the same basis and flowed from each other in terms of points in law, evidence, witnesses, reasoning and decisions, and all but the Kulkalem case were heard sequentially, without a jury, by BC Supreme Court Justice Denis Murphy. The Gonsalves case was tried on November 5–8, 1923, and the others layered on it.

The lawyers acting in subsequent cases sat in on the Gonsalves case on behalf of their clients and agreed that after the lead case, new witnesses would be called sparingly. The case against Mary Dunbar took less than half an hour to present on November 9. Three days later the Mariah Kulkalem case was adjourned indefinitely, pending negotiations for a settlement out of court. The case against Agnes Cummings and her sister Margaret West was heard on November 15.

The cases centred on the concept of adverse possession, whereby occupation that went unchallenged for a specified period of time overrode legal ownership. Occupation had to be open, actual, exclusive, undisturbed and continuous over a specified time period in order to maintain a claim for adverse possession. Occupation had to be so blatant that any owner paying due attention to his property had every opportunity to begin legal measures within the statutory time period to have the occupier removed. By virtue of the Government of Canada joining the action, the time period for adverse possession was set at 60 years, as opposed to the 20 years demanded by the City of Vancouver.

The prosecution had to demonstrate one of two things. Either the defendants had not been in possession 60 years prior to the initiation of the cases, April 21, 1863, or they did not remain in continuous and undisturbed possession since then. Persons in adverse possession could claim one from the other, but where property was handed down, lines of succession had to be intentional and deliberate. The defendants had, conversely, to demonstrate two things: that they had been in adverse possession by April 21, 1863, and that their predecessors and themselves had remained in continuous and undisturbed possession over the entire 60 years. Seven lines of succession, corresponding to the uses of Brockton Point over time, informed the trials.

South side, west to east

1

Policeman Tom to Robert Cole to Thomas Cole

2

Joe Silvey to Joe Gonsalves to Alfred Gonsalves

3

Shwuthchalton to Peter Smith to Peter Smith

4

Gregorio/Joe Fernandez to Tomkins Brew to Mary Dunbar

5

Shwuthchalton to Peter Smith to Edward Long and Mary Smith Long De Costa

6

John Baker to Nine O'clock Gun

North side

7

Klah Chaw/Dr. Johnson/Hjachalachth to Joe Mannion to James Cummings, Agnes Cummings and Margaret Cummings West

The plaintiffs' case was based on three key documents. Extensive research in the BC Provincial Archives had turned up no new materials to those used in the Deadman's Island case.[1]

So, to prove title, the plaintiff introduced the British government dispatch of 1884 acceding to Canada's request to return the peninsula, an act upheld by the Privy Council's decision of 1906 in the Deadman's Island case. To demonstrate 60 years' possession, the plaintiff introduced the instructions of January 1863 to Royal Engineers Lance Corporal George Turner for surveying Burrard Inlet. The third key document was a map of the peninsula plotted from Turner's field notes made in March 1863. Drawn especially for the trials by a city employee, the map was, with the concurrence of the defence, equated with the notes themselves.

The key date of April 21, 1863, was just a month after Turner had surveyed the peninsula from the water, which put the map drawn from his field notes at the heart of the prosecution's case. By then individuals could pre-empt land not set aside for other purposes, and a handful, including John Morton and Attorney General Henry Crease, had usurped most of it around Burrard Inlet. Otherwise, no written record existed of people's locations. During the trial, the lawyers for the plaintiff pointed out time and again that the map showed only one habitation on the tongue of land. Turner had marked "Indian house" on the bluff at Chaythoos where Supple Jack lived.[2] The plaintiff, however, claimed that the house belonged to Aunt Sally, the woman whose family still resided about a kilometre east of Chaythoos near the site of Whoi

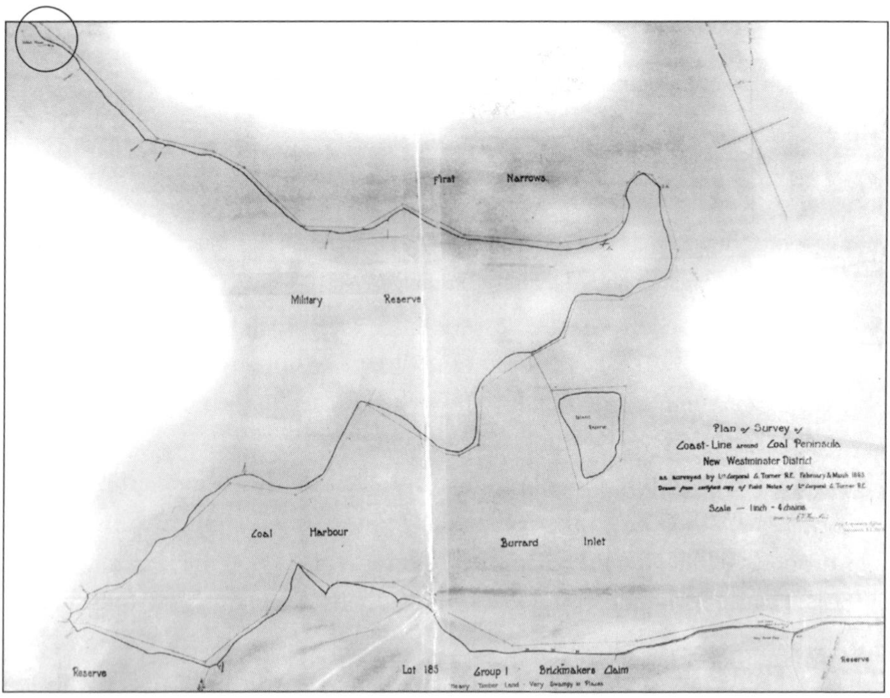

The centrepiece of the prosecution's case was the map of the peninsula drawn from Royal Engineers Lance Corporal George Turner's field notes of 1863, showing just one habitation, an "Indian house" (circled) in its far upper left corner. Library and Archives Canada RG 125 Vol 523 File 5074 (cropped)

Whoi. No one challenged the Turner map or this erroneous assertion, leaving the prosecution free to argue that the peninsula was thereby, with this exception, virginal space just a month prior to the beginning of the 60-year time period necessary to prove adverse possession.

In line with the thinking of the dominant society, both sides equated adverse possession with cleared spaces and dwellings, even more so with their deliberate containment by fences or other means. Early on, the plaintiff introduced two detailed maps of Brockton Point drawn by the Vancouver city engineering office on April 14, 1923. Consistent with space having to be individually owned, each of the defendant's locations was separated from the others, whereas in practice the families intermingled. From their perspectives, Martha Smith's lilac tree belonged to all of the families.

Not only did space have to be contained, time had to be measured chronologically. It is therefore particularly ironic that the cases were compromised by the presiding judge's repeated references to "the Cariboo gold rush." Historically, the Cariboo gold rush is associated with the years 1861–66, when miners moved north from the Fraser River. Despite the centrality of chronological time to adverse possession, witnesses were repeatedly queried as to whether particular events they recalled happened before, during or after "the Cariboo gold rush," as opposed to what calendar year they occurred. The most unfortunate aspect of the judge's using a symbolic representation for chronological time was that he himself appeared confused as to precisely what date he had in mind and then reprimanded witnesses for getting it wrong.

> On November 5, 1923:
>
> DEFENCE: My lord, when was the Cariboo Gold Rush?
>
> COURT: '60 and '61, '59 was the discovery and then '60 and '61—
>
> November 6, 1923:
>
> COURT: That couldn't be, you see, because the Cariboo gold rush was in 1858, the first time white people went up the river at all, and they did not go to Cariboo until '61.[3]

Apart from the reconstructed Turner map and the other prosecution documents, both sides depended on oral testimony. It was extremely difficult to find witnesses. Few newcomers lived at Burrard Inlet in 1863, two years before Hastings Mill began operation. Of the even fewer who had observed Brockton Point, barely any were physically and mentally able to testify. Each side marshalled an array of elderly persons with supposed first-hand knowledge of events. In order to ensure that memories were their own, it was agreed that witnesses would not be allowed in the courtroom except when testifying.

The prosecution had a far easier task than the defence. Individuals only needed to testify under oath that they had seen no signs of occupation at some date subsequent to April 21, 1863.

The defence had to locate people old enough and local enough to testify both to occupation prior to April 21, 1863, and to its ongoing character. To have made the case absolutely, witnesses for each defendant would have had to demonstrate continuous and undisturbed occupation by both predecessors and the defendant over the entire 60 years, in practice an impossible task.

The defence located two very respectable newcomer witnesses in 82-year-old Edward Trimble of Corvallis, Oregon, and 79-year-old Thomas Fisher of Vancouver. Born in Iowa, Trimble first saw Burrard Inlet in December 1862, when, he testified at the Gonsalves trial, there were three houses.

> The 23rd of December [1862]. I came from Victoria. I was going to Cariboo. I went up in the steamer to Westminster ... I wasn't in here more than about two hours. Just passing in a boat ... [that] came in for mail and passengers from New Westminster. On account of ice in the [Fraser] river, she couldn't get in there [to New Westminster], and she came in here [to Burrard Inlet].
>
> I seen three houses. I saw three over here on the [Brockton] point and a few houses over on the north side about Capilano Creek as far as I know ... [The houses were] standing right where they are now. There is [now] Pete Smith living there and Joe Gonzalves and his son Alf.[4]

Thomas Fisher arrived in Burrard Inlet from England in 1867 in his early 20s, but was willing to reflect further back in time. His account rang with authenticity, particularly in describing the three houses he saw at Brockton Point.

> You see when we came up here to load the ship [in the spring of 1867] the ship never arrived and we tried to get a job ... Well, this man at Hastings Mill they said he had dropped dead—he died or dropped dead and a man there by the name of Ben Wilson he said, "boys, if you are doing nothing there is a 'little job' for you here," and we said "what is it?" And he said, "there is a man here dropped dead and I will give you $3.00 apiece if you will take him and bury him," and we thought we would take that chance, so I asked him, "where shall we bury him?" "Well," he said, "there is a good place over there on that [Brockton] point."
>
> Anyhow we went there and when we got there to the Point and tied up there were three little wharves there where these Portuguese were and a float on that side of logs and one on this side and we tied up there and this man came down. I did not know who he was. He was a stranger to me. We never found out who he was. And he said, "what are you doing here, boys?" We buried the man. We dug a hole and put him in.
>
> These wharves were down this way and the houses were up there. There were four that I know of ... [The wharves were] right in front of the house, from the beach up. I would judge they were 24 or 30 feet long out in the water. These wharves were divided up among the men. They built their wharves to land their boats—and their fish. You see they used to fish for codfish and dog-fish and they used to take the livers out and throw them there. There was another man there—he was in a shack [up in the woods]. I don't know who he was and I never seen him.
>
> Right here [nearest the point]—there was a man named Portuguese Joe—his right name was Joe Fernandez and the next man who was living there was—well, we called him Portuguese Pete—that is Peter Smith. I knew him well. And the next one up here was a man by the name of Joe Silva; and this one here, I don't think there was anyone living in that at all, but there were four shacks there. [As for Joe Silva] I used to see him there all the time. He used to go dog-fishing.
>
> They had a bit of garden there and there was a few little fences up there, but they were not fenced altogether in—just a piece of a fence in an angle

> there ... One of them, I believe [Fernandez], was fenced. And the one this way, Portuguese Silva—Joe Silva—his was partly fenced. There was a fence around his place partly, but not altogether ... There was a piece of fence around the back of it—around here like that—that is where the fence was.
>
> I think by the look of those there shacks [in 1867] they must have been there five or six years, because they were all weather-beaten and the wharves looked as if they had been put up for sometime, that they had there. [They were built of] just lumber. Boards. At that time the Hastings Mill you see had no foreign market—no local market—and they used to throw a lot of that lumber overboard. Lots of lumber that had pitch seams in it, they would not take them as cargo and what could they do with them? There was no local market.
>
> [As to Brew's house] his was on the right hand side towards the Narrows—Brew's house was.[5]

Except for Trimble and Fisher, defence witnesses were Aboriginal. The prejudices of the time made it important to demonstrate credibility. The situation was so charged that the defence put the priest from the Mission Reserve on the stand as a character witness: "I am the Parish Priest from North Shore, of the Indian Reserve," he said. "The first time I met him [witness Thomas Abraham] was 22 years ago [or about 1901] ... I met her [witnesses Celestine and Emma Gonzales] at the same time. I think they are good. You can trust to them—what they say. They are good."

Not only were Aboriginal witnesses almost always challenged by the prosecution as to the credibility of their evidence, they required interpreters between Squamish and English, which exacerbated the power differential in the courtroom and the inherently confrontational nature of the law. In practical terms, no one knew what was being added, subtracted or amended. Both sides sought intermediaries who could be held accountable by virtue of being in the public eye. The principal interpreter in the Gonsalves case was Andrew Paull from the Mission Reserve, validated as being, with a touch of exaggeration on the part of the plaintiff, "secretary of all the Indian organizations in British Columbia—of the BC and Squamish Indians." Earlier that year the Squamish people had amalgamated, with the exception of the Burrard Reserve. Paull was secretary of the newly organized Squamish Band, as it was termed. Chief Joe Mathias of the Capilano Reserve served as interpreter at the Cummings sisters' trial.

The difficulties of translation, together with uncertainty as to what the judge intended by his repeated references to "the Cariboo gold rush," made for sometimes confused testimony. Thomas Abraham, who was blind and said to be 110 years old, had lived on the north shore of Burrard Inlet during the 1860s. The first day his testimony was translated into English in the third person.

> He remembers the time the white people were there—were rushing from Westminster to go to Cariboo. He was a big man then at that time.
>
> There were people living there [in Stanley Park] all the time—living there. He said people lived there long time ago at Why Why—for a long time—for generations. Aunt Sally lived [there] ...Yes, he knows Sally. He is older, he said, Sally is younger than himself. She died last year.
>
> The people came in there first—the fishermen, he says, first came into Stanley Park, and then there was a big [gold] rush afterwards from Westminster ... The old man says he doesn't know exactly the name, but there were two or three houses there at the time. He says there was a white man living in there—that is what he says. He says three or two [houses]—no, three or four, he says ... (Witness holding up fingers indicating four). Four. He says four. He puts up four fingers. They were houses right in Stanley Park.
>
> Joe Silva's house was on that [west] side [of the Nine O'clock Gun]. He knows it. Joe is living there now. His name is Joe. Yes, it is Joe live in it—Joe Gonsalves lives there. Yes, this is the man who lives there (indicating Joe Gonsalves).
>
> Yes, he knows him [Peter Smith, and he lived there at the time of "the Cariboo gold rush"].

On the second day, the substance of Thomas Abraham's testimony changed somewhat. With a much more experienced Squamish interpreter, Andrew Paull, who was present at the demand of the

SO OLD HE FORGETS
WHEN HE WAS BORN
TOM ABRAHAM, aged Squamish Indian, who is a witness for the Stanley Park squatters.

Thomas Abraham acquired the most personality of any of the witnesses. Not only did he give his testimony in "a Squamish dialect," but from time to time, the press reported, he stamped his umbrella stick on the floor of the witness box to make his point.[6]
Province, November 6, 1923

plaintiff, Abraham's voice shifted to the first person.

[As to whether any Portuguese lived on the inlet at the time of "the Cariboo gold rush"] that is where they lived. At the park. I think about four. There was one at first and then on the arrival of these others they would build the houses ... [As for the first house] it was Shwuthchalton's son-in-law's [Peter Smith] ... [Next was Joe Fernandez] and then he made a store. The store and his place where he lived was in the one, under the one roof, the place where he lived adjoined the store.

It was when the [Hastings] mill was working that these [other] people arrived who have now died. I don't know their names. [One of them was] Policeman Tom's son-in-law [Robert Cole]. It is impossible for me to know the English names ... [As to the house's construction] they put one board on top of one another like that. The ordinary fir, the ordinary material made for houses. Mill cut.

They arrived here and immediately resided at the park. They came by way of a boat and immediately resided there. A big boat. From town [New Westminster]. They were paddling it. It is a boat that could be manned by men and a sail hoisted up to convey themselves from one place to another.

Overall, the Aboriginal witnesses, as well as the others, handled themselves well in recalling events from two generations earlier. A number of elderly Squamish women were among the most effective defence witnesses. A woman identified only as Celestine, aged 77 and so born about 1845, had no difficulty describing aspects of her young adulthood at Whoi Whoi:

> I used to live in Whawha. I remember, I was a young girl [at the time of "the Cariboo gold rush"]. I was very small … [I was] 15 years [when I got married, or in about 1861] … My niece was married a little after me and it was about the time of her marriage that that house was built. Peter Smith's house. I seen lots of white people, but one was called Joe Silva. I think Joe was the first one. There were those three houses that were the first ones to be built. Joe Silva and Peter Smith and another old man called Joe. That is the man they called Fernandez, called by that name. Old man Joe [owned a store] …
>
> They [houses] were right on top of the bank not far from high water mark. Only Joe's house [had posts], the water would come around the posts a little bit.

Eighty-year-old Emma Gonzales had been born at Capilano on the north shore of Burrard Inlet and was still living there. Her surname came through her long-time marriage to Peter Gonzales, a Chilean who had jumped ship at Burrard Inlet in 1875, as did numerous of his countrymen during these years. She was able to trace the lines of succession of both the Smith and Cummings families back to specific Squamish individuals. Her recollection of Peter Smith's father-in-law was very similar to that of Thomas Abraham.

> Yes, I do [remember "the Cariboo gold rush"]. These people that resided eventually at Stanley Park were those people that had been to the Cariboo. Peter Smith is one, Joe Fernandez, Joe Silva. Soon after their arrival from Cariboo they build houses at the Park. Three [houses]. Old man Peter Smith was one. This house here is Joe Fernandez's house [pointing to map], this is Peter Smith's house and Joe Silva. Joe Fernandez [is next]. Peter Smith [next] and Joe Silva was the third one … It is when they came back from the Cariboo Rush that they built these houses.
>
> There was an Indian man [Shwuthchalton] that would split the cedar logs for them and they used that to build their houses … [Shwuthchalton lived with] his son-in-law, Peter Smith. That was all made from primitive material, and it was after that they used lumber from the mills. No mill there then …

That is the way I seen them as I am telling you. You see when these primitive boards became ancient they tore them down and build another house of mill lumber right on the very same place … I think the Indian boards were there about 10 years. The mill lumber was there 50 years and 10 years before that it was primitive made boards.

They were getting fish, fishing, and they would get the fish oil and sell the fish oil—dog-fish. They have been there long before they started to sell oil [to the sawmills] … They were all Portuguese.

In the Cummings trial, Emma Gonzales asserted a comparable line of succession for that family.

[As for Dr. Johnson] she says she knows him. [In the Indian language they called him] Klah Chaw … He was there [before "the Cariboo gold rush"] because that was his home …[As for Joe Mannion] she says she knows him. She says she knows [the woman he had for his wife] … She says she knowed her Indian name … [As for her father] it was this old man—called Johnson—Dr. Johnson [or] Klah Chaw. It was this Klah Chaw. They called him Dr. Johnson. She says she knows [where he lived in the park]. She says it is the Cummings family [that lives there now].

Also at the Cummings trial a Squamish woman identified to the court as "Mrs. (Chief) Joe Capilano" described what she remembered of Klah Chaw.

She knows Dr. Johnson. She says she never visits him, but she sees the old Dr. Johnson when she used to dig clams near to the beach there … [As for the well Dr. Johnson dug] she says she knows it. She says I went there and got some water from the well. She says [she did so] when I was a big lady—when I was old enough.

[As for Joe Mannion's house] she says she knows it … She says the neighbours he had was his father [-in-law] Klah Chaw ... She says she knows when Jim Cumming came and stayed in the house.

Ambrose Johnson, whose Squamish name was Tesamis, had an even closer link to the past, for his sister had been Joe Mannion's wife.

He could thereby trace the continuity of succession from his father Klah Chaw to the Cummings children.

> His Indian name is Tesamis. He is aged [65 or 67] … He says, I was a little bit of a boy [when Joe Mannion came to the country]. He says he cleared near to the house, he says—just around it. My older sister [was Mrs. Mannion]. He says about 10 years they were staying together ... He says—Joe Manion, he says, was [then] living in Gastown. He had a hotel in Gastown here. He says, yes, my sister just used to come down when she gets her provisions from her husband. She stayed on in the Park, where her husband built a house for her. That is where she was living. That is where these Cummings children are living now today … I was present there, me and my father, when my sister had a deal with Cummings.
>
> … That [house of Mannion] is where the Cummings children are living in. He says two women and one young man.

The task for the defence was made more difficult by the haste with which the trials were conducted. It is tempting to speculate that one reason for haste was that the prosecution wanted no unpleasant surprises to emerge in the courtroom. To avert even the possibility, the prosecution met before the trials with several of the defendants in circumstances that might be seen as not quite above board.

Most problematic was the Vancouver city solicitor's visit to Peter Smith's home at Brockton Point explicitly for the purpose of gathering evidence. At the trial he described the encounter.

> [I had a conversation on] September 13, 1922 … in his house. Mr. Rawlings [Vancouver parks superintendent], Captain Jones, [Brockton Point] lighthouse-keeper, were both with me at the time we went out there … for the purpose of getting such information as we could with a view to submitting it to Ottawa. The Parks Board had requested our Department to take up the question of getting these squatters out of the park. As we deemed it advisable to get whatever information we could relative to that and submit the whole matter to the Department at Ottawa …
>
> [Asked in cross-examination why Peter Smith was so communicative] I don't know. He didn't seem to show any reticence at all. He was quite free

and frank … [As to whether he was told the reason for getting information] no … [As to why he was not told] because it was not in my mind at the time. There was no idea of ejectment in my mind at the time. What was in our mind was the submitting of facts to Ottawa for their consideration. We were pressing Ottawa to get the people moved off there and we were trying to get Ottawa convinced to move in the matter. They were regarded by us as squatters, yes. But what, if I remember correctly, was in my mind at the time, was to get information to impress the necessity on Ottawa of doing something in the matter as soon and as quickly as possible. Up to that time we had no accurate information as to how long they had been there or anything about it. I went there to get all the information I could …

[Again asked whether the motive for talking to Peter Smith was disclosed] I think that during the conversation, in the early part of it at any rate, that I had said something to Smith that we were desirous of getting them to move off, and we were approaching Ottawa in the matter and I wanted to get all the information I could to submit to Ottawa to see what they would do. I didn't say anything that would make him feel harsh towards me at all. If I went to Smith and told him "I want to get all the information I can 'because we are going to fight you tooth and nail,'" he would not have given it to me.

Peter Smith's wife Martha gave another view of the visit. Having learned during her residential school years that she had to stand up for herself and her family because no one else would, she forcefully laid bare the duplicitous character of the visit.

Mr. Rawlings and Mr. Williams and Mr. Jones came to the door and Mr. Jones introduced them to me. One was the city solicitor and the other was the Parks Commissioner or something like that, and they wanted—well, they said something about buying the place or something to that effect, you know. And I said, "You don't need to say anything to me about it because my husband is here and he is in bed sick." And they said I was all right—whatever information they wanted they would get it out of me; and I said "You had better come and see him." But my husband he was too sick. He was propped up in the bed at the time—I don't remember just what was said at the time, but of course I was right in the room. He had dropsy pretty bad at the time.

Martha Smith sitting by her daughter Ada outside their Stanley Park home, about the time of the trials. Courtesy Herbert Smith

> He was not fit to be seen or for anyone to visit him. There was no one allowed to see him at the time.

Martha Smith was asked explicitly whether or not she had been told the purpose of the visit. She responded without hesitation.

> DEFENCE: Did they make notes in your presence?
>
> MS: No, they had nothing.
>
> DEFENCE: And they told you they had come there to see about buying the place from you?
>
> MS: Yes.

Legally it is permissible to interview witnesses on a formal basis prior to a trial. The substance of what is termed an examination for discovery can then be admitted as evidence. In the examination for discovery, Peter Smith absolutely and proudly denied the information supposedly got from him during the earlier visit to his house. In doing so the retired longshoring foreman indicated his firm grasp of the issues at hand.

> [I was] born at Brockton Point. It was not Stanley Park at that time. Brockton Point is where I was born. [My father was] Smith—Peter Smith … [As to nationality, he was] Portuguese. [I am] Portuguese.
>
> Since my father died I have been there all the time. My family lives there. It has never been vacant …
>
> [As to who lives on the property within the fence] our family is there. [There is] just the one [house]. Of course my father had a boat-house further down that way. He built a boat-house where he kept the boats. Further down towards Cole's place and I keep my boats there, too. The building is there. [As to whether it is on our property] no …
>
> [As to whether my father came only in 1872] I can tell you who gave you that. That is some of old Jones, the light-house keeper's talk. That is some of his talk, I know. It is not correct. It is absolutely wrong.
>
> I claim my father's rights.

Peter Smith was too ill to testify in court, so the court went to him.

As the defence lawyer explained, he "is a confirmed invalid suffering from very serious heart trouble for years." In a much publicized and photographed aspect of the trial, the entourage trooped to his house at Brockton Point on November 7, 1923, in order, as the defence lawyer put it, "to take his evidence from his bed there in the Park." The actual setting was a couch in what one newspaper described as "the small, spotlessly clean kitchen of a little grape-vined-clad cottage nestling in the shade of the forest giants of Stanley Park" and of "the great gnarled cherry and fig trees" that the family had so long ago planted there.[7]

The press report said that Peter Smith, "between moans, gasped out his story," as "a young woman sat beside him, whispering soothing words as he turned and twisted, groaning from the agony of his pain-wracked body." The minute book, or presiding judge's notes, indicates that Peter Smith was given just four minutes—from 11:26 to 11:30 a.m.—to be sworn in, tell his story and be cross-examined. The entire trip to "the scene of the action," as Justice Murphy put it, was intended to last just half an hour in total, and the entourage still had to meet with Joseph Gonsalves, who lived next door, and to examine "the site known as Aunt Sallie's" near Lumberman's Arch, before breaking at noon for a two-and-a-half-hour lunch.[8] All the same, a very sick Peter Smith, who died six months later at Brockton Point at age 51, was not to be stilled. He was determined to get his points across rather than have the earlier account remain on record.

> [My father's name was] Peter Smith … [He came to British Columbia] in '58. He went up the Fraser River. He went up the Cariboo Country. He came back here in '60, built here in '60 … [He was the original person] on this very property, yes …
>
> [As to nicknames by which my father was known] oh, Portuguese Pete; in them days they all had nicknames, the old timers.
>
> [He lived] right here. Not this house, but the one in the middle. There were split shakes. I have seen some of them, pieces of split shakes; don't come at me too hard.
>
> My father always here. [My father died] eighteen years ago … He left a will, a will. Is that the paper you want? That paper was destroyed. Fred Allen,

the man who kept a feed store in town, he kept it, and his safe was blown open by somebody, and the paper was destroyed. I never see it. I know the witnesses [to the will] ... [My father willed to me] his rights and a little money ... Well, he died, and I came in [to his house] next day ...

[When I was a boy, there was a fence] right from here, behind this tree here. Went to the Nine O'clock Gun there; there was a fence ... It was pretty old when I see it that I can remember ... [My father had a garden] around this way, all fenced in. [When they built the road] they moved one part of my fence, one end of it. Well, that part, that was straightened out a little bit in pieces ...

[This house was built] eighteen years ago. [As to who built it] I did ... I built it right adjoining it.

The Cummings sisters were far less effective defence witnesses at their trial 10 days later. Their years at residential school had denied them the detailed knowledge children were assumed to have about their parents. Agnes had been taken away at the age of 13 for more than seven years, Maggie at age seven for almost a dozen years. They had both been forced out of their homes as children, whereas Peter Smith was virtually full grown before spending a single year at Coqualeetza. The sisters' reticence, consistent with the school's demand for deference, worked to their disadvantage.

PLAINTIFF: When did your father first take up that property?

Agnes Cummings: I could not tell you.

PLAINTIFF: You haven't any idea. Is your father living?

AC: No.

PLAINTIFF: When did he die?

AC: He died in 1897, I think it was.

PLAINTIFF: Well, when did your mother come to live there? Do you know that?

AC: I don't know. I guess about two or three years after father did. I don't know exactly.

PLAINTIFF: Well, you haven't any idea when your father first came here?

AC: No …

PLAINTIFF: How long were they there?

AC: I could not tell you.

PLAINTIFF: Eh?

AC: I could not tell you…

PLAINTIFF: Well, you claim the property now, do you?

AC: Yes.

PLAINTIFF: And you claim it on what reason and on what grounds? Have you got any title deeds to show for it?

AC: No.

PLAINTIFF: Or anything like that?

AC: No.

PLAINTIFF: Well, on what ground do you say you are entitled to be left there undisturbed?

AC: I could not say.

The Gonsalves father and son did the best job as witnesses on their own behalf. Joe Gonsalves indicated clearly and precisely the line of succession that he considered extended from Joe Silvey to himself to his son Alfred.

> [I came to Stanley Park in] '74. It was in July … I stopped right there. I went there and stopped there. I got the place from Joe Silva right at this very corner. Myself has been there and nobody else, and my son and my daughter that is married, she lived there about six years. I make my home there since I came, but there are a few years back my daughter and my wife were there, till about 12 years ago I took my wife up to Pender Harbour. My daughter stayed [at Pender Harbour the first] six years and my son came down, and I came down myself at times, and we reckoned that [Brockton Point] to be our home, and I have my furniture there, I have my stove and everything in the place—the place never has been abandoned. I always lived there, we reckoned that to be our home.
>
> I am living in that place now. My son built that [new house], but it is on the same ground the house was, and besides the one my son built there is part of the other house now there. Nobody ever lived there except my family.

The most articulate of the defendants was young Alfred Gonsalves, who genuinely believed that he had a claim to the place that had always been his home.

> I was born in 1891 [in Stanley Park]. [My father Joe Gonsalves is] Portuguese. [He came to British Columbia] in 1874. When he first came there he settled there [in Stanley Park]. There was no town or anything, and that is where he first settled … [My father left] sixteen or eighteen years [ago, or about 1905–07], but he has been up and down, and there has always been somebody living here.
>
> The three generations [down to my children are] living right on that place … We always thought we had some right to it after living there so long. We always had in mind somebody—would live in it. [When my father left] he said we had always been raised there, and we should go on from generation to generation and keep the place. Not completely to me alone, because I have five sisters, whoever wanted to live there, we could all live there … [He has not turned the house over to us] because he lives there himself, occasionally stays there … It was very lately that they [siblings] got married, and until then they were all living there. Within five or six years back. My brother [Albert] got married. He was living in town and lived there. He is not here now, but we both lived there. He is away.

The families of Brockton Point had done what they could to make their case. The witnesses on both sides had spoken, to the extent that the adversarial system that is the law permitted them to do. All that was left was to await the judge's decision.

Chapter 9

The Several Faces of the Law

The totem poles erected after the victory in BC Supreme Court in 1923 near Lumberman's Arch quickly became the Stanley Park tourist attraction they remain to the present day. The next year the Canadian all-star soccer team posed in front of the poles. Stuart Thomson photo, City of Vancouver Archives, CVA 99-1357

The Cummings trial on November 15, 1923, ended the first stage of the legal action against the Brockton Point families. Two years later the plaintiff came out triumphant, but not before being given a jolt. While the BC Supreme Court judge sided with the City of Vancouver and the Government of Canada, the appeal decision did not do so. It would take a decision by the Supreme Court of Canada to dispossess the families.

The BC Supreme Court judge trying the cases without a jury was

Denis Murphy. He was, at one and the same time, both like and the antithesis of the defendants. He was just as deeply enmeshed as were any of them in the social fabric of British Columbia. His Irish Catholic father had arrived in 1858 with the gold rush but, rather than take an Aboriginal wife, had brought a sweetheart from home to the ranch and roadhouse he established on the way to the Cariboo goldfields. Determined to give their children every advantage, his parents educated Denis, born in 1870, and his siblings at Catholic private schools and the Catholic University of Ottawa. Returning with a "passionate faith in the power of disciplined intelligence to improve mankind," Murphy thereafter sought to uplift British Columbia.[1] Whereas the defendants were content to be ordinary, Justice Murphy was determined to lead his native province to the go-ahead future he and others like him envisaged for it.

Justice Murphy did not waste anyone's time once the cases were concluded. Final arguments in all three began on the morning after the Cummings trial. City Solicitor McCrossan spent two hours laying out the case for the plaintiff. The defence lawyers took just 15 to 20 minutes each on behalf of their clients. McCrossan responded briefly, whereupon Justice Murphy immediately rendered his oral judgement. He noted in his minute book: "Judg't for Plf. for possession in all cases. Question of costs reserved. Court adj: 3:55."[2] It is difficult not to conclude that he had already made up his mind by the completion of the Gonsalves trial a week before, if not earlier.

In Judge Murphy's view, the onus lay on the defendants to show continuous and undisturbed possession from April 21, 1863. The principal reason they had not done so, he concluded, was that the Aboriginal evidence on which the defence principally relied could not, almost inherently, be trusted.

> Dealing first with the six cases [Gonsalves, Smith, Long, De Costa, Cole, Dunbar], whose root of title is alleged to be either in Smith or in Silva [Silvey]; on the first point, as to whether it has been proven that possession has existed for 60 years, the only testimony adduced to prove that, apart from the Indian testimony, is the evidence of Trimble … I cannot accept this as satisfying the

> onus which rests upon the defendant.
>
> Three Indians give evidence that these houses were there for a period that would constitute adverse possession. Now with regard to the Indian evidence I must say it was unsatisfactory. I don't think the Indians intended at all to deceive the Court. Naturally they were very old people and could fix dates by the Cariboo gold rush. They contradicted themselves—two of them at any rate, very materially …
>
> With regard to West and Cummings, the same thing applies. With regard to the 60 years' possession, that depends altogether on Indian testimony.[3]

The Aboriginal evidence dismissed, Justice Murphy turned to the map drawn from the Turner field notes. In his view, no testimony he heard sufficiently challenged or contradicted this paper document, which had been constructed precisely for the purpose he now attached to it.

> As against that [Indian testimony] I have the map and it seems to me that is evidence which, even if the onus were not on the Crown, would conclude this case, on the point of 60 years' possession. That map was under instructions to shew any occupancy, by this man Turner, and he does show the occupancy of Aunt Sally and shews no other … If there were any such extensive clearing as would justify the Court in decreeing that these people own this extensive piece of land, as shown by the map, it would be a physical impossibility for a surveyor, such as Turner, to have failed to see it.

The Parks Board celebrated by erecting, "at a cost of $1,199.15," the totem poles in its possession. A few short weeks after the victory over unwanted Aboriginality, the imagined counterpart of that Aboriginality was in place. The totem poles were, the press wrote excitedly, "the first step towards the erection this year of a replica of an Indian village of the British Columbia coast on the cleared space west of 'Auntie Sally's' cottage which adjoins the Lumberman's Arch," the site of Whoi Whoi. The village would be named for "the Kwagwelth Indians" of northern Vancouver Island.[4] The Squamish presence at Whoi Whoi was to be overlaid with the material culture of a wholly different indigenous people.

At the time of the decision, defence lawyer Long intimated that no appeal would be made, since he was "satisfied that every source of reliable information about the old days in Stanley Park and Vancouver had been tapped."[5] But the defendants soon hired new lawyers, who filed notices of appeal in March 1924.

As well as very general reasons to do with the judgement being against the weight of evidence, the lawyers in the Gonsalves case argued on appeal that "an action cannot be brought by one who is not in a position to immediately re-enter."[6] By virtue of the Government of Canada having leased the peninsula to the City of Vancouver, it could not fulfill the basic principle of adverse possession of re-entering the property to regain possession. Only the lessee had that right; therefore the city's 20-year measure should apply. The only defendant not to appeal was Tommy Cole, who agreed to become a tenant of the city in return for being allowed to stay in his house. That decision too was short-lived. Acting in his capacity as secretary of the amalgamated Squamish Band, Andrew Paull sought to have Cole "properly compensated" for his property on the grounds that he was, like the Kulkalems, "a Squamish Indian." Although Cole had, with Department of Indian Affairs approval, become a member of the Squamish Band, he had done so only after the trial started, and the request was denied.[7]

On October 7, 1924, the BC Court of Appeal allowed the appeals in all the cases by a majority judgement. Chief Justice William A. Macdonald backed his lower-court counterpart. The other two judges, Archer Martin and A.E. McPhillips, favoured the defendants. Whether or not it influenced their decisions, all three viewed British Columbia with a more distanced gaze than did Justice Murphy. Born in Ontario, they were less vested in the province needing to have a particular history and destiny. Chief Justice Macdonald was known for his "air of old-world courtesy and grace" and passion for virtually all of the sports enjoyed at Brockton Point. At the other extreme, Archer Martin had a reputation as irascible. A fellow lawyer claimed that "he found difficulty in agreeing where, on occasions he should have, with the views of other people be they Judges, counsel, or otherwise."[8]

The chief justice's reasons echoed those of the lower court, whereas the other two judges contested the principal points of the decision. They wrote independent reasons for appeal, which are most usefully considered in tandem. Unlike the BC Supreme Court justice in his oral decision, they both took great care to cite legal precedent, as was common practice, in what were far longer and more complex written decisions.

The two appeal judges considered that the defendants had actual possession, putting the obligation on the plaintiffs to show that they had a better title. Justice McPhillips wrote, in reference to the lead case:

> It must be conceded that the defendant, who is acknowledged to be in possession of the land, is entitled to remain in possession thereof against all except those who can shew a better title, and can prove that they or their predecessors had earlier possession of which they were wrongfully deprived (Bract. Fo. B, 31a, 52a, 434b, 435a; *Doe d. Hughes* v. *Dyeball* (1829), M. & M. 346; *Doe dem. Smith and Payne* v. *Webber* (1834), 1 A. & E. 119; *Asher* v. *Whitlock* (1865), L.R. 1 Q.B. 1; *Perry* v. *Clissold* (1907), A.C. 73) ... Here, as I have said, there is the entire absence of there having been earlier possession in either of the plaintiffs to the possession of the defendant; in truth, it would not appear that it would be possible to make out any earlier possession. Then, proceeding to another view of the matter, even if it was admitted that the Crown (Imperial) up to 1884 and the Crown (Dominion) from that time onwards, could be said to be rightfully entitled to the land and no steps were taken to assert those rights within the period prescribed by statute, their remedies would be barred and their title extinguished (Stat. 3 & 4 Will. IV., c. 27, s. 34 (Imperial); Statute of Limitations, R.S.B.C. 1911, Cap. 145, Secs. 41, 49) ... In any case, the evidence is ample in its terms to show that there was adverse occupation of the land in question for the full period of 60 years and more, and there was that continuity of possession entitling the defendant to insist upon and to be admitted to be the owner of the land, the Crown being barred and title in the Crown in the land (0.354 acres) extinguished.[9]

As well as turning the relationship of defence to prosecution on its head, the two appeal judges emphasized two related factors. The first was context. An obligation existed, legal precedent demanded, to take into account the conditions of everyday life at the time the first newcomers made it to Brockton Point. The emphasis on clearings and fences was misguided.

Justice Martin wrote in respect to the Gonsalves case:

> This clearing was originally, and, indeed, barring the said road, still is, simply nothing more, relatively, than a small niche, so to speak, chopped into a primeval forest, which at the time and for many years after, till 1887, had no communication other than by water with civilization, and hence there would be little reason, in the earliest years at least for erecting fences or taking other steps to define possession against trespassers or adverse claimants, but simply some sort of rough definition of their claims as between the squatters themselves …
>
> The title set up by the defendant begins with an impregnable possession of 49 years [date of arrival of Alfred Gonsalves's father Joseph], and goes back to the very beginnings of law and order in the old colony of British Columbia, to its birth in fact, and whatever view the Courts may have taken as regards the encroachments of squatters upon private property or mere speculative squatters upon the public domain, in Western Canada at least, neither under the Hudson's Bay Company nor under the Crown direct, has the squatter as a settler upon public lands in the pioneer days of occupation been looked upon with disfavour, but on the contrary, he has been favourably regarded by the powers that be as a settler who was assisting in the building up of the country though in an irregular manner at the start …
>
> I see no reason why the Crown or the Courts in this Province should regard these ancient pioneers of Stanley Park in a less favourable light than similar pioneers have been regarded in other parts of Canada. The long and conspicuous occupation by this defendant since the trail was cut through Stanley Park of a piece of property fronting on what is the principal scenic road in the Canadian Pacific (over which innumerable persons have travelled, including myself, many scores of times) has been so public and notorious that it is difficult to believe it was contrary to the wishes of the Government …[10]

The second related factor had to do with jurisdiction over Stanley Park. By getting the Dominion of Canada to join in the action, the City of Vancouver got the time period tripled for proving adverse possession. Justice McPhillips in particular did not accept the ploy.

> When the roadway was made around the park in 1889 [*sic*], the defendant and the others in the immediate neighborhood in adverse possession to the Crown, and the City of Vancouver, were not proceeded against as trespassers, all that took place was the moving back (towards the sea) of the fences. This roadway was built by the City of Vancouver and is still maintained by the City of Vancouver. It is clear that there has been 34 years of adverse possession as against the City of Vancouver of the land in question. Therefore it would not appear that the City of Vancouver itself has any position enabling it to dispute the title of the defendant, as but 20 years are necessary to give title by prescription against the City of Vancouver. The Crown, however, is joined in the action and the City of Vancouver attempts through the Crown to displace the title of the Defendant.
>
> ... The question [is] as to whether the Crown is entitled to bring an action of this kind, having dispossessed itself of possession of Stanley Park to the City of Vancouver, and having executed a lease there of to the City of Vancouver ...
>
> Even were I in error as to the 60 years of adverse possession this action could not succeed, as it is beyond question that the 20 years only which is necessary to be established in this are made out, i.e., adverse possession of 20 years against the City of Vancouver (Statute of Limitations, R.S.B.C. 1911, Cap. 145, Sec. 16), the Crown having demised the land to the City of Vancouver in 1887.

The two appeal judges dissected the lower-court decision in detail. Judge Murphy had dismissed the Aboriginal testimony in favour of the Turner map. Justices McPhillips and Martin did the reverse. They separately discounted both the Turner survey and resultant map. "I cannot place any weight upon the triangulation survey," Justice McPhillips wrote in respect to Gonsalves's holding. "The area of land in question cannot be said to be extensive, as in this action all that is claimed is an area of 0.354 acres, a very small parcel indeed, and at the time of the survey the area was primeval forest, and occupation might pass unnoticed by a surveyor directing his attention primarily to the coast line."

Justice Martin pointed out, quite correctly, that the location of the single habitation on the Turner map was not, as the plaintiff claimed and the defence accepted as the basis of the four cases, where Aunt Sally lived. More important, in Martin's view, Turner had had no instructions to put down habitations on the peninsula in the first place. His mandate was quite different.

> The learned Judge places great reliance, to the extent even of styling it as going to "conclude this case," upon the map of Lance-Corporal Turner, R.E. …
>
> This [equation of the occupancy marked on the map with the house of Aunt Sally] is a most important misconception about the situation of the house of "Aunt Sally," the local Aboriginal matriarch, who died in 1922 (whose title was admitted), which I drew attention to when the matter came up during the argument before us, viz., that her house, though admittedly very ancient, is not shewn at all upon the plan, as it would be if current "occupations" were properly noted thereon, because her house is unquestionably situate[d] near the Lumberman's Arch at the end of a cross road by the side of the old Indian Village, formerly called Wha Wha, anglice, "Why, Why," yet the only house shown upon the plan is that marked "Indian House," on Exhibit 9, [situate[d] to the west of Wha Wha a distance of three-quarters of a mile at least …
>
> But Corporal Turner did not, in fact, receive any instructions to note "occupations" on this military reserve. Those relied upon to support such a view are contained in the "memo of Cptn. Parsons, R.E.," of the 26th January, 1863, given him by Colonel Moody [of the Royal Engineers], but when examined carefully and properly understood they do not apply to this military reserve (now Stanley Park) at all, but to the other localities therein mentioned, which are quite distinct therefrom, viz., the town reserve, the naval reserve, the Burnaby and Crease properties, and claims or surveys to the east up to "the village which has been laid out en bloc," not one of which relates to this reserve, in regard to which what Corporal Turner properly did was only to make a "survey of coast-line round Coal Peninsula," as his endorsement correctly recites …

It follows that even if Turner's map is admissible in evidence (which I doubt ...), it in no way supported the plaintiff's case.

Having dismissed the Turner map, Justices McPhillips and Martin assessed the quality and substance of the trial testimony. In scrutinizing the Aboriginal testimony, Justice Martin took into account the lower-court judge's repeated references to "the Cariboo gold rush." By using 1858 as a generic beginning to the gold rush, as did his colleague Justice McPhillips, Martin created the longest possible intervening time for men to put themselves down at Brockton Point prior to the key date of 1863.

The fact that this greatly-relied-upon evidence of the principal witness for the plaintiffs [Turner map] has thus completely broken down greatly influences consideration of the adverse view that the learned judge took of the evidence of the Indian witnesses, because he very largely discredits them on the ground that Turner's map was "against" their evidence, but if the evidence sought to be derived from the map had been shewn to him to be based on no foundation, I feel sure he would have viewed the evidence of the Indians in a very different light. He correctly says that three of them "gave evidence that these houses were there for a period that would constitute 60 years' adverse possession," which if credited would really "conclude this case," but he does not regard their evidence as satisfactory ...

In the first place, it is to be observed that while it is true that the evidence of the Indians would be fixed by the first great gold rush when the white man came into their midst, yet that gold rush occurred in 1858, and not two and three years later, in 1860–61, which were the years of the gold rush to Cariboo, hundreds of miles away, and this point is of importance, because it throws back the ages and memory of several witnesses at least two years earlier ... It would obviously be this first influx of white miners, and in particular the advent of the soldiers [Royal Engineers] for the first time, to their vicinity and hunting grounds that would indelibly impress itself upon the memory of the aboriginies: rushes two and three years later far away on the upper reaches of the river would not affect them to nearly the same degree, if at all, and the failure to distinguish between the two historical events has led to confusion and indefiniteness in examining the witnesses' evidence accurately and drawing conclusions, though the exact truth is to the advantage of the defendant when clearly understood.

After a specially careful examination of the evidence of the Indian witnesses (and speaking in the light of a judicial experience with witnesses of all kinds throughout this province of more than 26 years) I know of no good reason in general for placing the testimony of our native Indians at all on a lower plane than that of the others, and in particularly I perceive none in this case for doubting the substantial accuracy of their testimony in all essentials. Indeed, in some respects it is remarkable and beyond expectation precise, one of them, e.g., Abraham, a patriarch of over 100 years of age (being older than the said Aunt Sally, an admitted centenarian), who was a "big man" at the time of the first gold rush in 1858, and living on the Inlet (Burrard), actually saw these three Portuguese fishermen (as they were primarily) (Joe Silva, Peter Smith, and Joe Fernandez) arriving at that time, and in the way he describes—in a boat with sails and paddles from New Westminster—and they immediately went to live in the park and put up four houses, which he saw them building; and another aged witness, Emma Gonzales, born on the same Inlet, gives the name of the Indian, Shwuthchalton (father-in-law of Portuguese Pete Smith), who built the first house and cut the shakes (i.e., large shingles and boards of varying sizes split by hand from clear cedar timber) out of which the houses or cabins of the newcomers were first constructed. I say "first" advisedly, because an important misconception has arisen about the original construction of these houses owing to some uncertainty caused by the evidence of two of the Indian witnesses, Abraham and Celestine (aged 77). The former, doubtless because of his great age, was obviously at the end wearied and confused by the ordeal of a public trial, and by his evidence having to be interpreted ... and by the way the questions were put to him on this head, which left much to be desired in clarity and exactitude.

In his separate judgement on the Cummings case, Martin was even more precise in respect to the Aboriginal evidence.

It appears that James Cummings, the father of the defendant, acquired the parcel in question from the wife of one Joe Manion, who was an Indian woman, Takood, the daughter of an Indian shaman, or medicine-man, named Klah Chaw (called by the whites "Dr." Johnson) after Manion went to live in Gastown, on the south shore, leaving the woman in possession of their home with her two children by him, the house having been built by Manion for her out of lumber from the mill in 1865 or shortly thereafter; this sale occurred some ten years after the house was built and occupied, i.e., circ. 1875, and was made by Mrs. Manion about a month after Manion left and though he had a hotel in Gastown he maintained relations with his family and supplied them with provisions as her brother, Ambrose Johnson, testifies (and Mrs. Capilano) as he does also to the arrangement for the transfer of the house to Cummings by his sister in the presence of himself and his father, Klah Chaw, in the house itself, which is still standing, and occupied by the defendant (who was born in it in 1883) where they were all staying together at the time, but after the sale they (i.e., Indians) went away leaving Cummings and his wife in possession of the place, and since that time, 48 years ago, the defendant's father and herself have been in possession and the old house, as built by Manion in 1865, still stands as enlarged and is occupied by the defendant, being a continuous unquestionable possession of about 58 years upon the original site (which fact the Court below accepted), and this, upon the authorities cited in the *Gonzalves* case, constitutes a very strong case to shift the onus at least, if that were necessary.

But, in addition to that, the evidence shows (to my mind beyond serious dispute) that the land upon which Manion built his house was part of the clearing and land in the possession of and occupied by his father-in-law Klah Chaw, since a much earlier period, antedating the gold rush of 1858, upon which clearing he was living in a house built of shakes, as Emma Gonzales testifies, and there can be no question here of any substantial error in its situation, because the shaman is a personage of the first, indeed sinister consequence among the Indians of this Coast and no habitation would be better known by the natives than his …

I only add that Turner's map has also no application in this case, which indeed further established its irrelevance because there can be no question whatever that Klah Chaw's house was in existence years before as well as after Turner's coast-line survey was made, and yet the conspicuous "occupation" close to the shore lines he was following, is not shown upon his map thereof.[11]

Justice Martin also noted that the defendants were modest in their expectations. The property of the lead defendant in the principal trial, Alfred Gonsalves, occupied just a third of an acre, and the other plots were comparable. The lessons of humility learned in the residential school rebounded, in the case of Peter and Martha Smith, Tommy Cole and the Cummings sisters, to their advantage. The families were not out to take advantage of the system. Their "moderation in the claim is not only in itself commendable but is an evidence of good faith." Justice Martin added, quite astutely, that the reason "they were so small is because the squatters were not tillers of the soil who required an extensive area, but fishermen, primarily, who derived their living from the sea in various ways."

As soon as the appeal decisions were announced in favour of the families in October and November 1924, the Vancouver city solicitor went into action. He emphasized to the Parks Board that it was "immediately necessary" to consider an appeal to the Supreme Court of Canada. Having ensured that the Canadian government was still on side, the appeal was launched on December 1, 1924. The lawyer acting for the City of Vancouver and Government of Canada needed to refute the majority decision of the BC Court of Appeal. He asserted that witnesses called by the defence had perforce not dealt with the entire 60-year time period. Missing segments, for example "the six years between May 1867 and July 1873," indicated that "the district was more or less of a temporary abode for various vagrant trespassers who came and trespassed for awhile and then moved on."[12] As opposed to adverse possession being set in context, he argued that "possessions must be so notorious that the squatter may be said to have 'his flag' flying over … every inch of the land so claimed." He was particularly concerned to discredit the Aboriginal testimony, about whom the previous decisions had disagreed so fundamentally.

> [Thomas] ABRAHAM, an elderly Indian, was next called by Respondent. His evidence, like that of all the Indian witnesses, was vague and imaginative, incredible in parts and at times self-contradictory … It is notorious that native

> Indians have no idea of time … This story [told by Abraham] would appear to be tinged with the Indian imagination …
>
> The testimony of Abraham is in line with most of the Indian evidence, much of which is vague and filled with manifest contradictions and inconsistencies, and it was unacceptable to the learned Judge [Murphy], who expressly characterizes it as unsatisfactory and contradictory.

As in the lower courts, the hearings before the Supreme Court were in three parts. The combined Gonsalves, Smith, De Costa and Long case began on May 5, 1925. Arguments wrapped up the next afternoon, whereupon the Supreme Court promptly allowed the appeal without giving written reasons.[13] The Supreme Court of Canada unanimously restored the decision in the BC Supreme Court. On October 26, the case against Mary Dunbar was similarly decided. The decision in the Cummings case was made on October 20, 1925, and although it was the same as the other two cases, it differed from them by virtue of there being written reasons.

The Supreme Court of Canada's reasoning in the Cummings case addressed four of the bases for the decision of the BC Court of Appeal. First, the defendants were obliged to show title, not the reverse. Second, the Government of Canada was a legitimate party in the case, which meant that the 60-year rule for adverse possession applied. Third, possession needed to be defined in terms of a clear and definite area, as opposed to being set within a historical context. Fourth, given that the original judge did not credit the Indian testimony, neither should the appeal-court judges or the highest court.

> The trial Judge expressly stated that he did not credit the Indian testimony which was tendered. As a general rule, under such circumstances, a Court of Appeal will always be slow to intervene in the result arrived at by the court below. Nothing that we have been able to find, nothing that counsel for the respondents directed our attention to was of a nature, in this case, to warrant a departure from this wise rule; and, in our view, the findings of the learned trial Judge therein ought not to have been disturbed.[14]

The only possible further appeal was to the Privy Council in London, a course that was not pursued. The reason may have been the implicit threat that if the families did so and lost, the city would take up their right to levy costs against them, which were considerable.

One of the most striking aspects of the trials and the decisions is the ability of the two appeal judges to think beyond the assumptions of the time and rule in the families' favour. It may be that because the appeal judges were not physically present in the courtroom, they did not assess the credibility of defendants based on how they looked physically or presented themselves socially in the formal venue of a courtroom. They did not have to contend with bodies that looked, moved and perhaps smelled different from theirs. The defendants and their Aboriginal witnesses conformed to the stereotypes held by many members of the dominant society during these years. Even some people outside the courtroom treated the cases with a kind of gentle disdain or at best simple ignorance. The Law Society of British Columbia, which maintains a record of cases through *British Columbia Reports*, referred in its background information on the Gonsalves case to "an Indian named Joe Silva." In recording the Cummings case, it wrote that the head of the Royal Engineers was "in charge of the Coast in the early sixties."[15]

There is no way of knowing at this historical distance what actually went through the BC Supreme Court justice's mind in making the original decision. But we do know that he did not cite case law or historical precedent, which was the usual practice and was to be expected had he considered the defendants and their witnesses his equals before the law. His sweeping dismissal of their testimony seems to have been influenced by beliefs about Aboriginal people. And he was not alone in his views. The City of Vancouver and Government of Canada argued before the Supreme Court of Canada that the appeal decision should be dismissed out of hand by virtue of Aboriginal people's supposed inability to grasp the concept of time and to differentiate between truth and imagination.

Two of the three appeal judges took Aboriginal people far more

The Aboriginal witnesses were in reality hardworking, respected members of the Squamish community. The woman identified in the court only as "Mrs. (Chief) Joe Capilano" was Johnny Baker's mother-in-law and Chief Joe Mathias's mother. According to her grandson Simon Baker, "she used to go in her dugout canoe from the Capilano Reserve across the narrows into Vancouver ... She'd tie up there and pack her clams, berries, baskets and mats to the Hotel Vancouver and round the West End, where all the rich people lived—the Rogers, MacMillans, McDermids, Bell-Irvings—all those people used to ask my grandmother to bring them fresh berries and clams." The writer Pierre Berton described how she "never once strayed from the path followed by her ancestors" and "refused to compromise the methods of her forebears."[16] As was her usual practice, Mary Capilano arrived to testify by canoe, paddling herself across Burrard Inlet. City of Vancouver Archives, PORT P37N96

seriously than did their lower-court counterpart or, later, the Supreme Court of Canada. They both validated their testimony and dared to question the authority of written evidence, in the form of the Turner map, over oral recollections. They chided the City of Vancouver for shielding itself against its own law, the 20-year term for expulsion.

However we might interrogate the decisions in retrospect—and it is tempting to mull over them at length—the deed was done. The Supreme Court of Canada had affirmed the status quo, much as the Privy Council had done two decades earlier in reference to Deadman's Island and by extension the peninsula. The families of Brockton Point were dispossessed.

Chapter 10
Dispossession

For the Brockton Point families, everyday life continued for a time much as it had before their legal dispossession in 1925. Two years later the eldest Gonsalves daughter Margaret photographed her parents, siblings Albert (Sonny), Myrtle, Isabel and Willard, with the family car in Stanley Park's hollow cedar tree, said to be 5.5 metres in diameter. Courtesy Willard Gonsalves

Having won in the Supreme Court of Canada, the City of Vancouver seemingly lost interest in the families it had worked so hard to dislodge. It was almost as if, having made the point, the city and the Parks Board did not need to flex their muscles any more, at least for a time.

The victors could have gone for immediate eviction. Instead, they sought legal dispossession, perhaps responding to mixed feelings among the general public about the appearance of undue haste. Herbert Smith still retains the writ of possession served on his widowed grandmother Martha, which marked the property "in occupation" now being taken away by the "picket fence" the family had put up around it. An editorial in the *Province* observed: "if there is no immediate need of the sites they occupy, it would be an act of courtesy and kindness if the squatters were allowed to remain in their homes until they choose to move or death calls them to happier hunting grounds."[1]

On July 6, 1925, two months after the decision, Martha Smith, Ed Long, Mary De Costa, Alfred Gonsalves and Thomas Cole all signed agreements to become tenants of the city. Their rent was set at $1.00 per month, and the city agreed to pay for all improvements. The Parks Board planned to have the "buildings razed upon the decease of their squatter occupants." A newspaper account emphasized how the city "has a kindly feeling toward these old-timers and does not propose to evict them from the houses they have lived in so long."[2]

The Parks Board minutes record that immediately after the city took possession, Martha Smith sent the city solicitor a letter requesting "the repairing and re-shingling of the roofs of her house and the attached building." Her many years at residential school had given her facility with written English and a realization she had to

Among the young people who came of age in Stanley Park was Rose Cole, photographed by the fence of her Brockton Point home.
Courtesy Robert Yelton

stand up for herself, since no one else would. At the end of October, the board grudgingly agreed to make temporary repairs at a cost of not more than $20, to be repaid in monthly installments. Martha Smith's determination set a precedent, and a number of other tenants requested and were granted similar repairs.[3]

The Parks Board's moderate approach has several explanations, apart from a "kindly" feeling. The board never had unanimous backing for ejecting the families. Some, including the popular local author Robert Allison Hood, found their residences as decorative as totem poles. In *By Shore and Trail in Stanley Park*, published in 1929, Hood described how "quaint little habitations ... harmonize delightfully with their setting and add picturesqueness and a pleasing touch of human association, which makes them, far from a detriment, a distinct acquisition to the Park."[4]

Over the short term, the Parks Board had a much more pressing priority than the Brockton Point residents: the status of the Kulkalem property. The case had been adjourned in November 1923. Because the city had argued, fallaciously, that the house on Turner's map had been Aunt Sally's, its case against her daughter broke down. The very same map that became the basis for the others' eviction worked to Mariah Kulkalem's advantage. Mariah Kulkalem said she would sell her land to the city for $18,000. The Parks Board countered with $14,000, and she proposed to split the difference at $16,500.

The question became who was going to pay. The Parks Board considered that since it was not the level of government that recognized Aboriginal rights, it should not foot the bill. The Canadian government did not agree.[5] After rumours floated that another buyer was waiting in the wings with a higher offer, intending to build "a modern apartment house in the middle of Stanley Park," the Parks Board obtained an option to purchase the property by November 21, 1925. As the date approached and no one agreed to pay the bill, Board Chair W.C. Shelly paid out of his own pocket.[6] A year later the Canadian government was shamed into reimbursing him. Immediately on taking possession of the property, "the buildings and fences were forthwith destroyed by fire and later the fruit trees were cut down and destroyed." Robert Cole, a young boy of 10 living at nearby Brockton Point, retained the image in his head all his life. "I watched them burn it. The fire department came down and poured gas all over it and lit it up and 'way she goes.'"[7]

Mariah Kulkalem's monetary feat was echoed by Margaret McPhee at Kanaka Ranch. Young Norman McPhee recalled how "my grandmother couldn't keep the store going after my grandfather died, and in about 1923 or 1924 she sold Kanaka Ranch." Eihu's granddaughter gave Cranes' Shipyards the right of purchase in exchange for $26,000 payable at the rate of $7,000 a year.[8]

Margaret McPhee's estate on her death in April 1925 totalled $23,530.20, an enormous sum at the time. Her will bequeathed $3,000 to her daughter Minnie, who was Major Matthews' informant, and $500 each "to my sister LUCY SMITH, Widow, residing at Capilano Reserve, North Vancouver," a disabled son of her half-brother William Nahanee, and a granddaughter. Indicating how closely intertwined were the families at Kanaka Ranch and Brockton Point, she left $300 each to Agnes Cummings and her sister Maggie West. The remainder went to Margaret McPhee's daughter Irene, "to be used by her to pay for the maintenance, education, advancement, and benefit of my grandson NORMAN DONALD McPHEE until he shall attain the age of twenty-one years," at which point he was to receive $4,000 outright. All his life Norman took satisfaction in how "my grandmother liked me best; maybe it was because I reminded her of her grandfather Eihu."[9] The legacy proved to be more symbolic than real: it was spent by the time Norman was old enough to attend the commercial school he had his sights on, and he got work at a Vancouver lumber mill.

Apart from the unexpected legacies to the Cummings sisters, everyday life for the families at Brockton Point continued much as before. During the second half of the 1920s, three other issues deflected the Parks Board's attention away from them.

The first of these related to Tim Cummings. No one had noticed, at the time the cases were going through the court system, that he had not been made a defendant. His sister Agnes explained how her brother

All his life, Norman McPhee affectionately recalled at "about age four or five sitting on the grass in front of my grandmother [Maggie Eihu McPhee], who's wearing a large flat hat." Courtesy Mabel McPhee

considered that "since he was not made a party to the arrangement which turned the property over to the City as a park, he was not required to abide by it and the dispossession order made by the sheriff did not apply to him." In talking with a reporter three decades later, Tim emphasized how "he had not been dispossessed of his ancestral rights like his sisters."[10]

If oral testimony can be accepted, it was Parks Board Chair Shelly who once again went for a quick fix. Young Robert Cole, who lived close by, remembered the Cummings family being offered a considerable amount of money to "sell prop'y to gov." Agnes recalled that Shelly "spread out thousands of dollars on their table and offered to buy the Cummings property of a third of an acre." According to Agnes, her brother Tim "accepted; and later, when the city took over the property, Mr. Shelly spent years getting his money back from civic treasury."[11]

The second issue that distracted the Parks Board from the Brockton Point families was its principal attention to Aboriginalizing the park. The Indian village was less easily realized than the erection of the totem poles. The Art, Historical and Scientific Society was split between those who wanted to transport "an original Indian village" from northern Vancouver Island, those who preferred "new wood" to "old boards" and those who sought a more exotic variant "built of skins or bark or teepees."[12]

In late 1925 the Squamish Band Council came out in opposition on the grounds that the village and its totem poles were not indigenous to the area. The village was "a replica of a northern Indian village," whereas Lumberman's Arch, the proposed site for its erection, had been a Squamish village. Not only was it "on this spot that Chief Capilano gave welcome to Capt Vancouver," but Whoi Whoi, which translates from the Squamish language as "a place for making masks," remained "sacred ground."[13] The Art, Historical and Scientific Society got cold feet and turned responsibility for the Indian village over to the Parks Board, which did not have much better luck with fundraising than had the society.

The third issue that deflected the Parks Board's attention from the

Deadman's Island in 1925 was filled with both land-based homes and floating houses. Walter H. Calder photo, City of Vancouver Archives, ST PK N24

Brockton Point families was, once again, Deadman's Island. Ludgate died in 1918 and his heirs did not pay the property taxes, so the island reverted to the Canadian government. The Parks Board asked for a lease to run concurrently with that for Stanley Park. It was early 1930 before all the legal hurdles were overcome and Vancouver could acquire a lease for the island, "on condition that it was used exclusively for park purposes."[14]

There was a hitch. The island had become home to a substantial village of fishermen whose houses were built on logs so that the structures floated above the shoreline at very high tides. "Mostly single men, Italians, Spaniards, French, Portuguese, and one Native woman and her husband,"[15] their number included Angelo Sarcia, whom Pierre Berton depicted sympathetically in a fashion reminiscent of life at Brockton Point and Kanaka Ranch.

> Diminutive, white-haired Angelo Sarcia is a link between the old days and the new. But Angelo is a rebel, too. A man who refuses to keep his feet on dry land any longer than he has to. A man who hasn't lived in a house since the turn of the century.
>
> In 1894 the Italian seaman anchored his houseboat off Deadman's island. He's been there ever since. And he's perfectly happy to spend the rest of his days in a home that sways gently backward and forward on its log float.
>
> Angelo was born to the sea, in the Italian port of Genoa, shipped around Cape Horn in an old sailing vessel, finally dropped anchor in Vancouver, refused to have anything to do with the Good Earth.[16]

The Parks Board's delivery of 60-day eviction notices had press support. Newspapers waxed indignant that "some [had] been there as long as 20 years without having to pay rent." The differences between them and other Vancouver residents, in particular the lack of running water and electricity, were highlighted: they did not belong. "Between 35 and 40 squatters" were finally given notice in November 1930, and in February 1931 the city finally claimed its prize.[17]

Despite the forced removals, Deadman's Island would not be integrated into Stanley Park. By this time the Depression had hit,

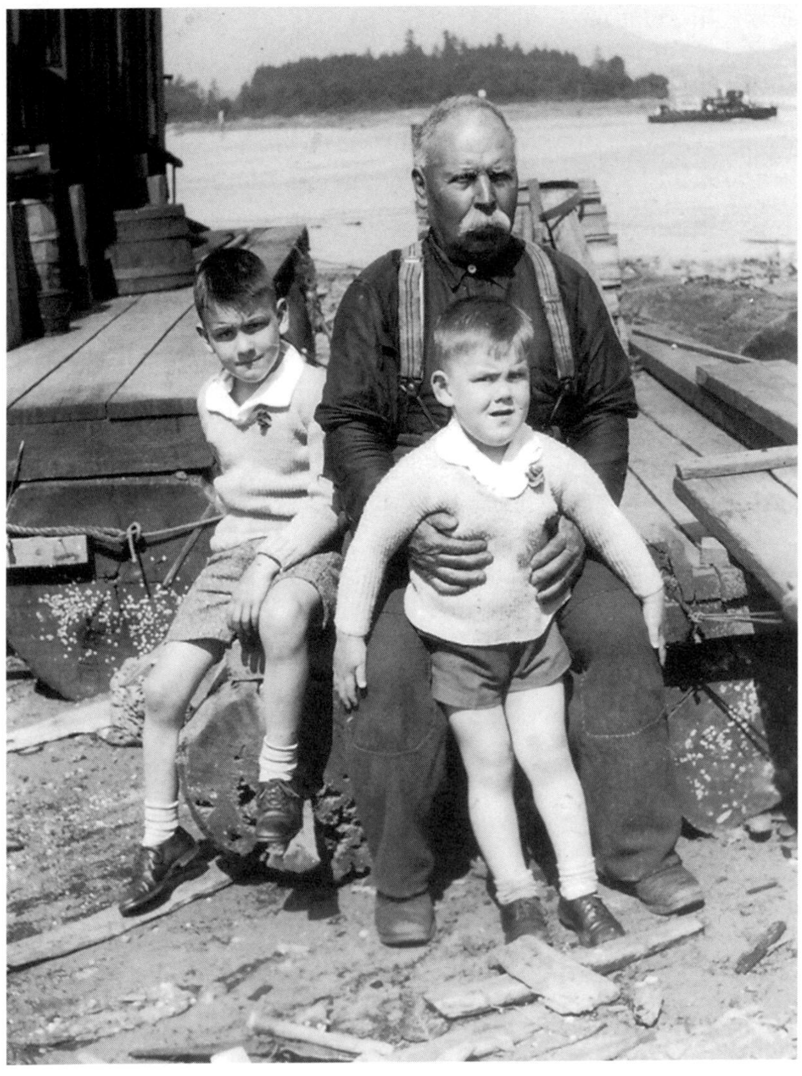

On being evicted from Deadman's Island, the ingenious Angelo Sarcia floated his houseboat across Coal Harbour to the foot of today's Cardero Street, adjacent to the former Kanaka Ranch and in sight of his former home. Tom Smith's eldest son Herb, born in 1928, cherishes memories of childhood visits during which he and his younger brother Ronny were fed spaghetti with endive salad and for dessert "CPR strawberries," which was Angelo's term for stewed prunes. Earlier in the day Angelo would pick up groceries at Woodward's on Hastings Street after a stop at the nearby Europa Hotel, to which he had his mail delivered.
Information and photo courtesy Herbert Smith

and then came the Second World War. The long-disputed island was transferred to the Department of National Defence in 1942 for use as a military base, a function that became permanent.

As soon as the Deadman's Island evictions were underway in 1931, the Parks Board turned its attention to nearby Brockton Point. The informal understanding that the tenants could stay there for the rest of their lives came under scrutiny. As a journalist put it on the eve of the Deadman's Island evictions, "the City, in its forward march, can afford no longer to be swayed by sentiment." Mary Dunbar had died in early 1930, but the remaining residents were not aging as rapidly as they might. While Mary De Costa was turning 60, and Tommy Cole and Tim Cummings were 50, the Cummings sisters and Martha Smith were still in their 40s, and Ed Long and Alfred Gonsalves were in their late 30s. The Parks Board was no longer willing to wait for their demise before getting the park of its imagination. The board was particularly proprietorial about the south side of Brockton Point, where "shacks border the shore line, ... constituting not only an eye-sore, but entirely shutting out one of the most attractive views in the Park." The board voted on February 26, 1931, to remove the five properties by June 1 in order to restore to "the people of Vancouver one of the finest obtainable views of the harbor skyline."[18]

Once again the tenants' supporters rallied. Mary Perceval, who had earlier written so fervently on Mary De Costa's behalf, appeared before the Parks Board asking for consideration to permit her to remain in the park for a few more years. Her second husband Joseph De Costa had died in 1926, depriving her of his longshoring wages, and now she was about to be evicted from the only home she had known.

The Parks Board relented, just a little. The Depression was hitting hard, and there would be reverberations if the families were thrown out on the street—literally. The parks superintendent was asked to see what could be done to find other accommodations, and he reported at the May 14 meeting on the possibility of houses acquired by the city for unpaid taxes being made available to the families until they had adjusted to their new situation and could manage on their own.

By the end of the month, arrangements were in place "to provide each family of squatters with a Tax Sale house, rent free, for a period ending December 31st, 1933."[19]

The families on the north shore had so far been absent from Parks Board discussions, and the parks superintendent recommended that they be allowed to stay until the end of 1933. Their view over Burrard Inlet was not as coveted as that toward the city itself.

As the three-month deadline for the departure of the south shore families approached, the Parks Board pulled back a little more. They would be offered their new accommodations rent-free for two years, later extended to four years at a monthly rent of $10. To qualify, the residents had to agree to leave immediately. As an incentive, the Parks Board bore the cost of removal of furniture and effects, which totalled some $500.

For all of the assistance, the consequences for individuals and families were very great indeed. Willard Gonsalves was a young boy of seven whose entire universe revolved around his small corner of Stanley Park.

> I was born on March 15, 1924, in Stanley Park. As a child I always lived, so far as I knew, in the park. I was the youngest down there. There were no other kids to play with. I had a red dump truck and a dog to play with. Tricksy was a little short haired white dog, black with white spots. She was a great little dog. I guess she got scraps from the table and bones. There wasn't any pet food then. The truck was well built of steel, about two feet long. I could get my knee in the box and scoot it along. That was a beautiful little truck.
>
> I used to go out in the rowboat by myself. I never had a life jacket. There was no boat traffic going by. I didn't go too far. I used to row around the little bay there. I would go out in a rowboat and I never got any big waves or anything. Boats never had any reason to come by. You could only get through Deadman's Island on high tide.
>
> All the kids in the family went to Lord Roberts School. I had a long way to go from Nine O'clock [Gun] to Lord Roberts. The people driving around us, they didn't know anything about us, so I didn't get a ride or anything. There weren't that many cars going around [Stanley Park] in those days. I

used to walk until, finally they got me a bicycle and I used to leave it at the confectionery store at the entrance to the park and then walk, so I wouldn't be riding in traffic.

I was pretty well seven [when we left Stanley Park]. They kicked us all out. They moved us all out together, one clean sweep. They bulldozed all the houses. They tore our Stanley Park house down.

My father was in the hospital when we left. He had gone down in his boat and suffered from lack of oxygen or something. I couldn't see anything wrong with him except he only talked about the early days. He always remembered the early days. He was out in New Westminster in the asylum.

It was just my mother who lived there by the time we left. There was nothing we could do about it, they moved us out. They wanted it for a park. They didn't want any people down there.

My dump truck, all steel, wheels and so forth, must have fallen off the moving truck when they moved us out. When we moved, it fell off the truck. That was all I had to play with.[20]

For the families forced to leave, the saddest aspect may have been the destruction of their lifelong homes by fire, as was the board's wont. On the morning of June 25, 1931, the fire brigade burned four of the houses on the south side, the remaining one slated to be moved a few days later. The image haunted Ed Long all his life, as did the trial, his daughter Marion explained.

Father was very upset that his house was burned. He never liked to talk about it. He was very, very upset by this, and he didn't want to discuss it with us. I can't imagine them watching something like that. I've watched a house burn down, and it wasn't even my own and I know how terrible it was.

Dad would never talk to the family about what happened at the trial. I thought the trial was fixed. They got the witnesses they wanted. I think they paid hardly anything for what they took, and I don't like talking about it still.[21]

From the Parks Board's perspective, "a new and attractive night view of the harbor is now available to the public by the evacuation from their old shanties." The board promised that "the area will be cleared and graded and made ready for the more permanent improvement scheme of the future."[22] All signs that the families had ever lived on the south shore of Brockton Point would be obliterated.

The residents went their separate ways. Tommy Cole moved his family across Burrard Inlet to the Mission Reserve, as his daughter Rose Cole later explained: "They offered us a house with a free year's rent near Hastings Park, but my dad wanted to come back to his people. They only gave my dad either a one-dollar or two-dollar cheque for the property. He couldn't believe it. He said he was going to frame it."[23]

The Smiths divided. Leaving her grown children in the house the city allotted to her at 2941 Trinity Street in east Vancouver, Martha Smith soon emigrated to Washington state, where she remarried. "She wanted a new beginning," according to her grandson Herbert. Mary Smith Long De Costa ended up living with a daughter in Burnaby. Mary's eldest son Ed Long was doubly dispossessed. In the autumn of 1924, at St. Paul's Catholic Church on the Mission Reserve, he had wed a young widow, Susie Thomas. Born on the Burrard Reserve, she was a member of the talented George family, being a niece by marriage of Joe Gonsalves's wife and a brother of the actor Dan George. By virtue of marrying a non-status person, she lost her right to live on the reserve. The actions of the Canadian state deprived both Ed and Susie Long of their childhood homes. Their daughter Marion recalled the circumstances: "When I grew up, my mother couldn't live on the reserve, and I would wonder. Susie tried to get a place for the family to live on the Mission Reserve, but was not allowed, so they moved to Third Street in North Vancouver."[24]

Willard Gonsalves remembered all his life his mother Lena's determination to hold the family together. For her in particular, the offer of a rent-free home was a godsend.

> It was the first part of '30 they moved us out. It was coming up on hard times too. My mother was a chambermaid in a hotel. She worked very hard. We never missed a meal.
>
> Father went back and forth to the asylum a couple of times. We would go

The dispossessed families each got on with their lives as best they could. In Seattle looking for longshoring work after his father's death, Tom Smith was introduced to a young American, Theresa Smith, as a lark because they had the same initials and last names. Following their wedding, the couple lived at Brockton Point and then on Trinity Street, where Tom's reputation as a tough, no-holds-barred longshoring foreman competed with his image as a doting father hugging his son Herb. Courtesy Herbert Smith

out to see him when he was working on Colony farm. It was quite a hike for a young feller like me and for my mother. My father died in the asylum in 1952.

I had been going to Lord Roberts, then we moved into Charles Street and I went to Woodlands School. When they got us out of the park, they gave us a house rent-free at 1531 Charles Street for four or five years. It was a great big house.

My brother Sonny was there at Charles Street for a while, then he went longshoring and moved out. My brother, he'd be out working, he was butchering, longshoring. Margaret worked for Kelly Douglas for a while, packing coffee or something. Isabel and Myrtle were still going to school. We all went to the same school. We had that great big house all by ourselves.

Then it was half rent, we had to pay half rent, and then full rent, so we moved to Victoria Drive and Pender. The other house was too big for us.[25]

For Willard Gonsalves and his brother, it was longshoring that came to mark their adulthoods. For three generations, the working lives of the men who made their homes at Whoi Whoi, Chaythoos, Kanaka Ranch and Brockton Point were characterized by hard physical labour.

It was taken for granted that boys of Aboriginal or mixed heritage would enter the paid work force as soon as they quit school to assist the family economy. Young Willard recalled:

> I was sixteen when I went to work. My mother was getting mother's pension for me, but couldn't stop me from going to work. As soon as I quit school, she lost that. I hated school, I hated it with a passion. I hated school with a passion, I couldn't pay attention. I quit in seventh grade. I guess everybody had a go at longshoring. I had a go at it. It was awful hard work. 140 pounds of wheat—we were loading it on ships on the waterfront. It came down [into the ship] in a pallet. They would put it on your back, and we had to walk between decks. We were in between decks. It was quite high. You had to step on the sacks of wheat. When you got up to the top with a sack of wheat on your back, two guys would take it off and put it right at the top. It was hard work, it was loosely packed wheat in the sacks too.[26]

Longshoring defined male adulthoods. The Smith, Long and Gonsalves families worked alongside men whose principal identity was Squamish. Numerous Bakers and Coles longshored, as did Chief Joe Capilano, August Jack Khahtsahlano and Andy Paull. Other men on the docks—Keamos, Nahanees, Nahus and others—continued to identify through the generations, at least in part, as Hawaiian. Fathers mentored sons, men each other. Ed Long remembered:

> In those days there was a great bunch of men on the waterfront. The greatest lumber handlers in BC and the whole world for that matter ... Pete Smith, Grant Campbell, Fred Corkell, a couple of Newman boys [sons of a German father and Squamish mother]. Old man Nahanee, he was one of the head guys. Bill Nahanee. That's the bunch that I would take my hat off to if they were alive today. The government ought to have done something for them while they were alive. They didn't get no pension or nothing at that time. There was old Mr. [Leon] Nahu, Bill Nahanee ... They were the greatest men that ever worked the lumber. They were really nice to us young fellows. They used to tell us what to do and be careful and everything else. Especially Mr. Nahu, the boss at that time ... They were gentlemen.[27]

William Nahnee's son Ed, whose ninth birthday party occasioned the memorable photograph, described how the occupation gave self-worth.

> All the characters fitted into a picture of fun. It makes for a real nice lively day. When you went home, you went home feeling good, and the next morning you got started and you were all there again and away you go again. That was the spirit in those days. If I had to live my life over again, I'd do the same thing. I don't care how dirty it was. We were a part of each other.[28]

These men's ways of life could not have been further away from the imagined Aboriginality still being pursued in Stanley Park. In 1934 a site was selected between Brockton Point and Lumberman's Arch for the long-sought Indian village. The new plan was even more far-fetched than its predecessors. "The Indians would make permanent quarters there, carrying on their native life." They would be on display, much like the animals in the park's zoo. The plan again came to naught, but the park did acquire some more totem poles. Two were Kwakiutl (Kwakwa̲ka̲'wakw), one originally erected at Alert Bay in 1899 and the other a replica of a pole carved in 1894. The third began its existence as a mortuary pole, or grave post, erected sometime before 1870 by the chief at Skidegate on the Queen Charlotte Islands to honour his father-in-law. The poles' authenticity did not prevent at least one of them from being "painted by the Art and Historical Society" a few years later.[29]

Some local Aboriginal people did what they could to counter the obsession with the BC north coast. Joe Mathias, who interpreted at the 1920s trial, carved a totem pole to commemorate the meeting with Captain George Vancouver off the peninsula in 1792. The pole's erection at Prospect Point during Vancouver's 50th anniversary celebrations in 1936 both claimed the art form as Squamish and gave a visible reminder of the one-time Squamish presence there. Mathias also got permission to construct a temporary building to sell "curios."[30] The sign in front termed it an "Indian Village," to which 10 cents admission was charged. Events had come full circle. The Squamish initiative was the closest Stanley Park would get to having an "Indian village."

The only "Indian village" to make it into Stanley Park was constructed for Vancouver's Jubilee in 1936. Vancouver Public Library, Special Collections, VPL 4941

Three years later August Jack Khahtsahlano, who spent much of his working life as a longshoreman, questioned why, as the son of Supple Jack, "they pay old 'Aunt Sally' for land at Lumberman's Arch, but they do not pay me." Perhaps as an accommodation, in 1944 August Jack travelled to the Fraser Valley "to purchase authentic Indian ware for the Parks Board to resell at the Brockton Point Stand." The *Vancouver News-Herald* promised Vancouver residents that "visitors to the curio stand at Brockton Point this summer will be regaled with Indian legends by Chief Khahtsahlano," who "will explain when the articles were made and the historical background."[31]

Stanley Park also continued to be modified in other ways consistent with the dominant society's ambitions for its city. In 1934 the Parks Board decided to replace the bandstand with a larger shell-type structure, whereupon a local businessman offered to sponsor it in his wife's memory as the Marion Malkin Memorial Bowl. At about the same time, the local Shakespeare Society began to create, not far from the Kiwanis Rose Garden, an area of plants and trees "natural"

In 1943 August Jack Khahtsahlano (left) and Chief Joe Mathias performed together at Stanley Park to large crowds. City of Vancouver Archives, Reded N13, with identification by Robert Yelton

to Elizabethan England and patterned on those at Shakespeare's birthplace of Stratford-on-Avon in England. The space was decorated with a Shakespeare Memorial and various commemorative plaques to actors who had performed in the genre. Coming full circle, the first performances held in 1940 at "Theatre Under the Stars" at Malkin Bowl were of two Shakespeare plays. It was not only Aboriginality and Shakespeare that were memorialized. In 1944 the Parks Board gave the Salvation Army permission to put up a plaque at Brockton Point both naming and claiming Hallelujah Point.

No action was more contentious than the construction of a road through the centre of the park. English business interests proposed to erect a bridge across Burrard Inlet from the north shore, where they owned property, to connect through Stanley Park to the City of Vancouver. The initial proposal had been rejected overwhelmingly in a 1927 city plebiscite. The Depression turned matters around, and in 1933 the Parks Board gave approval. The prospect of employment for men on relief overcame all other considerations. However, only some men were deemed worthy of road construction in Stanley Park, the contract stipulating, due to pressure from labour organizations, that "no Asiatic person shall be employed in or upon any part of the undertaking or other works."[32]

For all of the changes going on, in the popular mind Stanley Park was pristine. A newspaper editorial of 1931 lauded "the greatest natural park on this continent" set in a "forest primeval." An editorial three years later gloried that Stanley Park "remains unspoiled," a continuing testimony to what the "city that has been carved out of the forest once was." The chair of the Parks Board contrasted "encircling civilization, with its smoke, its poison-breathing motor cars" against Stanley Park as "a haven of forest refuge and quiet peace for nature-lovers in the very midst of bustling civilization." There "the busy world of commerce becomes faint and musical, and the roar of the great city's traffic is stilled." In honour of Stanley Park's 50th anniversary, the mayor of Vancouver effused: "Not in all the wide world is there a more picturesque and delightful haven where children may romp, aged find rest, and troubled find solace, than in its one thousand acres of primeval forest, interspersed with patches of smooth green sward."[33]

This supposed Garden of Eden had had its virginity returned, but not entirely so. Whether or not Tim Cummings's uncertain legal position was the key, or their house's location on the less desirable north side of Brockton Point made the difference, the City of Vancouver let the family stay year after year. Tim remembered how "people complained that the fish nets and boat houses spoiled the view across the harbor to Vancouver."[34] He and his sister Agnes divided the family house and to some extent went their own ways, as did their widowed sister Maggie, who lived next door from about 1931 with Harry Pells, an insurance agent originally from England. Whereas Maggie did dressmaking in

For a brief time period Agnes Cummings had her own car, but she could not afford the upkeep and soon she was once again walking every day to the bus stop at the park's entrance. Courtesy Keamo family

her home, Agnes was employed as a "tailoress" by various downtown businesses, becoming so respected at her craft that she made it into most Vancouver city directories. In the late 1930s Agnes went into partnership with two others to form the Customs Tailor Coop located at 653 Granville Street, later known as Custom Tailors.

Forced out of longshoring by his poor eyesight, Tim got a small pension. To pass the time he did a little fishing, used his telescope to monitor ships coming through Burrard Inlet into port, built five steps down to the beach and generally kept the cottage and grounds neat. Whatever the activity and wherever he went, his dog Rex followed him. Sometimes one of Tim's friends would come and read the newspaper to him. One of his most important daily activities was to hoist and lower the red ensign that he proudly flew in front of the house to signal his patriotism. As his niece affectionately recalled, "Tim had a flag, every morning he would run it up and at night bring it down, at ten he had to watch the news, he was real British in his outlook."[35]

Aggie and Tim's niece Olive Keamo O'Connor treasured her

When ships such as the Empress of Canada *headed into Burrard Inlet, they passed just outside of Tim Cummings's door and the nearby lighthouse.*
BC Archives, I-31454

family's weekly treks to Stanley Park, a practice that she passed on to the next generation. Olive was a single mother of five, having decided that her irresponsible Irish husband was better in the absence. During the Second World War, when she worked long hours, her four young daughters would head off on their own from their east side home. Her daughter Annie, named after her grandmother, has retained a vivid memory of these weekly highlights.

> I could already smell the berry pies baking in the old wood and coal stove as we approached my auntie Aggie's cabin. As usual, it was Sunday and we had come from Church on the streetcar to the entrance of Stanley Park. It was a long walk through the park, but always worth it.
>
> Uncle Tim would always wait by the front gate watching for us. He built a large flagpole just by the gate and would faithfully be standing under it as we managed to run the last part in great anticipation. Auntie Aggie would

be waiting by the front door and would give us each a big hug. I can still remember the smell of her powder and her very soft cheeks as I kissed her hello.

After we arrived, we would help with the dinner preparations, picking peas from the garden and shelling them, what a delicious taste, so fresh and green and sometimes a turnip or two. Part of the routine was to check on the pumpkins to see how big they were, then it was on to the berry bushes, sometimes blackberries or raspberries or loganberries for the pies. Auntie Aggie also had the most beautiful flower garden and when you entered the cabin, you were met with the overwhelming smell of sweet peas or roses or lily of the valley.

Usually Mom would arrive about this time, a quick hello and we were off to the beach, our favorite part. Usually the tide was out at this time of the day so we were able to turn over the bigger rocks and watch the crabs scurry around and grab the odd one. We would go swimming if it was a particularly hot day, but the water was very cold and you wouldn't stay in very long.

The call to dinner was always a welcome sound. We always had pot roast and fresh veggies. I remember when my aunt bought a pressure cooker, what a frightening experience that was. The next step in the dinner plan was for one of us to whip the cream using the old hand beaters, that seemed to take hours so no one volunteered quickly, usually we were appointed. Finally out came the roast and the dinner was underway. Usually we would save the pies for later.

At the end of the day we would fold into the soft big sofas in my aunt's living room while Mom and she would drink tea in the kitchen. The fresh ocean air and long day would creep in and one or all of us would fall asleep, happy and content. Time to go home and make the long trip to the streetcar again. My uncle Tim would lead us through the short cut [road] with only his flashlight to guide us through the dark trail, but we always felt safe. We would catch the streetcar and go home. Another wonderful day at the park had come to an end.[36]

The Cummings siblings gave comfort not just to their sister Annie's family, but to others for whom Brockton Point or Kanaka Ranch had

Agnes and Tim Cummings took pride in their home and perhaps for that reason permitted a newspaper reporter to photograph their neatly kept kitchen.
City of Vancouver Archives, CVA ST PK 249.4 N273.4

once been home. Norman McPhee, who as a child at Kanaka Ranch built forts on nearby Deadman's Island, would take his wife Mabel to visit Aggie and Tim. Mabel recalled once finding them canning salmon in the yard. They did the best they could, given their spartan living conditions, but, Mabel mused, "it was so primitive." Tommy and David Cole's younger half-sister Rosa was also a visitor, even though she lived as if she were white. In stories that circulate in the family, Tommy passed Rosa on the street in North Vancouver, reminded her that he was her brother, and she refused to respond.[37]

Even though Rosa never acknowledged her Aboriginal heritage, she was determined that her daughter Elsie understand and appreciate her Stanley Park origins.

> I do remember Tim Cummings. I remember going there when I was five or six [in 1939–40]. He and Aggie lived in the main house on the other side of Brockton Point. I remember this long hallway and you took one step down and that was where Tim lived. He had more or less a room where Aggie had

Malkin Bowl charmed young Elsie Kerr just as it has many thousands of Vancouverites for over two-thirds of a century. Jack Lindsay photo, City of Vancouver Archives, CVA 1184-1963

pretty much the rest of the house. Next door there was Harry [Pells] and Maggie, who lived just a few feet away.

I remember staying with them on the weekend, and we went up over the lawns of Stanley Park and there were these stage shows. It was awesome. It was a stage with a shell over it. We sat up on the stands [of Malkin Bowl] and watched. It was, like, Cinderella or Seven Dwarfs. And we would walk back and sleep there on mattresses on the floor.

They were my aunts and uncle all these years. They said, "that's your uncle Tim and your aunts Aggie and Maggie." I knew who they were, and I didn't know. They were still there in 1950 when I went there with my boyfriend to show him where they lived. My aunt Aggie was still there to welcome me.[38]

James Grant Keamo/Campbell's Hawaiian roots gave the extended family a distinctly multicultural outlook. When the Hawaiian entertainer Hilo Hattie visited Vancouver in 1945, she was welcomed by the Keamo clan. One of the photos taken with her has, in the back row, Aggie Cummings, Olive Keamo O'Connor, Hilo Hattie, Olive's brother-in-law Fred Lambert, Maggie Cummings and her husband Harry Pells; and, in the front row, Olive's daughter Marion, her nephew Jack Keamo and her daughters Ruthie and Annie. Courtesy Keamo family

So far as possible, the Cummings siblings made their lives on their own terms, down to Tim cutting wood in the well-used backyard into old age.
City of Vancouver Archives, ST PK P249.2 N273.2

The cost to the Cummings family of staying in the park was that they were treated as curiosities. As a summary statement in the City of Vancouver Archives puts it, "the cottage was without running water, no electricity; it was considered 'interesting' to the tourist passerby.[39] All her life Olive remained upset by the way in which her aunts and uncle were treated.

> It was a beautiful little paradise. It was also very primitive. They drew water from a well at the end of the garden. They had an outhouse, which was a little scary to go down to at night. There was no electricity, and they cut wood from the beach for their heat and cooking. They had no electricity even though electricity was installed at the Brockton Point Lighthouse and on the other side of them at the grandstand keeper's house [of the Brockton Point Athletic Grounds]. No running water, no light, no heat. And yet, they had lights at Brockton Point and at that grandstand on the other side [of the road].[40]

Everyday life could go on because the extended family rallied. Olive's young daughter Ruth was designated to assist her aging aunt Aggie.

> I was chosen to go to my Aunt Aggie's house in Stanley Park on weekends to extensively help her with her housework. I would take the bus from East Hastings Street where we lived to downtown Vancouver and meet her at Eatons. It was a very big deal for me at that age and I looked forward to the personal attention I received from my aunt and the delicious lunch at Eatons cafeteria. We would then take the bus to the entrance of the park and walk to my aunt's house with the shopping bags full of meat, etc. that she wanted for the weekend meals. When we got there we would have afternoon tea with Uncle Tim where they would discuss the garden and what work was to be done today.
>
> She would then teach me housework—mopping the living room and making her bed (which had to have mitred corners) and dusting. I would put on her old gramophone records of "Here we go down in our ships to the sea." I played it over and over again to spur me on to the energy level I needed to complete my tasks.[41]

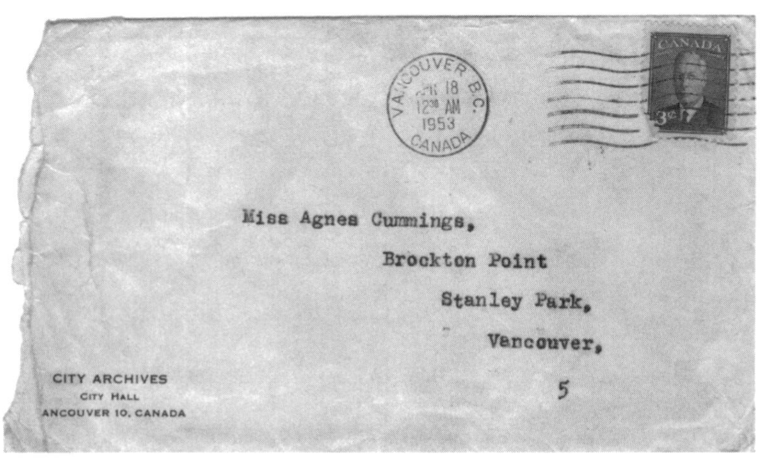

Despite the uneasy relationship with the various levels of government, all their lives the Cummings siblings received mail addressed to them in Stanley Park.
Courtesy Keamo family

The lonely vigil at Stanley Park got lonelier with the passage of years. Maggie died in 1945 in her mid-50s, Agnes in 1953 at the age of 70. Tim Cummings lowered the flag in front of the house to honour the sister with whom he had lived all his life, except when he was sent away to Coqualeetza Residential School. He fretted that the flag was wearing out and, when a young archaeologist excavating nearby paid him a visit in September 1955, he "hinted for a new 3 1/2′ x 7′ Canadian flag."[42] Tim acknowledged to two other visitors that life had become a bit lonely at Brockton Point.

> Tim Cummings, the 74-year-old squatter who rents three-quarters of an acre of Stanley Park for $5 a month, mopped up the spilled tea on his plate with the heel of his fried egg sandwich. His face is a leathery mahogany. His bare arms still ripple with muscle formed from many years of working on the docks.
>
> To our first glance Tim Cummings's estate, at the north end of the Brockton Point Cutoff, seemed to have changed not one whit, and certainly it is no less the glorious triumph against progress than it was when Tim was born there in 1881. The wash on the [four-roomed] shingled cottage still rambled from green to blue from shingle to shingle. There was the outside convenience that Tim calls his post office, and there was the white flag pole with its red ensign, limper now, but then, so is Tim.
>
> The ugliness of the weather-beaten structure is softened by the profusion of flowers, patches of orange-red rhubarb, strips of neatly trimmed grass and the budding pear and apple trees surrounding it. "The fruit trees, the pear and the winter apple, they're getting old you know," he said. He seemed just a little angered by the trees giving up so easily.
>
> Tim, a short man with grey short-cropped hair and a trace of a Scottish accent, today lives alone in the cottage. "Gets lonely, you know." Despite the loneliness, he prefers the quiet of a cottage which has no electricity (a kerosene lamp supplies his light), plumbing or a telephone. Tim Cummings says he will never move from the Park.[43]

Tim Cummings did not get his wish to die as he had lived in Stanley Park. In December 1957 he had to be hospitalized after a heart attack, and he died 10 weeks later, away from his beloved home. The Parks Board was ready to pounce. Less than 24 hours later it announced that his house would be torn down the next week.

The ensuing debate brought into the open, perhaps more than ever before, the Parks Board's long-standing animosity toward the families of Stanley Park. On March 12, the *Vancouver Sun* pointed out, more forcefully than any newspaper had done in the past, that Tim Cummings and the other families predated the park itself.

> He died Monday. And on Tuesday it was announced that his place would be torn down next week. His place, that was a home in the wilderness before the wilderness was ever a park. Before, indeed, there was even a city to have a park.
>
> There are times when there is too much engineering and not enough humanity about our Park Board. Presumably a crew will go in next week and tear down the cottage, a bulldozer will knock over the fence, the boysenberries, the lilacs. Tim's little "post office," the lily of the valley bed. "But its site will always be 'Tim's place' to us," a parks official said.
>
> It will be to a good many thousand citizens, too, who like the look of it, incongruous in its age and quaintness, defiant under its proud red ensign ... Could it possibly become a museum to display pictures and relics of old Vancouver, to get them out of their archival hiding places and out where visitors and citizens do go, where they could pop in and see them. Tim was a longshoreman; maybe his place could be devoted to the waterfront's past.[44]

Major J.S. Matthews, the city archivist, weighed in a day later. He joined a growing chorus of voices opposed to the Parks Board's peremptory attitude. "I believe the board is called the board of parks and public recreation. It should be called the board of parks and public desecration."[45] The scattering of Tim Cummings's ashes from the seawall in front of his cottage only added to the allure of the property. Having backed down, the board returned to the issue a year later to discover that its members were split between those who would maintain the cottage, those who would demolish but commemorate, and those who would obliterate. In April 1959 the board voted to preserve the main part of the building, and eight months later they agreed on a sum of money for that purpose.

Principle and practice did not correspond. For whatever reason, the cottage was removed from its original site and placed adjacent to the totem poles, which had been moved to their present location at Brockton Point. The same Parks Board official who had sought the immediate destruction of the cottage four years earlier now declared that it looked incongruous and needed too many repairs to become a historical site. The decisive meeting of the Vancouver Parks Board took place in mid-November 1963. The *Vancouver Sun* reported:

> Parks Board passed the death sentence Monday on the shack at Brockton point, where the park's last squatter, Tim Cumming, lived for most of his 77 years.
>
> George Wainborn was the only commissioner to oppose destruction of Tim's place Monday. "This shack has some historic value," he said. "I feel that it should be preserved as a tourist attraction. We should do something with it, perhaps convert it into a souvenir shop for selling Indian art."
>
> George Puil described the shack as hideous and suggested it should be demolished. "Many people have threatened to push the cottage into the harbor," he said. His suggestion was accepted, five votes to one.[46]

The double edge of race came to the fore the next day. The ambivalence that had marked Tim Cummings's life in no way receded with his death. Maisie Hurley, editor of BC's principal Aboriginal newspaper, *Native Voice*, took pains to ensure that neither Tim nor his cottage was acknowledged as Aboriginal. "Cumming was the son of a white man and not entitled to live on Indian land," she said, according to a report in the *Sun*. "Tim Cumming's shack in the park is not a suitable memorial to the association of Indians with Stanley Park."[47] The patriarchal law of the day that denied him status overrode all other considerations. Hurley's stand indicates clearly the great extent to which external precepts had become internalized as the accepted measure of Aboriginality. Two weeks later the cottage was torn down.

Despite denying her hybrid heritage, Tommy Cole's half-sister Rosa kept all her life a photo taken on the beach outside of the Cummings family homes at Brockton Point. Rosa (right) and her children Alva, Myrtle, Gladys and Gertrude pose with Harry and Maggie Pells and Aggie Cummings. Courtesy Elsie Kerr

In death as in life, Tim Cummings and his siblings were in-between. They were not white enough to be white. They were not Indian enough to be Indian. They were, at best, acceptable as Aboriginal stand-ins when the real thing could not be had, as in residential school and as a tourist attraction. There was no space for the Cummings family cottage in death, just as there had been no space for them and the other Brockton Point and Kanaka Ranch families in life.

AFTERWORD

Back to the Lilac

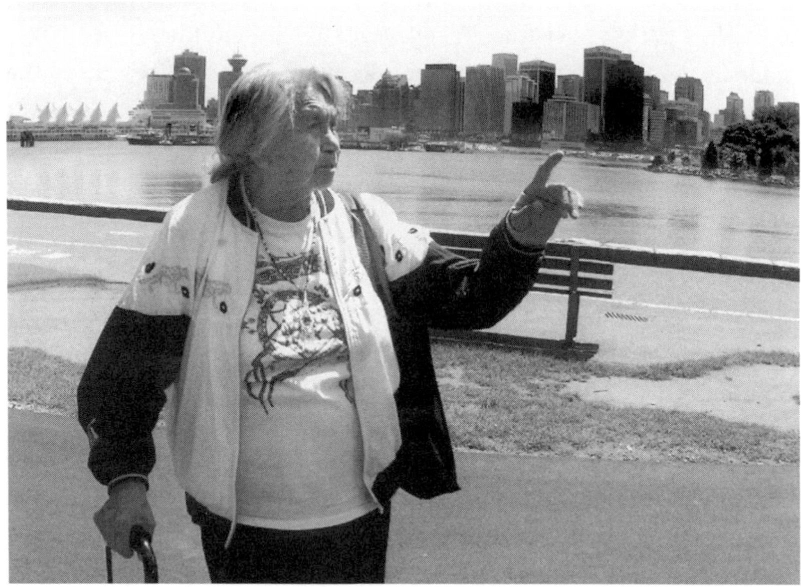

In June 1998, two-thirds of a century after her family was forced out of Stanley Park, Rose Cole Yelton had no difficulty locating the site of her long-ago home just east of the road on the south shore of Brockton Point.
Jon Murray photo, *Province*, PRV0604-Park-08

With Tim Cummings's death in 1958, over two-thirds of a century after the imposition of Stanley Park, the City of Vancouver finally got its way. The families who made their homes on the peninsula were gone, and it could be returned to its pastoral state. The sole element overlooked in doing so appears to have been the lilac Martha Smith planted when she was a bride just out of residential school. Today, in all of Stanley Park, only the lilac and a small plaque for Chaythoos hidden away on the beach east of Prospect

Point recall the Squamish and hybrid families who got there first. Only the lilac makes visible Stanley Park's secret.

At the one level, the families' dispossession from Whoi Whoi, Chaythoos and Brockton Point was a blip in the process whereby Stanley Park became the much loved entity it remains today. Their presence on the peninsula and at nearby Kanaka Ranch disturbs us on a deep emotional level, in line with the way we have been encouraged to think of parks as pristine. We are grateful that no Indian reserve was made in 1876 and that the Brockton Point families lost in 1925 in the Supreme Court of Canada. Be it Stanley Park or Central Park, we want our parks to originate in nature and not in human greed. At another level, the families' dispossession makes larger points that we should find disturbing.

The events attest that the law is not the neutral arbiter of right and wrong that we might have it be. Prior to 1884 the peninsula appears to have had no legal status. The common understanding, that it was a military or government reserve, has never been demonstrated, despite numerous searches through government records in Victoria, Ottawa and London. The most likely reason is that the peninsula was never formally so declared. Colonel Moody of the Royal Engineers undoubtedly intended to do so, but almost certainly did not follow through. He himself did not consider the peninsula or, for that matter, the other reserves off limits for purchase. Just a year after he returned to England in 1864, a company backed by him applied to colonial authorities to buy part of the peninsula, a request that was granted as a matter of course, as was a revised request to purchase the naval reserve to the east. The new province of British Columbia assumed authority over the peninsula from its colonial predecessor in line with the provisions of the British North America Act. As well as dealing with prospective purchasers, British Columbia made the decision in 1876 to refuse to permit an Indian reserve at Whoi Whoi and Chaythoos.

But the province did not own the tongue of land, or so the former mother country decided in 1884. Pushed by the Dominion of Canada to hand it over, Britain acquiesced, despite being unable to determine that it had ever acquired the peninsula. Canada's ownership from 1884 onwards was upheld in the Privy Council's decision of 1906 over Deadman's Island, which retroactively pushed the date of acquisition back in time to Colonel Moody. The Privy Council could not conceive that the actions of those in authority, be it Moody on the periphery or Britain itself were any less than honourable.

No obligation was ever put on any government—Britain, Canada, British Columbia, Vancouver—to demonstrate a clear line of succession in ownership, comparable to that demanded of the families of Stanley Park. The 1884 handover of the peninsula to Canada should have negated, it would seem, British Columbia's earlier refusal, based on an assumption of provincial ownership, to deny an Indian reserve. In the dispossession trials, the Brockton Point families were held to a more rigorous standard to demonstrate adverse possession than was the state to prove ownership.

In accounting for the law's partiality, we do not have far to go. Explicitly, the decisions on an Indian reserve and dispossession had nothing to do with race. The Whoi Whoi and Chaythoos families were denied a reserve because they supposedly arrived after the peninsula had already been claimed by others. Indigenous ways of life counted for naught. The dispossession trials were conducted, to read their transcripts, as if no distinctions based on colour existed, whereas the presiding judge and then the Supreme Court of Canada had no such scruples in assessing the evidence. Aboriginal testimony was deemed "unsatisfactory" compared with newcomers' written sources. "As against that I have the map" is how the BC Supreme Court judge put it in deciding the case. Dispossession, whatever form it took, was all about race.

Skin pigment as a marker of belonging was central to colonialism. The paler shades that newcomers saw in the mirror they equated with the right to dominate. Their acts of subjugation confirmed to them that they were inherently superior. Indigenous people were made the authors of their destiny, doomed by biology. The families of Brockton Point and Kanaka Ranch posed another challenge, and that was their hybridity. They occupied the real and psychological distance that newcomers sought to put between themselves and British Columbia's first peoples. Persons who dared to cross racial boundaries personified a facet of colonialism that most newcomers sought to deny or put in the past. They preferred a neat division between "us" and "them" into which hybrids did not fit. Mary See-em-ia won a victory at Kanaka Ranch because her home lay outside of Stanley Park's boundaries, but it was very likely more partial than had her family's skin tones blended in with those of newcomers. The repeated attempts to reduce the offspring of Whoi Whoi and Chaythoos, Kanaka Ranch and Brockton Point to their Aboriginal heritage were successful only so far as they were voluntary, as with the moves to the Squamish reserves. Long years in residential school did not diminish a sense of belonging among the second and subsequent generations that crossed newcomers' easy division based on skin colour. Whatever their life courses, none of them became the stereotypical Indians of the dominant society's imagination.

Sadly, the need persists for those in positions of authority to conceive Stanley Park in their own image. The families who got to the peninsula first are still forgotten, or erased. In May 2004 the Vancouver Parks Board adopted unanimously "as a reference for future decision making" a lengthy Commemorative Integrity Statement prepared by Parks Canada to reflect Stanley Park's status as a National Historic Site. In acknowledging the presence of Aboriginal people "virtually up to the park's establishment in 1888," it does so as "archaeological sites," relegating them to a kind of prehistory. A historical paragraph begins: "When Stanley Park was established in 1888, a number of European and First Nations residents were reported to be living on the land set aside for the park. In several cases, these residents had established homes in the early 1870s [*sic*—1860s], where they resided for as long as several decades [*sic*—70 years]." Not only is the information incorrect, the rest of the paragraph describes only the acquisition of Aunt Sally's house by "a concerned citizen" [*sic*—the chair of the Vancouver Parks Board] with no mention of the earlier refusal to grant an Indian reserve or the dispossession trials. The bulk of the 61-page statement details Stanley

Park's "cultural resources of national historical significance" (including "designed" gardens and bodies of water, playing fields, "rustic" elements, totem poles, monuments and memorials). The last section turns to "cultural resources not directly linked with commemorative intent." Among elements whose presentation must "not overwhelm or detract from the presentation and understanding of the site's national significance" are Whoi Whoi, Chaythoos, "sites of former shantytowns and squatters' residence, where pilings may still survive," a "former Chinese pig farm, near Coal Harbour" and three gravesites, described as "former Chinese cemeteries," "European burial place at Brockton Point" and "the burial site of sailors at Brockton Point."[1]

If still cast aside by the Vancouver Parks Board and by Parks Canada on behalf of the federal government, the families of Whoi Whoi, Chaythoos, Kanaka Ranch and Brockton Point have not forgotten their history. The ties that bound families to their places of belonging continued long after their dispossession. August Jack Khahtsahlano's two decades of conversations with Vancouver archivist Major Matthews kept Whoi Whoi and Chaythoos in living memory long after Lumberman's Arch and Prospect Point became newcomer playlands. Virtually until his death in 1958, Tim Cummings emphasized to visiting reporters how, "at one time, the Cummings family used to have lots of neighbours." In his autobiography, published in 1994, the Squamish elder Simon Baker paid respect to his grandfather John Baker and even more so to his grandmother Mary Tsiyaliya for managing the family's transition from Brockton Point to the Mission Reserve. A member of the Cummings family in the fourth generation, Anne Fowler, wrote in 1999 about her long-ago Sundays at Brockton Point: "Many years have passed since then, but I still drive around Stanley Park and stop in front of what used to be their cabin. I am filled with the memories of the happiest days of my childhood and if I close my eyes, I can almost feel my Auntie Aggie's soft cheek brush mine."[2]

Memories do not only survive in written form. Descendants who were once children in these places of belonging have carried with them through their lifetimes images of what might have been. In 1998

Tommy Cole's daughter Rose took a newspaper reporter to see where she grew up on the south shore of Brockton Point. She was still upset: "It's a heartbreak. We never wanted to go back because it just made us feel so bad that we had to move out of there." Ed Long's grandson explained to me how he had tried to find out more. "I wish I had talked more to grandpa but he'd get so upset whenever it was mentioned. He never used to like to talk about the past. He was such an honest man, he was a standup man. Imagine, losing your house!"[3]

The descendants who persuaded me to write their stories have sought to ensure that the past is not forgotten. All his life Norman McPhee continued to "think about my grandmother Maggy and my great grandmother Mary Eihu who fought so hard to keep Kanaka Ranch." Olive Keamo O'Connor, who links back to both Kanaka Ranch and Brockton Point, was absolutely determined that, as she put it at the end of our first meeting, I would reverse the still upsetting image of how "I'd be out with my five children" visiting Aggie and Tim Cummings, and "the sightseeing bus would be going around on Sunday, 'look on this side, and you'll see a family of squatters.'"[4]

Descendants continue to identify strongly with their families' one-time homes. Herbert Smith, whose great-grandfather was among the earliest newcomers to set down at Brockton Point, still takes pride in being a toddler there. "I remember everyone in the park asking my name."[5] Willard Gonsalves reflected on visits to his childhood home: "I used to go back to Stanley Park and look her over. I used to go to see Tim Cummings when I could. My mother always liked taking a ride around Stanley Park. She missed it, we lived there quite a few years. The Salvation Army would sing where we used to live. They called it Hallelujah Point. We went back there and saw the Salvation Army having their revival, and this was where we lived. I always thought they should have called it Gonsalves Point, not Hallelujah Point."

The Gonsalves family's sense of belonging has remained so strong that when one of them died, it was their wish to have the ashes scattered there. Willard Gonsalves remembered, "My oldest sister Margaret got married and moved to Edmonton. Every time they came here, they

The location where families lived on the south shore of Brockton Point was commemorated on the centennial of Canadian Confederation as Hallelujah Point. The plaque, which still stands, honours the Salvation Army for "erecting a rugged shelter … in the silent atmosphere of early Burrard Inlet." Nearby is a large statue of the runner Harry Jerome as BC Athlete of the Century, 1871–1971. The families who lived there are forgotten.
Courtesy the author

took a ride around the park and sat under the lilac tree. When she died about four years ago [1998], her husband brought her ashes out. They put them under the lilac tree that Martha Smith planted so very long ago."[6]

Martha Smith's lilac need not stand alone. For all of the conscious obliteration, the spaces are still there, none more so physically than the long-ago graveyards at Brockton Point, Chaythoos, and perhaps elsewhere in the park. The spaces where the forgotten families were born, lived, died and were laid to rest want to be remembered. The vegetable garden maintained by Supple Jack's wife Qwhaywat at Chaythoos has long since disappeared. So has the cherry tree Mary See-em-ia's granddaughter Minnie planted from seed at Kanaka Ranch. Only the lilac set out by Peter Smith's wife Martha at Brockton

Point survives. Each of the locations testifies to ways of life that are part of our common heritage. Only when we are given the opportunity to value the past as well as enjoy the present day will Stanley Park's secret be no more.

Notes

Abbreviations: BCA (British Columbia Archives), BCR (*British Columbia Reports*), BCSC (British Columbia Supreme Court), CC (Colonial Correspondence), CVA (City of Vancouver Archives), DIA (Department of Indian Affairs), LAC (Library and Archives Canada), NA (National Archives U.K., formerly Public Records Office), SCC (Supreme Court of Canada), VCC (Vancouver City Council), VPB (Vancouver Parks Board), VPL (Vancouver Public Library)

Preface: The Lilac Still Blooms

1. As examples, "The Myriad Songs of Stanley Park," *Vancouver Province*, April 10, 1909 ("primitive simplicity," "unspoiled"); "Trapped Game in Vancouver's Park," *Victoria Colonist*, April 10, 1910 ("witching savagery," "an impenetrable jungle"); June 20, 1927, VPB minutes, CVA ("a natural forest," "a woodland retreat"); "Stanley Park," *Vancouver Sun*, November 30, 1931 ("the greatest natural park on this continent," "the forest primeval"); "Concessions in the Park Are Opposed," *Vancouver Sun*, March 11, 1936 ("1000 acres of primeval forest"); "Park Preservation," *Vancouver News-Herald*, October 30, 1939 ("unspoiled").
2. Eugene Kinkead, *Central Park 1857–1995: The Birth, Decline, and Renewal of a National Treasure* (New York: Norton, 1990), 78. The dominant perspective, reflecting contemporary newspaper descriptions, originates in Egbert Viele, "Topography of New-York and Its Park System," in James Grant Wilson, ed., *The Memorial History of the City of New York* (1893), v. 4: 556–57, cited in Roy Rosenzweig and Elizabeth Blackmar, *The Park and the People: A History of Central Park* (Ithaca: Cornell University Press, 1992), 64.
3. In drawing from Major Matthews' conversations, I have edited them as little as possible, mostly making spelling and punctuation consistent. Where a person returned to the same topic at different points in the same or different meetings, I have sometimes combined conversations. In doing so, I have used ellipses (…) sparingly, only as needed to indicate that relevant material on the same topic has been left out.
4. James Nahanee, conversation, November 12, 2002.
5. I have not separately footnoted such usual sources as vital statistics, obituaries, entries in directories, pre-emption records, census data, or VPB minutes unless quoting directly from them.
6. J.S. Matthews, conversation with August Jack Khahtsahlano (hereafter referred to as August Jack), July 14, 1937, in J.S. Matthews, comp., *Conversations with Khahtsahlano 1932–1954* (Vancouver: CVA, 1955), 78. In 1933 the Chiefs of the Squamish Indian Council endorsed and adopted Matthews's principal spellings (388).

Chapter 1: The Aboriginal Presence

1. Jim Franks and Andrew Paull, conversations with Major Matthews, respectively November 20, 1932, and January 10, 1922, CVA, Add. Ms. 54.
2. Andrew Paull (Qoitechetahl), conversations with Matthews, December 15, 1932, and January 10, 1933. All Matthews conversations not in Matthews, *Conversations*, are in CVA, Add. Ms. 54.

3. June 1, 1891, VPB minutes; Vancouver Board of Works, Report for the year ending December 31, 1888, p. 30, cited in "Excerpt" typescript, Stanley Park file, Add. Ms. 54.
4. Charles Hill-Tout, "Notes on the Skqomic [Squamish] of British Columbia, a Branch of the Great Salish Stock of North America," *Report of the British Association for the Advancement of Science*, 70th meeting (1900), reprinted in Ralph Maud, ed., *The Salish People: The Local Contribution of Charles Hill-Tout*, v. 2: *The Squamish and the Lillooet* (Vancouver: Talonbooks, 1978), 53, also 29–30; Charles Hill-Tout, letter to Matthews, August 2, 1932, in CVA, Add 54; Leonard Ham, Stephanie Yip, Peter Gose and David Rozen, *The Evaluation of Archaeological Sites in the Greater Vancouver Regional District: Proposals for Management, 1979* (Victoria, BC, 1979).
5. George Vancouver, *A Voyage of Discovery to the North Pacific Ocean and Round the World 1791–1795*, ed. W. Kaye Lamb, v. 2 (London: Hakluyt Society, 1984), 580–83.
6. Clause 2, letters patent to James Douglas, September 2, 1858, in *Papers Relative to the Affairs of British Columbia*, part 1 (London: Her Majesty's Stationery Office, 1859), 3; Jimmy Sievewright in *Vancouver Sun*, June 13, 1958; also R.W. Harrison, "Shots Missed Him in Gold Rush Days," *Vancouver Sun*, August 30, 1947.
7. R.C. Moody to Douglas, Off Vancouver Island, January 28, 1859, enclosed in Douglas to Sir E.B. Lytton, Colonial Secretary, Victoria, February 4, 1859, 60, in *Papers Relative to the Affairs of British Columbia*, part 2 (London: Her Majesty's Stationery Office, 1859), 60.
8. Moody to Douglas, Victoria, August 8 and 11, November 10 and 12, December 8, 1859, January 28, February 8, March 3, 1860, BCA, GR 2900, v. 1; Colonial Office memos on Moody to Douglas, August 8, 1859, November 10, 1860, NA, CO 60/5–6.
9. Douglas to Lytton, Victoria, February 19, 1859, and enclosed proclamation, February 14, 1859, NA, CO 60/4; Douglas to Lytton, Victoria, January 14, 1860, and enclosed proclamation, January 4, 1860, CO 60/7.
10. Moody to Douglas, New Westminster, December 12, 1859, February 1, 1860, BCA, GR 2900, v. 7, enclosed in Douglas to Duke of Newcastle, Colonial Secretary, December 23, 1859, NA, CO 60/5; Newcastle to Douglas, London, February 28, 1860, enclosing Moody to Newcastle, New Westminster, December 13, 1859, NA, CO 60/5; R. Lambert Baynes to Douglas, Esquimalt Harbour, January 9, 1860, Douglas to Baynes, Victoria, January 11, 1860, W.A.G. Young, Assistant Colonial Secretary, to Moody, Victoria, January 11, 1860, Moody to Douglas, New Westminster, February 1, 1860, all enclosed in Col. Crossman to Inspector General of Fortifications, Victoria, July 21, 1881, NA, CO 42/770; December 18, 1859, January 9, 11, 1860, entries, Baynes, Pacific Station Journal, NA, ADM 50/309; Baynes's map of proposed naval reserves, 1860, BCA, P616.8aj/B361lbu/1860, also January 9, 1860, CVA, Add. Ms. 202, exhibit d32D, neither of which marks out the peninsula. Douglas assured Baynes that the requested lands would "be reserved as requested by you until the wishes of Her Majesty's Government can be ascertained," and Baynes promised to "strongly urge the Lords Commissioners of the Admiralty to secure [them] for Naval purposes." The journals of Baynes and of his successor as head of the Royal Navy's Pacific Station, which minute all incoming correspondence, and the record book of Admiralty correspondence contain no subsequent references to the naval reserves, suggesting strongly that the Admiralty never accepted the

reserves on behalf of Britain (Baynes, Pacific Station Journal, 1860, NA, ADM 50/309; Sir Thomas Maitland, Journal, 1860-63, ADM 50/310; Index of Admiralty Correspondence, 1859–60, ADM 12/658 and 674).

11. Moody was clearly aware of the expectation, inserting notices in February 1860 in respect to "reserved lots" in New Westminster (Moody to Douglas, New Westminster, February 7, 1860, BCA, GR 2900, v. 7) and being reminded by the Colonial Secretary in letters of April 5 and August 2, 1861, of the necessity of "publishing in every District lists of the Indian and Government Reserves" (William Young, Colonial Secretary, to Moody, April 5, 1861, and George Good, For the Colonial Secretary, to Moody, August 2, 1861, in British Columbia [Attorney General] v. Canada [Attorney General], Case on Appeal, 299–301); also testimony of George Turner, June 22, 1904, Alexander Richard Howse, January 7, 1901, June 23, 1904, in British Columbia (Attorney General) v. Canada (Attorney General), Case on Appeal, 32, 326, 350, 353, 359, CVA, Add. Ms. 202.
12. Undated Royal Engineers map, exhibit 4, maps volume, CVA, Add. Ms. 202. One assistant recalled how "reserves were made in the Land Office without—I think at the time without any reference to publication." Another took pride in how "Colonel Moody selected the Military" reserves "as protection against invasion." He remembered an "index plan, showing the reserves," but if one existed, it soon disappeared. George Turner, June 22, 1904, Alexander Richard Howse, January 7, 1901, June 23, 1904, in British Columbia (Attorney General) v. Canada (Attorney General), Case on Appeal, 32, 326, 350, 353, 359, CVA, Add. Ms. 202.
13. Moody to W.R. Spalding, Justice of the Peace, New Westminster, January 20, 1860, BCA, GR 1404, file 5; Moody to Douglas, New Westminster, November 27, 1860, BCA, GR 2900, v. 8.
14. Letter from "A Farmer," *British Columbian*, February 21, 1861, also February 13, 1861; Young to Moody, Victoria, April 5, 1861, in British Columbia (Attorney General) v. Canada (Attorney General), Case on Appeal, 300–301. Both the North Road from New Westminster to Burrard Inlet and Douglas Road to Burnaby Lake, named after Robert Burnaby, ran to or through Moody's properties.
15. Moody's four letter books of outgoing correspondence to Douglas indicate he understood the obligation to consult about reserving land for town sites, schools, and other public purposes. Correspondence Outward, Lands and Works Department, Original Letter Books, v. 7–10 to the Governor and Colonial Secretary, 1859–63, and v. 1–4 general, BCA, GR 2900; Colonial Office: British Columbia, Original Correspondence, 1858–63, NA, CO 60, v. 4–17; for examples of ongoing consultation, Moody to J.W. Trutch, July 8, 1859, v. 1; Moody to J.J. Southgate, July 21, 1859, v. 1; Moody to Douglas, December 8, 1859, February 7, 1860 [two letters], v. 7; August 1, 1861, v. 9; Douglas to Lytton, Victoria, January 27, February 18, 1860, v. 7.
16. F.W. Howay, who spent a lifetime meticulously researching primary sources on British Columbia's early settlement history, reluctantly concluded "the material in reference to the formation of reserves on the [Burrard] inlet, whether naval, military, townsite, or Indian, is extremely vague and indefinite" (F.W. Howay, "Early Settlement on Burrard Inlet," *British Columbia Historical Quarterly* 1 [1937], 103). Having read through all of the potentially relevant materials I could locate in the

CVA, BCA and NA (former Public Records Office) in London, I agree with Howay's assessment.

17. Moody to Captain Parsons, January 26, 1863, Exhibit 8 in Canada (Attorney General) v. Gonzalves (1925), BCSC, Case on Appeal, in LAC, RG135, v. 522, and VPL, SC971.133, v. 22ca.
18. Turner, June 22, 1904, in British Columbia (Attorney General) v. Canada (Attorney General), Case on Appeal, 325, 329.
19. Chartres Brew to Charles Good, Acting Colonial Secretary, February 4, 1864, BCA, GR 1404, file 5.
20. H.P.P. Crease, "Burrard Inlet with pencil notations," BCA, S616.8(87)/B968/1863. A notation on the pencil sketch in Crease's hand at the edge of the map reads: "Going out (off of mill) 13 Aug 63." I am grateful to Randy Bouchard and Dorothy Kennedy for bringing this important map to my attention.
21. Robert Burnaby to his brother Tom, Victoria, July 21, 1859, in Anne Burnaby McLeod and Pixie McGeachie, *Land of Promise: Robert Burnaby's Letters from Colonial British Columbia, 1858–1863* (Burnaby: City of Burnaby, 2002), 102.
22. The birthdate is deduced from August Jack's baptism at age one month in January 1881. Bouchard and Kennedy kindly shared their copies of the Oblate records with me.
23. August Jack, conversations with Matthews, July 7, August 8, 1932, April 20, 1939, in Matthews, *Conversations*, 11–12, 16, 113.
24. Incorporation papers, British Columbia and Vancouver Island Spar Lumber and Sawmill Co., Ltd., November 30, 1865, BCA, GR 1404, file 5; Moody to Crease, undated, December 3, 1867, Ludlow, England, September 9, 1870, and December 22, 1873, BCA, GR 2879, box 37, file 16; Edward Stamp to A.N. Birch, Colonial Secretary, New Westminster, May 17, 1865, BCA, CC, GR1373, reel B1343.
25. Birch to Stamp, New Westminster, May 10, 1865, also Joseph Trutch, Chief Commissioner of Lands and Works, to Crease, New Westminster, September 6, 1865, BCA, Add. Ms. 120.
26. J.B. Launders to Colonial Secretary, June 3, 1865, BCA, CC, GR1373, reel B1343.
27. Launders to Colonial Secretary, June 7, 1865, BCA, CC, GR 1373, reel B1343.
28. Indenture between Joseph Trutch and British Columbia and Vancouver Island Spar Lumber and Saw Mill Company Ltd., November 13, 1865, BCA, GR 1404, file 5.
29. C. Bryant, "Early Methodism in Vancouver," *Western Methodist Recorder* 6, 11 (May 1905). Bouchard and Kennedy generously shared this article.
30. Dick Isaacs (Que-yah-chulk), conversation with Matthews, October 14, 1932, in Matthews, *Conversations*, 178.
31. Charles Montgomery Tate, conversation with Matthews, July 1, 1932, in Matthews, *Conversations*, 171–75. It is unclear who Tate meant by Chief Thomas. Bouchard and Kennedy have found no other references to a person by this name as a chief in the vicinity. Tate was ordained a minister only in 1879.
32. Matthews, *Conversations*, 77.
33. Crease, "Burrard Inlet with pencil notations."
34. The confused state of the records is indicated by another 354-acre "military reserve" being listed as "north of First Narrows, Burrard Inlet," where there were only the Squamish reserves. Robert Beaven, February 11, 1901, and "Return of Government Reserves, 14th Jan. 1873," in British Columbia (Attorney General) v. Canada

(Attorney General), Case on Appeal, 106–107, 285.
35. "Government Takes Action," *Vancouver World*, May 1, 1899.
36. Joseph N. Thain to Joseph Trutch, Lieutenant Governor, Victoria, April 1, 1876, BCA, box 2, file 14/727/76. A man who joined the office of Lands and Works in 1875 could not recall the peninsula ever being referred to as a "Military Reserve" except in Turner's field notes. W.S. Gore, February 12, 1901, in British Columbia (Attorney General) v. Canada (Attorney General), Case on Appeal, 149–50.
37. November 13, 1876, A.C. Anderson diary, BCA, Ms. 559.
38. Censuses taken November 10–20, 1876, enclosed with report of the British Columbia Reserve Commission, 1877, in DIA, RG10, v. 3645, file 7936, on reel C-10113; also enclosed with James Lenihan, Indian Superintendent, to E.A. Meredith, Deputy Minister of the Interior, January 19, 1877, in DIA, RG10, v. 3642, file 7624, reel C-10117.
39. Census of the Skwamish taken November 10–20, 1876, enclosed with report of the BC Reserve Commission, 1877, in DIA, RG10, v. 3645, file 7936, reel C-10113; supplemented by LAC, RG88, v. 494, and RG10, v. 10,010. The nature of the writing makes it impossible to determine spellings with absolute certainty. I have been assisted by Randy Bouchard's transcriptions of the multiple versions of the census for comparison.
40. November 16–17, 1876, Archibald McKinlay diary, BCA, E/C/M21.
41. Gilbert Malcolm Sproat to A.C. Elliott, Provincial Secretary, In camp, Howe Sound, November 27, 1876, in BC, Provincial Secretary, BCA, GR 294.
42. November 16–17, 1876, McKinlay diary.
43. McKinlay and Sproat to F.G. Vernon, Howe Sound, November 27, 1876, BCA, GR 2982; also Sproat to Elliott, In camp, Howe Sound, November 27, 1876, and Joint Indian Reserve Commissioners to Elliott, In camp, Howe Sound, November 27, 1876, in BC, Provincial Secretary, BCA, GR 294.
44. August Jack, conversations with Matthews, January 12, 1934, April 20, 1939, April 10, 1943, March 25 and May 8, 1944, in Matthews, *Conversations*, 35–36, 114, 144–46.
45. August Jack, conversations with Matthews, April 29, 1940, March 25, 1944, in Matthews, *Conversations*, 125, 145.
46. August Jack, conversations with Matthews, January 12, 1934, August 5, 1936, April 20, 1939, April 10, 1943, March 25, May 8, 1944, in Matthews, *Conversations*, 35–36, 62, 114, 144–46.
47. August Jack, conversation with Matthews, January 12, 1934, in Matthews, *Conversations*, 31, 33–34.
48. August Jack, conversations with Matthews, January 12, November 23, 1934, December 23, 1936, in Matthews, *Conversations*, 34–36, 41, 69.
49. Elizabeth Silvey Walker, conversation with Matthews, November 28, 1938, in Matthews, *Conversations*, 213–14.

Chapter 2: Kanaka Ranch

1. John Barrow, ed., *Captain Cook's Voyages of Discovery* (London: Dent & Sons, 1906), 434. On the Hawaiians see Jean Barman and Bruce McIntyre Watson, *Leaving Paradise: Indigenous Hawaiians in the Pacific Northwest, 1787–1898* (Honolulu: University of Hawai'i Press, 2005).

2. Minnie McCord Smith, conversations with Matthews, July 20, 1936, April 2, 1937.
3. Ibid.
4. Mabel McPhee, conversation, November 12, 2002.
5. William Nahanee, conversation with Matthews, September 12, 1941.
6. Walter Keamo, conversation with Matthews, April 18, 1952.
7. Herbert Nahu, conversation with Matthews, April 1, 1940.
8. Alice Patterson Crakanthorp, conversations with Matthews, March 21 and 28, 1935, and cited in Muriel Crakanthorp, conversation with Matthews, November 9, 1937, in CVA, Add. Ms. 54.
9. Walker, conversation with Matthews, April 22, 1940; Tomkins Brew to Forbes Vernon, Chief Commissioner of Lands and Works, Burrard Inlet, June 25, 1876, in BCA, GR 868, box 2, file 14/1429/76.
10. James Nahanee, conversation, January 2, 2003; Fred W. Alexander, conversation with Matthews, December 1, 1933, in Matthews, *Early Vancouver*, v. 3, typescript in CVA.
11. William Nahanee, conversation with Matthews, September 12, 1941.
12. Minnie Smith, conversation with Matthews, February 8, 1937, and letter to Stanley Park commissioners, February 9, 1937, CVA, Add. Ms. 54.
13. Minnie Smith, conversation with Matthews, July 20, 1936.
14. Minnie Smith, conversations with Matthews, July 20 and 29, 1936, April 2, 1937.
15. Minnie Smith, conversations with Matthews, July 2, 1936, April 2, 1937.
16. Minnie Smith, conversations with Matthews, February 8 and April 2, 1937.

Chapter 3: The Families of Brockton Point

1. Mary Silvey Buss, conversation with Matthews, June 29–30, 1936.
2. Walker, conversations with Matthews, October 27, 1938, September 23, 1943, in Matthews, *Conversations*, 209–10, 224; August 17, 1939.
3. Walker, conversation with Matthews, October 27, 1938, in Matthews, *Conversations*, 210.
4. Jim Franks, conversation with Matthews, undated, in Matthews, *Conversations*, 29.
5. Adapted from Canada (Attorney General) v. Gonzalves (1925), BCSC, Proceedings at Trial, courtesy of Willard Gonsalves, and Case on Appeal. Subsequent testimony not otherwise identified is adapted from this case and these two sources.
6. March 5, 1866, in Robert Brown, "The Land of the Hydahs, a spring journey north," in BCA, ms. 794, v. 2, file 10.
7. Adapted from testimony, BC v. Canadian Pacific Railway (1904), BCSC, in Joseph Mannion file, CVA, Add. Ms. 54.
8. On October 3, 1878, the Galiano preemption was officially "cancelled for cessation of occupation." Preemption of Maryanns Point, Galiano Island, March 23, 1867, in BCA, GR766, box 7, file 79/982.
9. Joseph Silvy to Chief Commissioner of Lands and Works, New Westminster, May 15, 1868, in BCA, CC, GR 1372, reel 1364.
10. Joseph Silvy to Chief Commissioner.
11. Walker, conversation with Matthews, September 23, 1943, in Matthews, *Conversations*, 224–45.
12. Walker, conversation with Matthews, October 12, 1943, CVA, Ms. 54.

13. E. Brown to A.T. Bushby to Colonial Secretary, New Westminster, December 28, 1870, in BCA, CC, GR 1372, reel 1312; Alice M. Russell, Assistant Provincial Archivist, to Theodore Bryant, Victoria, October 31, 1932, in Matthews, *Early Vancouver* (Vancouver: Brock Webber, 1932),v. 2, 98.
14. Silvey, conversations with Matthews, October 27, 1938, July 17, 1939, October 12, 1943, in Matthews, *Conversations*, 209, 211, 212–13, 216, 225.
15. Walker, conversations with Matthews, November 28, 1938, August 17, 1939, in Matthews, *Conversations*, 212–13, 217–18.
16. Walker, conversation with Matthews, October 27, 1938, in Matthews, *Conversations*, 199.
17. Adapted from testimony, BC v. Canadian Pacific Railway (1904).
18. Adapted from testimony in Canada (Attorney General) v. Cummings, SCC, Case on Appeal, copy in LAC, RG125, v. 123.
19. Adapted from testimony in Canada (Attorney General) v. Cummings, SCC, Case on Appeal.
20. Tomkins Brew to Forbes Vernon, Chief Commissioner of Lands and Works, Burrard Inlet, June 25, 1876, in BCA, GR 868, box 2, file 14/1429/76.
21. Simon Baker, *Khot-La-Cha: The Autobiography of Chief Simon Baker*, compiled and edited by Verna J. Kirkness (Vancouver: Douglas & McIntyre, 1994), 17.
22. Walker conversations with Matthews, October 27, 1938, November 28, 1938, CVA, Ms. 54.
23. Buss, conversation with Matthews; Buss, CVA genealogy form, October 15, 1934, CVA, Add. Ms. 54.
24. Walker, conversation with Matthews, November 28, 1938, in Matthews, *Conversations*, 214.
25. Margaret Mannion Christie, conversation with Matthews, July 26, 1934.
26. Minnie Smith, conversation with Matthews, April 2, 1937.
27. "Old Timer" [Joseph Mannion], "Vancouver in the Days of Yore," *Vancouver Province*, January 6, 1912.
28. Walker, conversations with Matthews, September 14, 30, October 17, 1943.
29. See Jean Barman, *The Remarkable Adventures of Portuguese Joe Silvey* (Madeira Park: Harbour, 2004).
30. Adapted from Canada (Attorney General) v. Gonzalves, Proceedings at Trial, and Case on Appeal.
31. Lewella Duncan, conversation, April 18, 1999; Jennifer Hopkins, "How Madeira was named," *The Press* (Sechelt, BC), November 5, 1991.
32. William Timothy Cummings, conversation with Matthews, February 23, 1939.
33. H.P.P. Crease, presiding judge, reporting on the case, August 10, 1877, BCA, Add. Ms. 55, box 2, file 8; Crease, undated draft, BCA, Add. Ms. 54, box 4, file 3; Register of inmates and Education register, New Westminster Penitentiary, LAC, Burnaby, RG 73, v. 277 and 294.
34. Les Himes, "Ed Long's Toted Planks 53 Years,"*Vancouver Sun*, September 27, 1957.
35. Alf Cottrell, "But Listen!" *Vancouver Province*, August 4, 1951.
36. Cummings, conversation with Matthews.
37. Minnie Smith, conversation with Matthews, April 2, 1937.
38. Calvert Simson, conversation with Matthews, December 14, 1937.

Chapter 4: Imposition of Stanley Park

1. Report of a Committee of Privy Council, February 25, 1880, in NA, CO 42/760, and *Correspondence and Papers in Reference to Stanley Park and Deadman's Island, British Columbia* (Ottawa: S. Dawson, 1899), 7.
2. George Walkem, Chief Commissioner of Lands and Works, to Joseph W. Trutch, Victoria, November 20, 1880, and W.S. Gore, Surveyor General, to Chief Commissioner of Lands and Works, Victoria, October 29, 1880, enclosed in above, NA, CO 42/770.
3. Ralph Thompson to Colonial Office, London, June 17, 1881, NA, CO 42/770.
4. Col. Crossman, Victoria, to Inspector General of Fortifications, Admiralty, December 10, 1881; Trutch to John A. Macdonald, Minister of the Interior, Victoria, November 22, 1880, NA, CO 42/770. The Chief Commissioner of Lands and Works became extremely frustrated in compiling the list, informing Trutch that "the old records of the department have, as far as time has permitted been examined, but no satisfactory information has been obtained as to the number of reserves, or as to how or by whom they were made." Chief Commissioner of Lands and Works to Trutch, Victoria, August 12, 1880, in British Columbia (Attorney General) v. Canada (Attorney General), Case on Appeal, 188.
5. Notation on Thompson to Secretary of State, Colonial Office, London, January 28, 1882; internal memo, Colonial Office, July 16, 1883.
6. "Reserve Lands of B. Columbia to be surrendered to Dominion Govt," War Office, July 27, 1883, NA, CO 42/773 and 776.
7. Internal memo, Colonial Office, London, February 29, 1884, NA, CO 42/778; NA, CO 42/778; draft minutes for Marquis of Landsdowne, March 20, 1884, NA, CO 42/778; also *Correspondence*, 7–8, and Exhibit 1, Canada (Attorney General). v. Gonzalves, Case on Appeal.
8. W.C. Van Horne, CPR vice president, to L.A. Hamilton, Montreal, January 12, 1885, CVA, Add. Ms. 54, Stanley Park file.
9. Ross to Sir Adolphe Caron, Minister of Militia, Ottawa, March 24, 1886, and attached note of response, *Correspondence*, 12.
10. May 12, 1886, VCC minutes and VCC to Dominion Government, May 17, 1886, in CVA, Add. Ms. 54; also "City Council Meeting," *Vancouver Daily Advertiser*, May 19, 1886.
11. L.A. Hamilton, letter to Matthews, April 11, 1932, CVA, Add. Ms. 54; Minutes of a Meeting of the Committee of the Privy Council, approved by his Excellency the Governor General on 8th June 1887, adapted from Exhibit 2 in Canada (Attorney General). v. Gonzalves, Case on Appeal.
12. Adapted from testimony in Canada (Attorney General) v. Gonzalves, Case on Appeal.
13. Cummings, conversation with Matthews.
14. Adapted from the testimony of James Clendenning in Canada (Attorney General) v. Gonzalves, and in Canada (Attorney General) vs. Cummings; Frederick Samuel Steel, genealogy form, August 30, 1945, CVA, Add. Ms. 54.
15. August Jack, conversations with Matthews, January 12, 1934, March 25, 1944, in Matthews, *Conversations*, 35, 145–46.
16. December 27, 1887, July 23, 1888, VCC minutes.

17. "The Opening of Stanley Park," *Vancouver News Advertiser*, September 27, 1887.
18. J. Lyle Telford, mayor of Vancouver, to Earl of Derby, October 2, 1939; "Incorporation & Dedication of Stanley Park," January 1956, both in CVA, Add. Ms. 54.
19. "An Act to amend the 'Vancouver Incorporation Act, 1886,' and the 'Vancouver Incorporation Act, 1887'," April 6, 1889, in *Statutes of British Columbia* (1889).
20. Frank Harris, conversation with Matthews, May 16, 1937, in Matthews, *Early Vancouver*, v. 4; June 16, 1937, in Matthews, *Conversations*, 276.
21. Minnie Smith, conversation with Matthews, February 8, 1937.
22. Walker, conversation with Matthews, November 28, 1938, in Matthews, *Conversations*, 213–14.
23. August Jack, conversations with Matthews, November 6, 1936, January 27 and March 15, 1937, October 31, 1939, in Matthews, *Conversations*, 67–68, 70–71, 123.
24. Vancouver Board of Works, Report for the year ending December 31, 1888, p. 30, CVA.
25. Cummings, conversation with Matthews.
26. Original document in Smallpox files, CVA, Add. Ms. 54.
27. Ibid.
28. March 28, September 17, 1888, VCC minutes.
29. March 28, 1889, July 17, August 13, 1890, VPB minutes.
30. Sarah Avison Harrison, conversation with Matthews, February 11, 1958, CVA, Add. Ms. 54.
31. October 25, 1892, VPB minutes; Robert Cole, conversation with Steele.

Chapter 5: Generational Transitions

1. March 28, 1889, VPB minutes.
2. December 14, 1889, October 25, 1900, VPB minutes.
3. Adapted from testimony in Canada (Attorney General) v. Cummings, SCC, Case on Appeal.
4. May 29, 1890, VPB minutes.
5. Mrs. Daniel Snell, conversation with Matthews, July 2, 1941; Hannah Elizabeth Greatrex, conversation with Matthews, August 25, 1943.
6. *William's British Columbia Directory, 1882–1883*, 235.
7. Baker, *Khot-La-Cha*, 17.
8. Behari L. Verma, "The Squamish: A Study of Changing Political Organisation," unpublished MA thesis, Department of Anthropology, Criminology and Sociology, University of BC, 1954, 112–13.
9. Baker, *Khot-La-Cha*, 17–18.
10. Baker, *Khot-La-Cha*, 19–20.
11. "Coqualeetza Industrial School, Admissions and Discharges," United Church Archives, Vancouver School of Theology. Information taken from the register is not separately footnoted subsequently.
12. Lavinia Clarke in Women's Missionary Society of the Methodist Church, *Monthly Letter* 10, 4 (April 1894), 4.
13. Laurie Nahanee Cole, conversation, April 2, 2002.
14. Exhibit 10 in Canada (Attorney General) v. Cummings (1925); Olive Keamo O'Connor, conversation, April 10, 2000.

15. "A Random Visit to the Coqualeetza (Indian) Institute," *Missionary Outlook* 15, 9 (September 1894), 135.
16. September 22, 24, 26, 27, 1894, Ebenezer Robson diary, BCA, R/D/R57.
17. February 12, 1895, Robson diary.
18. December 13–15, 1894, Robson diary.
19. February 26, 1895, Robson diary.
20. February, 13, March 28, November 10, 15, 17, December 1, 1895, January 19, 1896, Robson diary.
21. February 21, 1896, Robson diary.
22. Alexander Sutherland, General Secretary of Methodist Church of Canada, to Superintendent General of Indian Affairs, Toronto, April 11, 1895, in DIA, RG 10, v. 6422, file 869-1, reel C-8754; November 14, 1895, Robson diary.
23. January 19, 1895, Robson diary; Report for Fraser River Agency in DIA, *Annual Report*, 1897, 80.
24. Report for Fraser River Agency in DIA, *Annual Report*, 1897, 80.
25. September 5, 1895, Robson diary.
26. "Review of Year's Work," Women's Missionary Society of the Methodist Church, *Monthly Letter* 12, 5 (May 1895), 5.
27. Report of principal of Coqualeetza in DIA, *Annual Report*, 1901, 420.
28. October 27–29, 1895, Robson diary.

Chapter 6: Life Goes On

1. Ruth (Mrs. John) Morton, conversation with Matthews, March 15, 1937.
2. Eihu file, CVA, Add. Ms. 54.
3. William Nahanee, conversation with Matthews, September 12, 1941.
4. John Morton to Ruth Morton, Vancouver, May 11, 1895, in BCA, Add. Ms. 336, 547-E-4, file 4; City of Vancouver, Fee Book 7365C, v. 21, p. 231, held in BC Land Title Office, New Westminster.
5. Minnie Smith, conversation with Matthews, July 20, 1936.
6. Mabel McPhee, conversation, November 12, 2002.
7. Maude Nahanee Thomas in Margaret Moran, ed., "I've Always Lived Here," *Indian Voice*, September 1975.
8. James Nahanee, conversation, January 7, 2003.
9. Tina Cole, conversation, June 29, 1993.
10. "Squamish Mission, North Vancouver, is Point of Interest," *Vancouver Province*, August 14, 1909.
11. Quoted in "Squamish Mission."
12. Thomas, "I've Always Lived Here."
13. Ed Nahanee, interview, November 6, 1973, in International Longshoremen's and Warehousemen's Union archive, UBC Special Collections; Ed Nahanee in *"Man along the shore!" The Story of the Vancouver Waterfront As Told by the Longshoremen Themselves, 1860s–1975* (Vancouver: ILWU Local 500 Pensioners, 1975), 55.
14. "Cecilia Nahanee (nee Johnny) 1880–1918," typescript courtesy of Laurie Nahanee Cole; Thomas, "I've Always Lived Here."
15. Verma, "The Squamish," 124; Thomas Lascelles, *Mission on the Inlet: St. Paul's Indian Catholic Church, North Vancouver, BC, 1863–1984* (privately printed, 1984), 44–45.

16. Louis Cordocedo, conversation, June 29, 1993.
17. Norman and Margaret McPhee, conversations, June 25 and July 5, 1991.
18 "Woman Took Heavy Dose of Poison," *Vancouver Province*, May 19, 1908.
19. Ellen Elizabeth Fowler at Josephine Marstrand Inquest May 19, 1908, in BC, Attorney General, Inquests, BCA, GR1327, file 76/1908, reel B2383.
20. I am grateful to Mabel McPhee for taking me there on June 27, 1991. At the time I had no idea who Seraphine was or why Mabel did so.
21. August Jack, conversation with Matthews, August 8, 1932, in Matthews, *Conversations*, 16.
22. August Jack, conversation with Matthews, October 31, 1938, in Matthews, *Conversations*, 107.
23. Report of principal of Coqualeetza in DIA, *Annual Report*, 1906, 449; report of Indian agent for BC in DIA, *Annual Report*, 1894, 203.
24. Marlene Smith, conversation, March 9, 1999; O'Connor, conversation, April 10, 2000.
25. R.H. Cairns, Principal, Report of Coqualeetza School, July 25, 1907, in United Church Archives, Toronto, Sutherland Papers, fonds 14, series 2, 78.083, box 25.
26. Leona Marie Sparrow, "Work Histories of a Coast Salish Couple," unpublished MA thesis, Department of Anthropology, UBC, 1976, 266; Charlie Anderson, "A beautiful place to grow up," *Vancouver Province*, June 21, 1998.
27. Elsie Kerr, conversations, September 15 and October 4, 2002.
28. O'Connor, conversation, April 10, 2000.
29. E. Burpee in Women's Missionary Society of the Methodist Church, Canada, *Monthly Letter* 15, 10 (October 1898), 6.
30. Wilton Hyde, "Last Man in the Park," *Vancouver Province* magazine, July 6, 1957.
31. Sarah Sprott to Sutherland, February 26, 1906, in United Church Archives, Toronto, Alexander Sutherland Papers, box 25, file 88, accession number 78.092c.
32. Report of principal of Coqualeetza in DIA, *Annual Report*, 1906: 449, 1907: 414.
33. Minnie Smith, conversation with Matthews, February 8, 1937.
34. Olive Keamo O'Connor, "Mom's Story," typescript, April 2000, courtesy of the author; O'Connor, conversation, April 10, 2000.
35. September 9, 1895, Robson diary.
36. January 4, 28, 1894, Robson diary.
37. "County Criminal Court," *Daily News Advertiser*, January 20, 1895.
38. January 4, 28, 1894, Robson diary.
39. Women's Missionary Society of the Methodist Church, *Annual Report*, 1896, 26–27.
40. Maggie Smith in Women's Missionary Society of the Methodist Church, *Monthly Letter* 14, 7 (July 1897), 3; Report of principal of Coqualeetza, DIA, *Annual Report*, 1897, 284.
41. Ed Long, interview, September 27, 1973, in International Longshoremen's and Warehousemen's Union archive, UBC Special Collections; Ed Long in *"Man along the shore!"*, 28.
42. Ed Long, interview.
43. Ed Long in *"Man Along the Shore!"*, 25–26; Ed Long, interview.
44. Memo, DIA, Ottawa, December 30, 1914, in DIA, RG 10, v. 6422, file 869-1, reel C-8754.

45. Willard Gonsalves, conversations, March 8 and April 21, 2002, supplemented by Willard Gonsalves, conversation with Steele, October 21, 1984, in CVA, Add. Ms. 954.
46. Gonsalves, conversations.
47. Eddie Nahanee in *"Man along the shore!"*, 56.

Chapter 7: Changing Times

1. *Vancouver, British Columbia: The Sunset Doorway of the Dominion* (Vancouver: Vancouver Tourist Association, 1903), 43.
2. General information on Stanley Park over time draws on Richard M. Steele's meticulous research, both as published—*The Stanley Park Explorer* (Vancouver: Whitecap, 1985)— and as lodged in VCA.
3. "Squatters' Rights Not Yet Settled," *Vancouver Province*, c. March–April 1918, in VPB; Scrapbook of newspaper clippings, 1911–25, CVA, 50-F-4.
4. Information courtesy of Marlene Smith, March 9, 1999, who shared Sarcia's personal documents in her possession.
5. Herbert Smith, conversations, January 23 and April 4, 2005.
6. British Columbia (Attorney General) v. Canada (Attorney General), Case on Appeal, 159; Justice J. Martin's decision in BCSC in British Columbia (Attorney General) v. Canada (Attorney General), 8 BCR, 256, 259.
7. British Columbia (Attorney General) v. Canada (Attorney General) (1906), [1906] *Appeal Cases*, 431–32; also *Canadian Reports [1906] Appeal Cases* (1912), 389–434.
8. "Raid," *Vancouver Province*, April 30, 1912.
9. Resolution of VCC, August 1, 1898, in *Correspondence*, 20.
10. November 8, 1911, June 25, 1913, July 10, 1907, VPB minutes. Bouchard and Kennedy have found no evidence that "Aunt Sally" lived on the peninsula prior to the early 20th century.
11. "Squatters Will Claim Rights," *Vancouver Province*, April 25, 1904; "Squatters in the Park," *Vancouver Province*, April 26, 1904; "Declares Occupancy Illegal," *Vancouver Province*, May 6, 1904.
12. March 24, 1909, VPB minutes.
13. "Minister Passes Mawson's Design," *Vancouver Province*, March 5, 1913.
14. August 11, 1915, VPB minutes; "Drowned in Effort to Save His Wife," September 20, 1915, unidentified clipping courtesy of Marlene Smith.
15. "Squatters' Rights Not Yet Settled"; February 13 and March 27, 1918, VPB minutes.
16. March 24, 1909, May 22, 1913, VPB minutes; "Squatters' Rights Not Yet Settled."
17. "The Myriad Songs of Stanley Park the Lure and Delight of Thousands," *Vancouver Province*, April 10, 1909; June 12, 1912, May 14, June 11 and 25, 1913, VPB minutes.
18. June 19, 1903, April 9, 1919, VPB minutes; Charlotte Gordon, "Proposed Indian Village in Stanley Park," *Vancouver Province*, January 14, 1922.
19. August 9, 1921, January 4, 1922, VPB minutes. Descriptions come from S.W.A. Gunn, *The Totem Poles in Stanley Park* (Vancouver: Whiterocks, 1965); "Totem Poles are Placed," *Vancouver Sun*, February 6, 1924.
20. Stephen Golder, "Indian Village in Stanley Park," *Vancouver Province*, magazine, April 12, 1925; Robert Allison Hood, *By Shore and Trail in Stanley Park* (Toronto: McClelland & Stewart, 1929), 69.

21. Mary Ashby (Mrs. Fred B. Holmes), letter to Steele, November 2, 1984, in CVA, Add. Ms. 954.
22. T.B. Jones, Barrister, to Minister of Lands, Vancouver, June 5, 1919, in DIA, RG 10, v. 4089, file 521,804, reel C10186.
23. Jones to Minister of Lands, Vancouver.
24. W.E. Ditchburn, Chief Inspector of Indian Agencies, to DIA, July 28, 1919, in DIA, RG 10, v. 4089, file 521,804, reel C10186.
25. October 11, 1921, VPB minutes.
26. "Claim Stanley Park is not Really Part of Vancouver City," *Vancouver World*, August 11, 1922 ; "Portuguese, No Indian," *Vancouver World*, August 18, 1922.
27. Israel I. Rubinowitz to Attorney General of Canada, September 11, 1922; Deputy Minister of Justice E.L. Newcombe to Rubinowitz, October 12, 1922, in LAC, RG13, Justice, v. 271, no. 1704; also Memorandum for Deputy Minister of Justice, September 21, 1922; to Attorney General of Canada, October 4, 1922.
28. October 11, 1921, VPB minutes.
29. Charles C. Perry, Indian Agent in Vancouver Agency, to Duncan Campbell Scott, Vancouver, February 8, 1923, in DIA, RG 10, v. 4089, file 521,804, reel C10186.
30. VPB *Annual Report*, 1921, 3.
31. April 4, 1923, VPB minutes; VPB *Annual Report*, 1923, 4; Deputy Minister of National Defence to Scott, May 12, 1923, in DIA, RG 10, v. 4089, file 521,804, reel C10186.
32. "Squatters' Rights Not Yet Settled."
33. George E. McCrossan, Vancouver City Corporate Counsel, to Perry, April 25, 1923, in DIA, RG 10, v. 4089, file 521,804, reel C10186.
34. Robert Cole, conversation with Steele.
35. Margaret Perceval to Mackenzie King and to H.H. Stevens, April 23, 1923, H.H. Stevens, MP, to Scott, April 30, 1923, F.A. McGregor, Private Secretary to Minister of the Interior, to Perceval, April 30, 1923, in DIA, RG 10, v. 4089, file 521,804, reel C10186.
36. Perceval to King and Stevens; also Perry to Scott, May 21, 1923, in DIA, RG 10, v. 4089, file 521,804, reel C10186.
37. M. Parkinson, "Indians in the Park" in "Letter to the Editor," *Vancouver Province*, July 18, 1923.

Chapter 8: To the Courts

1. "Squatters are Losers in Suit," *Vancouver Province*, November 17, 1923.
2. Major Matthews concluded that the mark indicated Supple Jack's house. See his annotation on the Turner field notes in Matthews, *Conversations*, 24G. Based on their exhaustive research, Bouchard and Kennedy reach the same conclusion.
3. Adapted from testimony in Canada (Attorney General) v. Gonzalves.
4. Ibid.
5. Ibid.
6. "Old Indian on Stand," *Vancouver Province*, November 6, 1923; also "Ancients Appear at Indian Trial," *Vancouver Sun*, November 6, 1923.
7. "Court Held in Stanley Park Shack," *Vancouver Province*, November 7, 1923.
8. November 7, 1923, Denis Murphy, minute book of cases, BCA, GR1935, v. 3.

Chapter 9: The Several Faces of the Law

1. "Judge Murphy," *Vancouver Sun*, May 3, 1947; "Loving Canada and Being True Citizens Means That Every Resident Should Study Canada and Live Up to National Ideals, Is the Plea of BC Jurist," *Vancouver Sun*, June 29, 1924; "Death Calls Pioneer Supreme Court Judge," *Vancouver Province*, May 2, 1947.
2. November 16, 1923, Murphy minute book.
3. Oral reasons for judgement in Canada (Attorney General) v. Gonzalves (1925) are taken from 34 BCR, 362–64.
4. February 6, 1924, VPB minutes; March 11, 1924, directors' meeting, minutes, Art, Historical & Scientific Association, CVA, Add. Ms. 336, file 546-F-1; "Totem Poles are Placed," *Vancouver Sun*, February 6, 1924.
5. "Squatters to Vacate Park," *Vancouver Sun*, November 17, 1923.
6. Canada (Attorney General) v. Gonzalves (1925), 34 BCR, 365.
7. "Vancouver Wins Appeal Against Park Squatters," *Vancouver Province*, October 20, 1925; Andrew Paull, Delegate from Squamish Nation, to Scott, April 8, 1925, Ditchburn to Scott, May 24, 1925, in DIA, RG 10, v. 4089, file 521,804, reel C10186.
8. "Hon. W.A. Macdonald," *Victoria Colonist*, October 4, 1946; Alfred Watts, "Mr. Justice Archer Martin," *Advocate*, July–August 1968, 142. A fourth appeal judge heard the cases but died before the decision, whereupon it was generally agreed to proceed with the three remaining judges.
9. Justice McPhillip's reasons for appeal in Canada (Attorney General) v. Gonzalves (1925) are taken from 34 BCR, 385–96.
10. Justice Martin's reasons for appeal in Canada (Attorney General) v. Gonzalves (1925) are taken from 34 BCR, 373–83.
11. Justice Martin's reasons in Canada (Attorney General) v. Cummings (1925) are taken from 34 BCR, 437–40.
12. October 14, 1924, VPB minutes; Canada (Attorney General) v. Gonzalves (1925), SCC, Appellants' Factum, LAC. Arguments are taken from this source.
13. Canada (Attorney General) v. Gonzalves (1925), [1926] 1 *Dominion Law Reports*, 51.
14. Ibid., 52–53
15. Canada (Attorney General) v. Cummings (1925), 34 BCR, 360, 434.
16. Baker, *Khot-La-Cha*, 2; Pierre Berton, "Magic in Their Souls," *British Columbia Digest* 1, July 1946, 91.

Chapter 10: Dispossession

1. "The Fate of the Squatters," *Vancouver Province*, November 18, 1923.
2. June 11 and July 16, 1925, February 27, 1930, VPB minutes; "Squatters are Ousted From Park," *Vancouver Province*, July 7, 1925.
3. September 24 and October 30, 1925, February 25, 1926, February 28, 1929, VPB minutes.
4. Hood, *By Shore and Trail*, 36.
5. February 6, 1924, VPB minutes.
6. "W.C. Shelly Bought Acreage to Prevent Commercial Venture Being Launched," *Vancouver Sun*, October 30, 1939; November 26 and December 10, 1925, VPB minutes.

7. November 26, 1925, VPB minutes; Robert Cole, conversation with Steele.
8. Norman and Margaret McPhee, conversations, June 25 and July 5, 1991; land registry deed between Cranes' Shipyards and Maggie Eihu, November 14, 1922, held in BC Land Title Office, New Westminster. I am tremendously grateful to Cheryl Wong for tracking down the land records for me.
9. Affidavit of Margaret Eihu or McPhee, May 8, 1925, BCA; copy of will courtesy of Mabel McPhee; Norman and Margaret McPhee, conversations, June 25 and July 5, 1991; Margaret McPhee, conversation, November 12, 2002.
10. "Lifetime Resident of Stanley Park, Agnes Cumming Dies at 69 Years," *Vancouver Province*, July 25, 1953; Hyde, "Last Man."
11. Robert Cole, conversation with Steele; "Lifetime Resident of Stanley Park."
12. Minutes, Art, Historical & Scientific Association, CVA, Add. Ms. 336, file 546-F-1.
13. "The Indian Village," *Museum Notes* (Vancouver Museum) 1, 2 (June 1926); 23 (October 23, 1935), directors' meeting, minutes, Art, Historical & Scientific Association.
14. January 21, 1930, VPB minutes.
15. February 27, 1930, VPB minutes; Elgin Neish, letter to Steele, Vancouver, July 23, 1984, CVA, Add. Ms. 954.
16. Berton, "Magic in Their Souls," 92.
17. "Deadman's Island Squatters To Get Order to Vacate," *Star*, February 28, 1930; "Squatters Lose Their Homes as Island Becomes a Park," *Victoria Times*, February 28, 1930; February 27, March 13, December 11, 1930, VPB minutes; "Squatters Given Final Warning," *Vancouver Sun*, November 21, 1930.
18. "Squatters Given Final Warning"; February 26, 1931, VPB minutes; "Stanley Park Squatters to be Evicted," *Star*, February 27, 1931.
19. May 28, 1931, VPB minutes.
20. Gonsalves, conversations.
21. Marion Long, conversations, November 16, 2001, March 2, 2002.
22. "Squatters Move from Park Area," *Star*, July 10, 1931; VPB *Annual Report*, 1931, 15.
23. Anderson, "A beautiful place."
24. Herbert Smith, conversations, Vancouver, January 23, 2005; Marion Long, conversations, November 16, 2001, March 2, 2002.
25. Gonsalves, conversations.
26. Ibid.
27. Ed Long, interview; Ed Long in *"Man Along the Shore!"*, 25–27.
28. Ed Nahanee, interview, November 6, 1973; Eddie Nahanee in *"Man Along the Shore!"*, 56.
29. January 27, 1934, meeting, Indian Committee, Vancouver Golden Jubilee Committee, CVA; VPB *Annual Report*, 1940, 5.
30. August 21, 1936, July 8, 1937, VPB minutes.
31. August Jack, conversation with Matthews, April 20, 1939, in Matthews, *Conversations*, 112; "Indian Chief at Brockton," *Vancouver News-Herald*, April 29, 1944.
32. November 9, 1933, VPB minutes.
33. "Stanley Park," *Vancouver Sun*, November 30, 1931; "Park Preservation," *Vancouver News-Herald*, October 30, 1934; "Park Preservation," *Vancouver News-Herald*,

October 30, 1934; R. Rowe Holland, "Forward" to Catherine Mae MacLennan, *Rambling Round Stanley Park* (Vancouver: Wrigley, 1935); J. Lyle Telford to Earl of Derby, Vancouver, October 2, 1939, in Stanley Park file, VCA, Add. Ms. Stanley Park file.

34. Hyde, "Last Man."
35. O'Connor, conversation, April 10, 2000.
36. Anne Fowler, "Auntie Aggie & Uncle Tim," *Dogwood Pavilion*, Fall 1999.
37. Mabel McPhee, conversation, January 17, 2003; Laurie Nahanee Cole, conversation, April 2, 2002.
38. Kerr, conversations, September 15, October 4 and 20, 2002.
39. "The Cumming Cottage," CVA, Add. Ms. 54.
40. O'Connor, conversation, April 10, 2000; O'Connor, "Mom's Story."
41. Ruth Ullrich, "Stanley Park," typescript dated July 27, 2003, courtesy the author.
42. "Flag at Half Mast in Park," *Vancouver News-Herald*, July 28, 1953; D.N., Abbott, "Stanley Park Site Surveys," in CVA, Add. Ms. 954.
43. "Park Squatter's Getting Lonely," *Vancouver Sun*, May 10, 1955; Hyde, "Last Man."
44. "Go Slow at Tim's Place," *Vancouver Sun*, March 12, 1958.
45. "Matthews Goes to Bat To Save 'Tim's Place,'" *Vancouver Sun*, March 13, 1958.
46. Fred Allgood, "Shack in Shadow of Board's Axe," *Vancouver Sun*, November 19, 1963.
47. Maisie Hurley, "Tim's Place Unmourned by Indians," *Vancouver Sun*, November 20, 1963.

Afterword: Back to the Lilac

1. May 17, 2004, VPB minutes; National Parks and National Historic Sites of Canada, *Stanley Park, National Historic Site of Canada: Commemorative Integrity Statement* (Ottawa: Parks Canada, November 2002), 2–3, 7, 13, 25, 42, 44–46, 52.
2. Hyde, "Last Man"; Fowler, "Auntie Aggie & Uncle Tim."
3. Anderson, "A beautiful place"; Michael Long, conversation, November 16, 2001.
4. Norman McPhee, conversations, June 25 and July 5, 1991; Olive Keamo O'Connor, conversation, April 10, 2000.
5. Herbert Smith, conversation, January 23, 2005.
6. Gonsalves, conversations.

Keamo, Josephine (daughter of James Keamo and Anne Nelson), 113, 121, 144
Keamo, Mona (daughter of James Grant Keamo and Annie Cummings), 123, **145**
Keamo, Olive (O'Connor) (daughter of James Grant Keamo and Annie Cummings, wife of Jack O'Connor), 16, 123, **145**, 147, 239-41, **244**-45, 256
Keamo, Walter (son of James Keamo and Anne Nelson), 51
Keamo family, 118, 234
Kenick (daughter of Shwuthchalton, wife of Peter Smith), 59, 62, 106, 111-12, 147
Kennedy, Dorothy, 167
Kerr, Elsie (daughter of Rosa Caros), 141-42, 242-43
Khaltinaht (Mary Ann) (granddaughter of Chief Capilano, daughter of Sumkawht, wife of Joseph Silvey), 59-62, 64, 67-69, 108
Khahtsahlano, August Jack (son of Supple Jack and Qwhaywat), **15**, 18, 29-31, 41-46, 92-93, 95-96, 136, 234, 236-**37**, 255
Khahtsahlano, Louisa, *see* Burns, Louisa
Khahtsahlano, Chief (Hahlch láh nuk) (father of Supple Jack), 30-31, 38-39, 44
Khahtsahlano family, 38-39, 102
Khaytulk, *see* Supple Jack
Kitsilano Reserve, *see* Snauq
Klah Chaw (Dr. Johnson, Mowitchman, Mowitch Jim, Hjachalachth) (father of Takood and Tesamis, father-in-law of Joseph Mannion), 59, 70-71, 76, 167, 187, 196-97, 215
Kulkalem, Chief Jim (husband of Aunt Sally), 176-77
Kulkalem, Mariah (daughter of Jim Kulkalem and Aunt Sally), 175, 177-78, 185-86, 223-24
Kulkalem, Sally, *see* Aunt Sally
Kulkalem family, 208, 223
Kwán itz, Thomas, 38
Kwatleematt, Kwahama (Lucy) (wife of Joseph Silvey), **73**
Kwe áh jilk (Que-yah-chulk, Dick Isaacs) (brother of Chém chuk and Aunt Sally), 34, 38-39, 167
Kweeahkult, Sam (son of Chief Capilano), 61, 67-68
Kwi oots, Thomas, 38
Lâ-lâh, Chief (son of Chief Capilano, uncle of Mary See-em-ia), 36, 53
Lee, Kitty, *see* Kitty Caros
Lock/Locke, David, *see* David Burns
Long, Edward (husband of Mary Smith), 80-81, 97-98, 106, 111, 148, 153-55, 178, 187
Long, Ed (son of Edward Long and Mary Smith, husband of Susie Thomas), 153, 159, 171, 178-79, 185, 206, 217, 222, 229, 231-32, 234, 256
Long, Henry (son of Edward Long and Mary Smith), 154
Long, Josepha (daughter of Edward Long and Mary Smith), 154-55
Long, Marion (daughter of Ed and Susie Long), 231-32
Long, Susie (Susie Thomas) (brother of Dan George, wife of Ed Long), 232
Long, William (son of Edward Long and Mary Smith), 154
Long family, 16, 103, 167, 234
Ludgate, Thomas, 163-66, 227
Lumberman's Arch, *see* Whoi Whoi
Lumtinaht (Louise) (granddaughter of Chief Capilano, sister of Khaltinaht), 61, 67-**68**-69

McCord, Maggie, *see* Margaret Eihu
McCord, Maud (daughter of Benjamin McCord and Margaret Eihu), 54, 94, 133, 135
McCord, Minnie (daughter of Benjamin McCord and Margaret Eihu, wife of William Smith), 15, 47-**49**, 54-57, 72, 75-76, 82, 94-95, 112, 127-28, 134, 145, 148, 224, 257
McCord, Seraphine (daughter of Benjamin McCord and Margaret Eihu, wife of Jens Marstrand), 54-56, 112, 115, 117, 133-**34**-36, 148-49
Macdonald, Chief Justice William A., 208-09
McPhee, Daniel (husband of Margaret Eihu), 54-55, 112, 126-27, 224
McPhee, Donald (son of Daniel McPhee and Maggie Eihu), 55, 132
McPhee, Irene (daughter of Daniel McPhee and Maggie Eihu, wife of Tommy Armstrong), 55, 128, 132-**33**, 224
McPhee, Maggie, *see* Margaret Eihu
McPhee, Mabel (wife of Norman McPhee), 16, 242
McPhee, Norman (son of Irene McPhee, grandson of Daniel McPhee and Margaret Eihu), 16, 132-**33**, 224-**25**, 242, 256
Malkin Bowl, 236-37, **243**
Mannion, De Vere (son of Joseph Mannion and Takood), 72, 76
Mannion, Joseph (husband of Takood), 59, 69-70, 72, 74-78, 82, 84, 187, 196-97, 215
Mannion, Margaret (Mrs. Dr. H.A. Christie) (son of Joseph Mannion and Takood), 72, 75-76, **77**
Marstrand, Jens (husband of Seraphine McPhee), 134-36
Martin, Appeal judge Archer, 208-16, 218, 220
Mathias, Chief Joe (son of Chief Joe and Mary Capilano), 174, 193, 219, 235, **237**
Matthews, Major J.S. (first Vancouver archivist), 14-15, 18, 21, 248
Mission Reserve, 34-37, 39, **44**, 55, 107-08, 127, 129-32, 140, 167, 192-93, 232, 255
Moody, Col. Richard, 24-28, 32, 64, 87, 165, 212, 218, 25-53, 261 fn 11-12 and 14-15
Moodyville Mill, 29, **31**, 39-40, 46, 69, 81, 127
Morton, John, 48, 50, 89, 124-27, 188
Murphy, Judge Denis, 186, 189, 201, 205-09, 211, 217-18, 220, 253
Musqueam Reserve, 37, 39, 60-62, 67, 69, 136, 140

Nahanee, Cecilia (Cecilia Johnny) (wife of William Nahanee), 127-28, 131-32
Nahanee, Ben (son of William Nahanee and Cecilia Johnny), 128, 130
Nahanee, Edward (Ed) (son of William Nahanee and Cecilia Johnny), **128**, **130**-31, 159, 235
Nahanee, James (son of Edward Nahanee and Margaret Joe), 15, 128-29
Nahanee, Joe (husband of Mary See-em-ia), 47, 51, 53-54, 127

Also by Jean Barman

THE REMARKABLE ADVENTURES OF PORTUGUESE JOE SILVEY

BRITISH COLUMBIA IS KNOWN for the colourful pioneers who helped build and shape the character of this weird but wonderful province. And few were as colourful as Portuguese Joe Silvey—a saloon keeper, whaler and pioneer of seine fishing in British Columbia.

Born on Pico Island, of Portugal's Azores Islands, sometime between 1830 and 1840, Joseph Silvey began whaling when he was just 12 years old. In 1860, when Silvey came to the BC coast on a whaling schooner, he decided to jump ship to try his hand at gold-mining.

From harpooning whales in small open rowboats, to serving up liquor to rambunctious millworkers, to being the first man to have a seine license in BC, Silvey was the Renaissance man of his generation. His friends were many, and included saloon keeper Gassy Jack Deighton for whom Vancouver's Gastown is named, his prestigious grandfather-in-law Chief Kiapilano (of the Capilano Nation) and a remittance man who liked to wear either his wife's clothes or none at all.

Although Portuguese Joe and his family prospered—he had 11 children with two wives and his many descendants still populate the BC coast—they also had their share of grief. Joe's first wife Khaltinaht died after a few short years of marriage; his eldest child Elizabeth was later kidnapped and forced to marry against her will; and his sixth child John was murdered in a rowboat while on his way to buy clams.

Historian Jean Barman brings to life the story of Portuguese Joe—the romance, the tragedy, and the adventure—with skill, piecing together interviews with Silvey's descendants, archival records and historical photographs to build an intriguing and entertaining portrait of Joseph Silvey, his family, and the time and place in which he lived.

1-55017-326-X · Paperback · 8.5 x 11 · 88 pp

Other Great Books *from* Harbour Publishing

Raincoast Chronicles: Fourth Five
edited by Howard White
Raincoast Chronicles have become a west coast institution—articles, stories, poems, drawings covering every imaginable aspect of northwest history and folklore. *Fourth Five* collects books 16 through 20 in one hardcover edition. The volume expounds on such diverse matters as supernatural deer, the cannery village of Ceepeecee, fishing-fleet superstitions and the coveted recipe for donkey boiler coffee. Writers include coast favourites Howard White, Doreen Armitage, Tom Henry, Dick Hammond, Vickie Jensen and Bus Griffiths, plus longer features by Pat Wastell Norris and Stephen Hume. The book is illustrated in characteristically extravagant fashion with drawings and archival photos.
1-55017-372-3 · Hardcover · 8.5 x 11 · 420 pp

Backstage Vancouver: A Century of Entertainment Legends
by Greg Potter and Red Robinson
What do Boris Karloff, Bing Crosby, Marilyn Monroe, Elvis, Jack Benny, Bob Hope, Goldie Hawn and Pamela Anderson have in common? They are all legendary entertainers who made stops in Vancouver, BC, leaving flakes of stardust behind. A wonderful horde of showbiz lore has accumulated over the decades but has been jealously guarded by industry insiders. *Backstage Vancouver* collects these rarely seen photographs for the first time, presenting them in a breathtaking pictorial hardcover.
1-55017-334-0 · Hardcover · 8.5 x 11 · 240 pp

Bijaboji: North to Alaska by Oar
by Betty Lowman Carey
Betty Lowman was 22 years old in June 1937 when she climbed into her beloved red dugout canoe, *Bijaboji*, and set out on a journey from Puget Sound to Alaska. Traversing some of the most treacherous waters on earth, the journey would have been a risky act for an extreme adventurer in any era; for a young woman in the conservative 1930s, it was a venture of almost unimaginable daring.
1-55017-340-5 · Hardcover · 6 x 9 · 288 pp

Mountie in Mukluks: The Arctic Adventures of Bill White
by Patrick White
During the 1930s, Bill White gave up trapping and joined the Royal Canadian Mounted Police, volunteering for arctic service. Bill started out crewing on the historic RCMP patrol ship *St. Roch* under the command of the legendary Captain Henry Larsen, but hungered for greater adventure and requested a posting ashore upon reaching Cambridge Bay. Adventure he found: *Mountie in Mukluks* includes hair-raising accounts of a near-death experience under the ice on a frozen river; of a 1200-mile dog-sled chase after an arctic murderer; and of numerous fascinating encounters with shamans, telepathy and an Inuit way of life that has now vanished from the earth. White's absorbing oral accounts of life in the old north, molded into lively prose by Patrick White, place *Mountie in Mukluks* among classics of arctic literature like *Kabloona* by Gontran de Poncins and *People of the Deer* by Farley Mowat.
1-55017-352-9 · Hardcover · 6 x 9 · 248 pp

Diary of a Wilderness Dweller
by Chris Czajkowski
In the late 1980s, Chris Czajkowski left her truck at the end of a logging road 300 kilometres north of Vancouver and hiked for two days on unmarked wilderness trails to the site of what would become her home. This is her account of building three log cabins, an ecotourism business and a life beside an unnamed lake 5,000 feet high in the Coast Range mountains. This new trade paper edition of *Diary of a Wilderness Dweller* shares Czajkowski's adventures from the beginning as she wields chainsaw and axe to forge a different kind of life.
1-55017-357-x · Paperback · 6 x 9 · 176 pp

These titles are available in bookstores or from:

INDIAN VILLAGE

BURRARD INLE

BEFORE THE